IMAGES
of America

BOWLING GREEN SINCE 1950

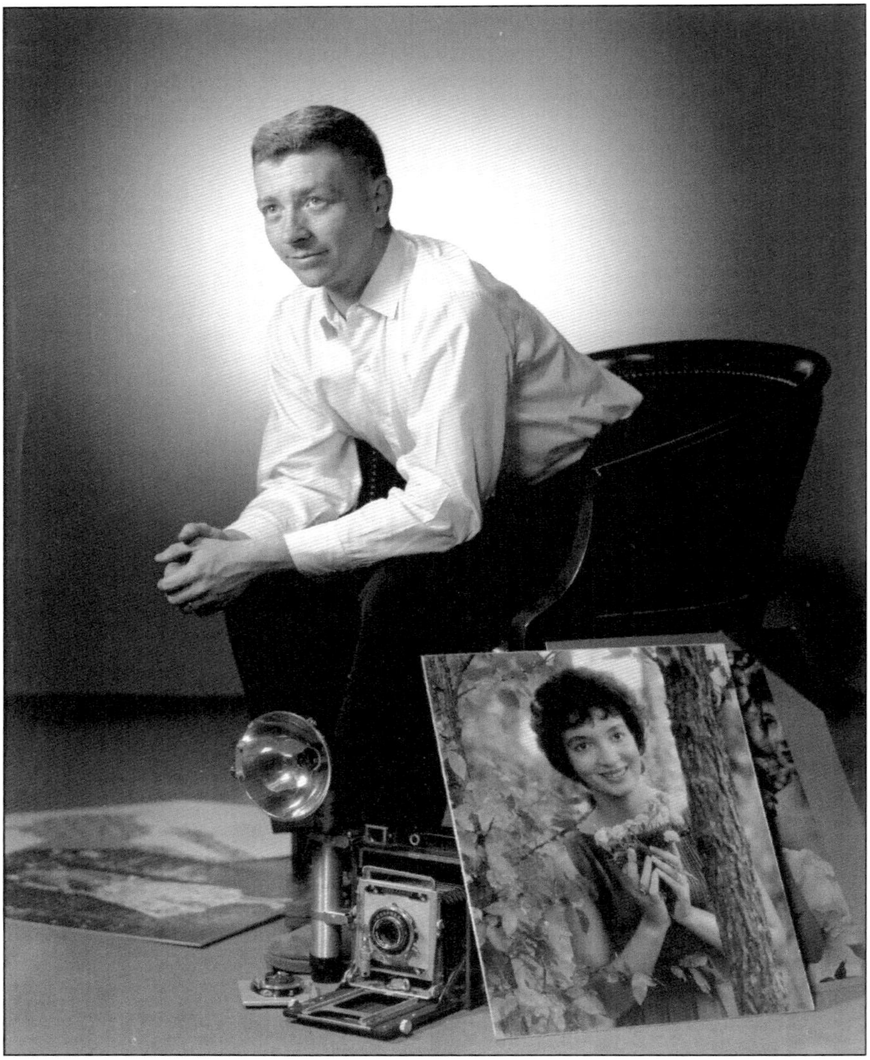

Master Photographer. For over five decades, Thomas Walter Hughes Jr. chronicled the life and times of Bowling Green, lending his unique vision and genuine love of people to every subject he photographed. Born in Savannah, Georgia, and raised in Franklin, Kentucky, his spicy blend of Kentucky rogue and Southern gentleman gave his work the inimitable style and wit for which he was known. (From the collection of Tommy Hughes.)

On the Cover: Anything, Anywhere, Anytime. The ambitious and all-inclusive motto of Ches Johnson Studio in 1951 reflected the deep-seated commitment to excellence of a thriving staff of photographers, photo finishers, and photoengravers who set out to document the life and times of Bowling Green for its citizenry. Ready in 1954 at any time to snap any shot, from left to right are (first row) Ray Bunch, Jimmy Conner, Marshall Love, unidentified, Gilbert Brown, Vaughn Talbott, and Tommy Hughes; (second row) Jewel Harrison, Jonell Stahl Price, Glenda Morrow, Frances Cole Hayden, Jackie Mosley, Frances Deckard, and Ches Johnson; (third row) Betty Reynolds, John Moore, unidentified, John Grider, and Lawrence Jones. (From the collection of Tommy Hughes.)

IMAGES
of America

BOWLING GREEN SINCE 1950

Amy Hughes Wood and
Portia Beck Pennington

ARCADIA
PUBLISHING

ISBN 978-0-7385-6677-1

Published by Arcadia Publishing
Charleston, South Carolina

Printed in the United States of America

Library of Congress Control Number: 2009933858

For all general information contact Arcadia Publishing at:
Telephone 843-853-2070
Fax 843-853-0044
E-mail sales@arcadiapublishing.com
For customer service and orders:
Toll-Free 1-888-313-2665

Visit us on the Internet at www.arcadiapublishing.com

To Franklin, Andrew, and Paul Wood, with love and appreciation.
—Amy Hughes Wood

To Bettye and Ted Beck—Mom and Dad—with thanks for the gift of history and with heartfelt gratitude for instilling in me the love of the written word.
—Portia Beck Pennington

Contents

ACKNOWLEDGMENTS

This book would not exist without the creativity and artistry of Tommy and Nancy Hughes. They embraced photography as both a career for Tommy and as a hobby for Nancy. They created a happy home and a successful business in Hughes Photography, and their constant commitment to spontaneous creativity in their work made this collection of photographs a lasting reality. Unless otherwise noted, all images are from the collection of photographer Tommy Hughes.

Many thanks go to Franklin Wood for his patience, wisdom, and technical support and to Paul and Andrew Wood for their accomplished research.

For moral support, cheers, laughter, and believing in the project (and in mom), much heartfelt gratitude goes to Tom Pennington, Hannah, Hallie, Mary Cullen, Beck, and Cassie Pennington.

Our editors, Luke Cunningham and Amy Perryman, have provided support and guidance throughout the process, from simple idea to finished book.

No project such as this can be undertaken without the help of others, and the community of Bowling Green has provided support, advice, research, and information that we could not have done without. Special thanks to Elizabeth Britt, Ray Buckberry, Harriet and Dero Downing, Barbara and John Grider, Cheryl Johnson, and Marshall Love for their time, expertise, and razor-sharp recall. The many resources of the Warren County Public Library and the Kentucky Library have also been invaluable to this project.

Finally, to the countless people of Bowling Green who have enthusiastically embraced the project and taken to the streets in their efforts to assist us in unearthing information about these photographs, bless you all. You have brought us your stories, memories, and special times, you have reconnected with each other in ways that have touched our hearts, and you have reminded us of what is so good about this place we are fortunate to call home.

INTRODUCTION

The quintessential American life can be measured and recorded in 10-year increments: A baby is born. At age 10, he or she is on the cusp of adolescence. By 20, the young adult is making life decisions; by 30, most youthful lots have been cast, and those often hasty judgments now provide the parameters of adult life. At 40, middle-agers begin to see the end results of their choices, and by 50, with the blessings of good health and an active mind, Americans are embarking on new adventures, many of which they never could have dreamed.

The development of a small American town is much the same. Bowling Green in 1950 was small, simple, and innocent—an *Ozzie and Harriet* kind of town with *Leave it to Beaver* fashions and moral codes. With two traffic lights and very little traffic, three brightly lit movie theaters, a bustling town square, and the genesis of an active industrial base, Bowling Green was poised for rapid growth and development. The recent establishment of Union Underwear Company, the return of young men and women from World War II hungry for advanced education and for a place to raise a family, and the foresight of town fathers who wooed business and industry to the area ensured that Bowling Green would fast forward from the 1950s into the 1960s and beyond, growing by leaps and bounds.

Growth—real, lasting growth—does not come without cost, nor is it experienced without some pain. The 1960s brought national turmoil and local sorrow, as Bowling Green grieved with the country for lost leaders, as the specter of war took native sons and daughters to foreign lands, and as Kentuckians were forced to recognize the ugly face of racism. Through the growth and through the change, the people of Bowling Green answered the hard questions together and created a 20th-century town of which they could be proud—a town where leaders such as F. O. Moxley and Wayne Constant could work simultaneously to motivate and inspire, to instruct and lead.

The 1970s were a period of some unrest both in Bowling Green and in the country at large. Life on "the hill" teemed with energy and conflict, as young students questioned authority and challenged tradition. Undeterred from his educational mission, Dr. Dero Downing faced hundreds of students at a late night sit-in, offered to meet with each individually the next day at his office, and encouraged them all to go to bed. Malls opened and interstate thoroughfares surrounded the city with fast, rapid transportation, bringing the world in and taking Bowling Green to the world.

One result of growth and a by-product of progress is a booming population, and the 1980s saw Bowling Green continue to swell with hundreds of new citizens as the promise of employment and education tempted settlers from throughout the country. With the opening of General Motors and with advances in health care, real estate, and agriculture, Bowling Green was cited as one of the fastest-growing cities in the state. Restaurants found Bowling Green families more than willing to dine out as society continued on the fast track and retail establishments flourished during this era of prosperity.

Heading into the last decade of the millennium, Bowling Green was older and wiser. The town celebrated its victories and mourned its defeats, with a concentrated effort to learn from past mistakes. Common tragedies bred common bonds as citizens struggled to recover following a cataclysmic hail storm and a harrowing downtown fire. Crime increased but so did philanthropy as Bowling Green continued to open its pocketbook and its heart to those in need. New Year's Eve 1999 saw a town with firmly planted roots and a strong grip on its history looking the new millennium square in the eye.

Since its founding in 1798, Bowling Green has never been a town to rest on its laurels. Throughout its history, the community has been known for its progressive, innovative drive and entrepreneurial spirit. Town fathers have been instrumental in luring rail service and industry, often making a personal financial down payment on the future. The descendants of those men and women have not forgotten and continue to invest in a county seat focused on progress—from a business incubator at Western Kentucky University to industrial parks poised and ready for development, Bowling Green refuses simply to tread water but marches steadfastly into the decades to come.

When photographer Tommy Hughes first came to Bowling Green in 1952, he was fresh from the Progressive School of Photography in New Haven, Connecticut. With a camera in his hand and a glint in his eye, he set to work capturing the town and its people. He signed on with Ches Johnson Studio, one of the largest and most well-known photography studios in the area. Hughes packed his camera and lights, boxes of large-format film, and unwieldy tripods and set to work.

Photography in the 1950s was an athletic pursuit, requiring of its practitioners the physical will of a champion, the eye of an artist, and the tongue of a diplomat. Presented with the challenges of one disposable flash bulb per picture and one exposure per shot, the photographer worked diligently to find the right shot before he ever pressed the button. An artful combination of light and dark, of illumination and of shadows, photography in the pre-digital age required a commitment of time and concentration. Hughes gave this and more to his continued development as a photographer dedicated to excellence and to his philosophy that there was always time for "just one more." Recognized in 1970 with top honors at the Kentucky Professional Photographers Association and published in nationally lauded *Life* magazine, Hughes's work was well regarded by his colleagues and by the public.

Fifty years after moving to town, a visually evocative history of Bowling Green and its transformation from sweetly rural small Kentucky hamlet to a primary anchor of economic, cultural, and educational growth had been brought to life in the negatives and prints Hughes had stuffed in boxes and closets—a treasure trove of Bowling Green memories just waiting to be discovered and now worthy of record for posterity.

One

The 1950s
A Nice Place to Live

Images from the past often take on the rosy glow of retrospection—the streets were cleaner, the sunlight brighter, the smiles truer, and the days longer, or so it seems.

Life in 1950 Bowling Green was, indeed, simpler. Fewer people meant fewer problems, and fewer problems meant less public discord. Citizens knuckled down to the task at hand, be it a job well done for an employer or a household well managed. Students were appreciative of the opportunity for an education, while the town at large was bursting with renewed postwar energy. Bowling Green was abuzz with life.

In spite of the ominously dark clouds of the Korean War and McCarthy-era hatred, Bowling Green moved ahead, too slowly for some citizens and too rapidly for others. Rev. J. Stuart Wake and his forward-thinking committee bravely recommended integration for Bowling Green City Schools, and Bowling Green Parks and Recreation was born under the leadership of Mayor C. W. Lampkin. Warren County agriculture suffered millions of dollars in losses during a deadly summer drought, and Duncan Hines became a household name.

Three television stations brought the outside world into Bowling Green's comfortable environs, and families gathered before a flickering screen engrossed in the comedy of Red Skelton or the drama of *The Rifleman*. The local newspaper printed the names and addresses of hospital patients, allowing concerned neighbors to help with food and a listening ear, while the Red Cross applauded generous donors by name. But the same newspapers minimized the lives of an entire segment of the community in segregated obituaries and in limited, equally segregated reportage.

Town fathers enacted Prohibition in an effort to rid the city of alcohol and alcohol-related problems, only to find that drunken driving arrests increased almost 200 percent. Local leaders considered the annexation of farmland into the city, a then-controversial proposition that forever changed the geography and the demographics of the community.

A simple town rich in complexities and contradictions, 1950s Bowling Green was a thriving center of commerce, agriculture, education, and spiritual life. Photographer Tommy Hughes willingly turned his youthful eye and inquisitive mind to the task of capturing that life.

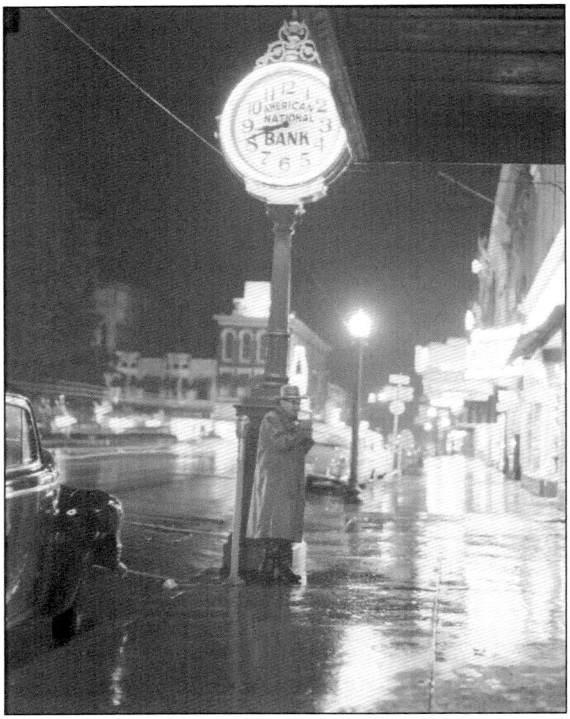

THESE LITTLE TOWN BLUES ARE MELTING AWAY. With true Frank Sinatra swagger, Vaughn Talbott paused for a solitary smoke in rainy 1954 downtown Bowling Green at the cosmopolitan corner in front of American National Bank at 922 State Street.

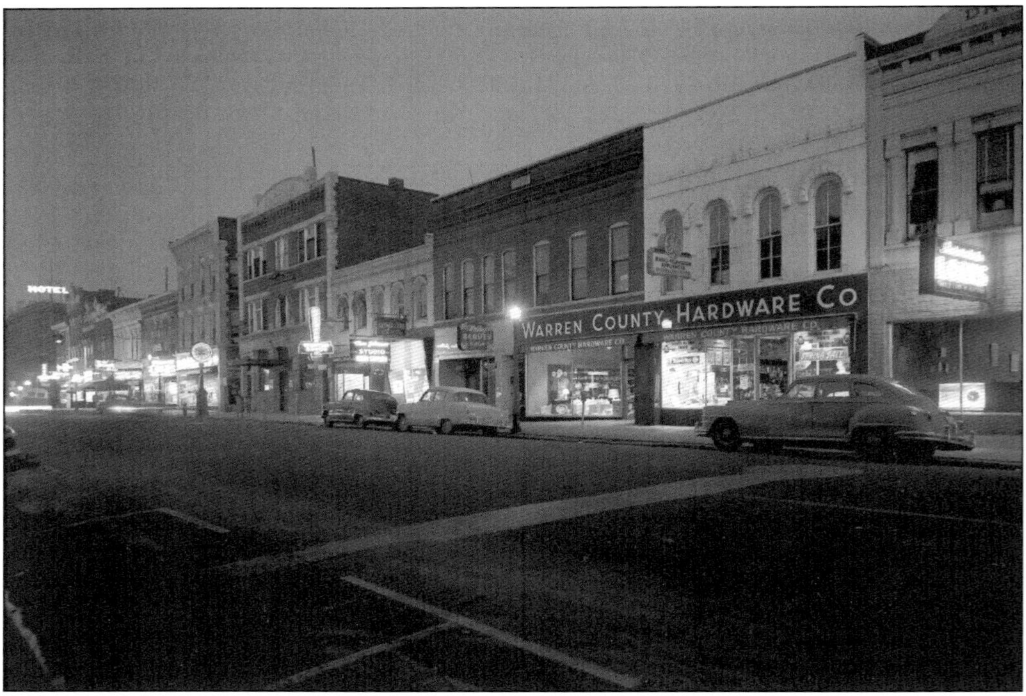

LIGHTS OF COMMERCE. The shining windows of Warren County Hardware at 934 State Street were aglow on this balmy spring evening in early 1954, while the clean, quiet downtown thoroughfare belied the hustle and bustle of a busy day drawing to a close.

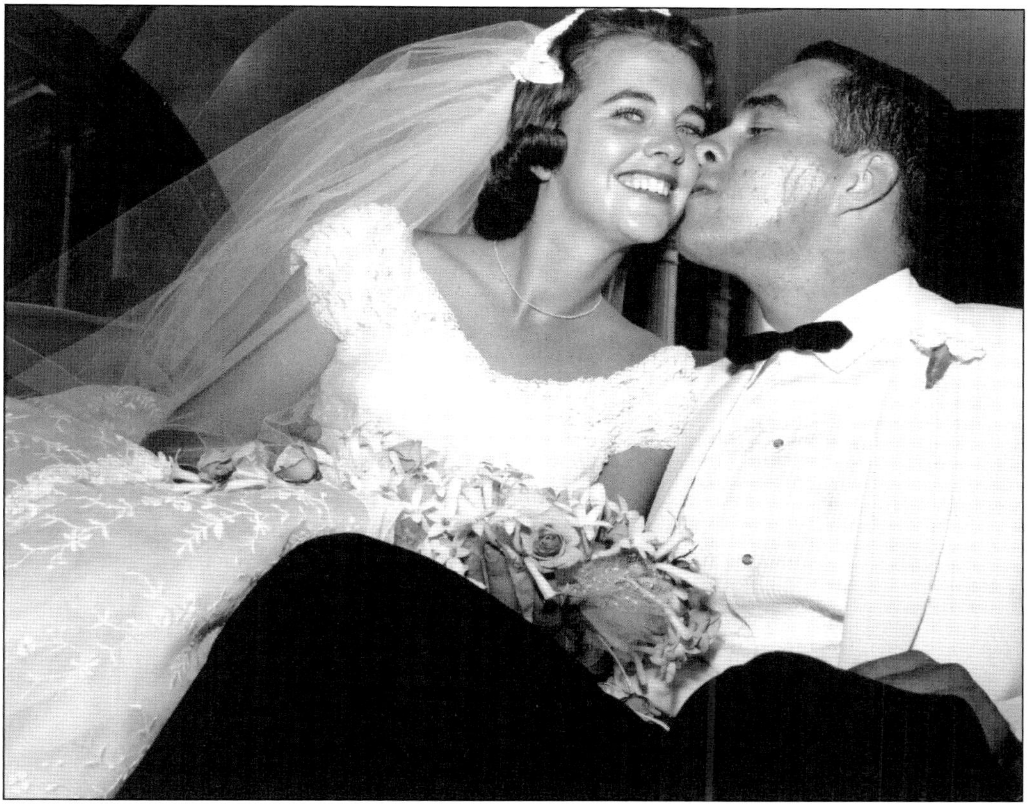

OH, HAPPY DAY! Patricia Grant and Richard Bertelson began a joyous new life together on August 31, 1957, at State Street United Methodist Church. Kentucky summer heat and humidity could not wither the high spirits and youthful passion of this day.

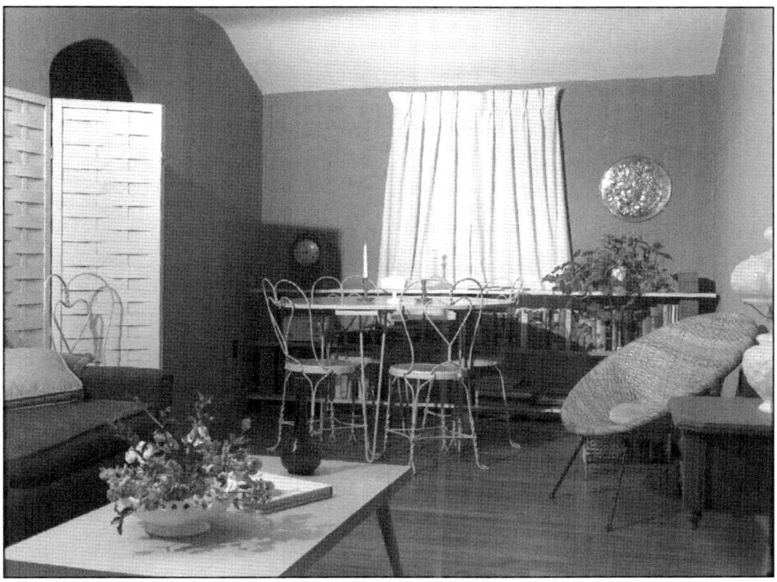

HOUSE BEAUTIFUL. A typical newlywed home of the 1950s was spare, simple, and spotless. Sweetheart ice-cream chairs, a cherished family clock, and an up-to-the-minute Papasan chair are eclectic reminders of timeless Kentucky roots combined with postwar, post-modern style.

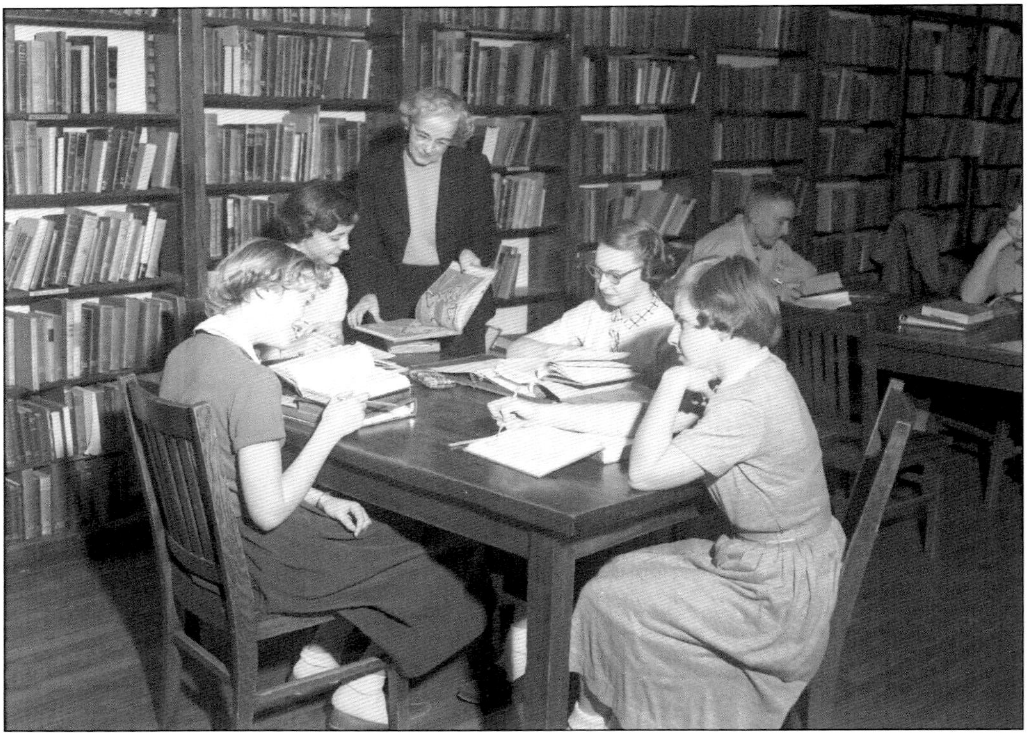

Women of Letters. Four studious young women consulted with Bess Ford, dedicated librarian at Western State College, in 1953. With bobby sox and penny loafers tucked under the table, one young scholar was ready to kick off her shoes and relax.

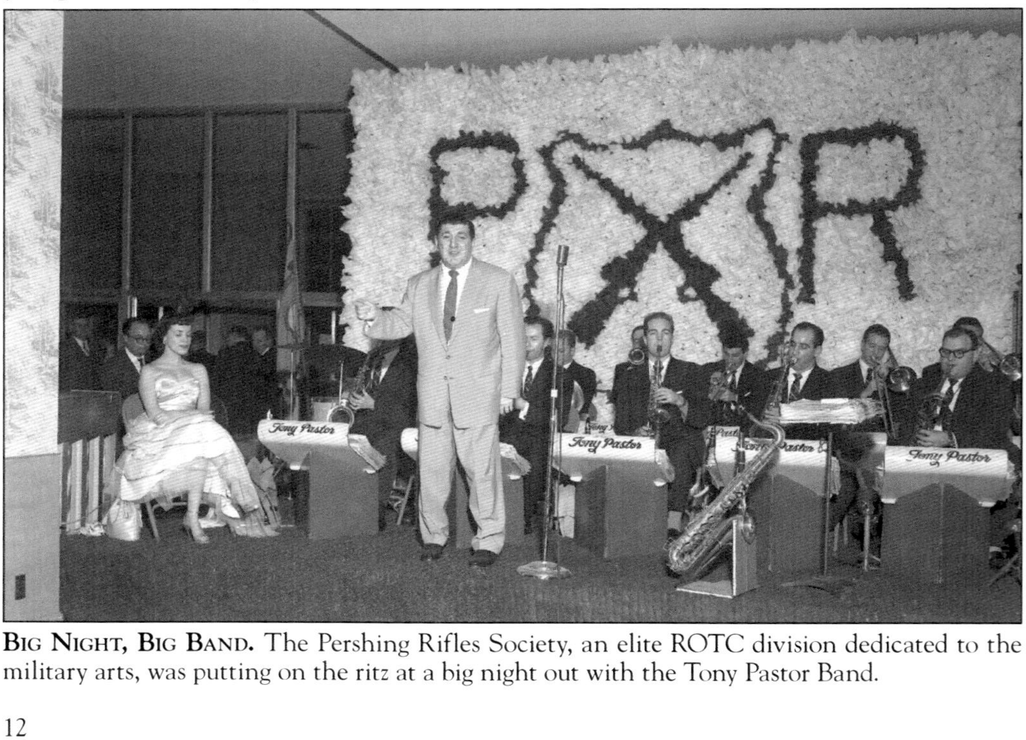

Big Night, Big Band. The Pershing Rifles Society, an elite ROTC division dedicated to the military arts, was putting on the ritz at a big night out with the Tony Pastor Band.

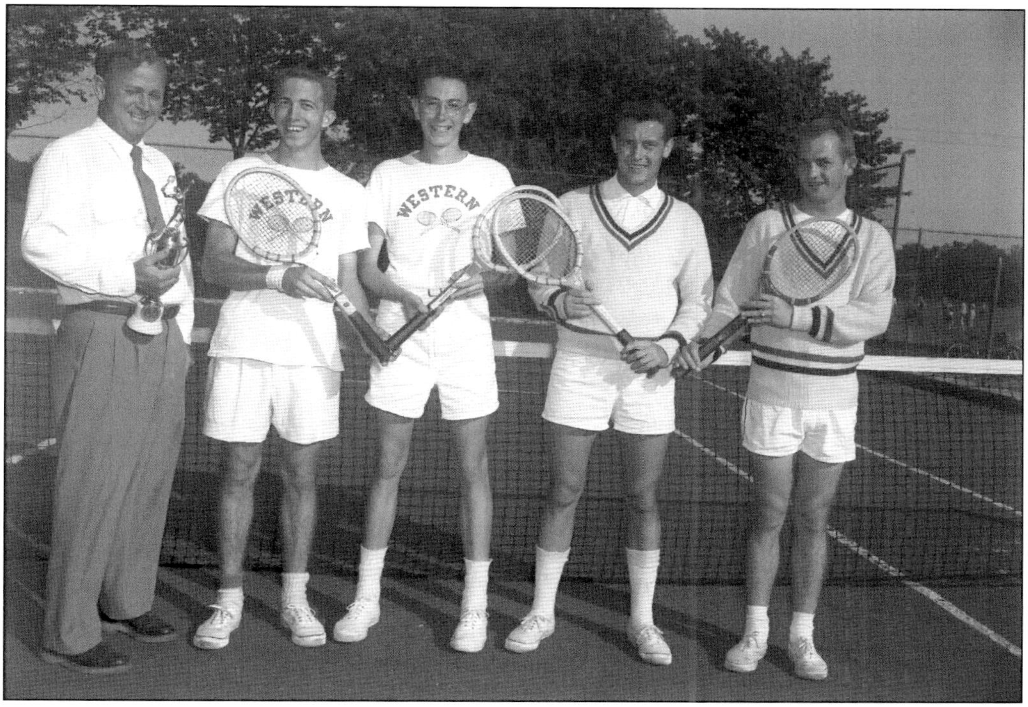

Men of the Court. Coach Ted Hornback (left) led his "netters" to on-court victory in 1954, when the Hilltoppers were a dominant force in the Ohio Valley Conference, winning first place in both *a* and *b* singles and doubles. Masters of the perfect touch lob and the smashing volley included, from left to right, Lynn Shanton, Harry Gray, C. L. Cutliff, and Marion Chestnut.

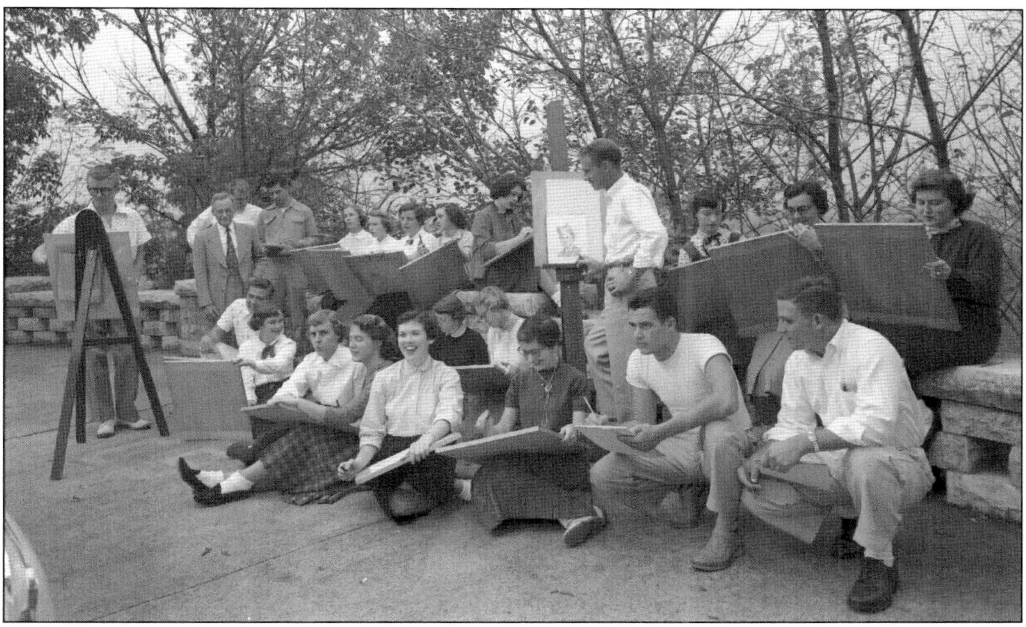

Fine Arts. The legendary Ivan Wilson (standing, with coat and tie) instructed his students in the finer points of art in this 1954 en plein air class atop the hill at Western Kentucky State College.

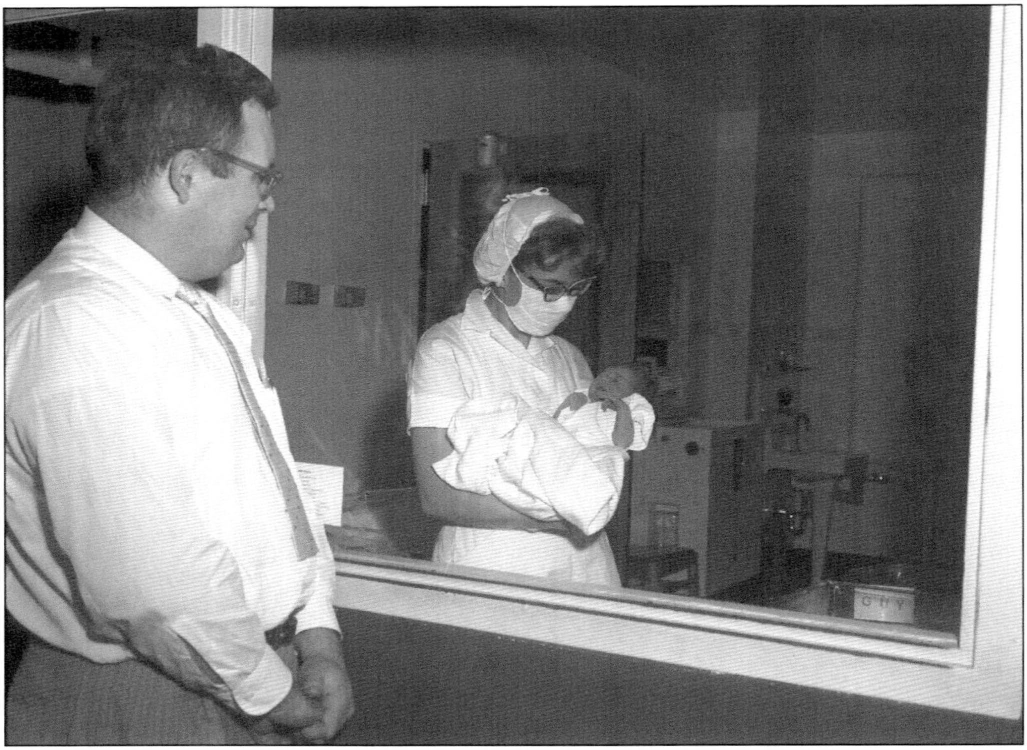

PROUD PAPA. Jenrose Pierce made her 1957 debut in Bowling Green at the County Hospital. Before he met his daughter for the first time, William Pierce went home to change from his work clothes to his very best Sunday shirt and tie, a show of respect for the auspicious occasion.

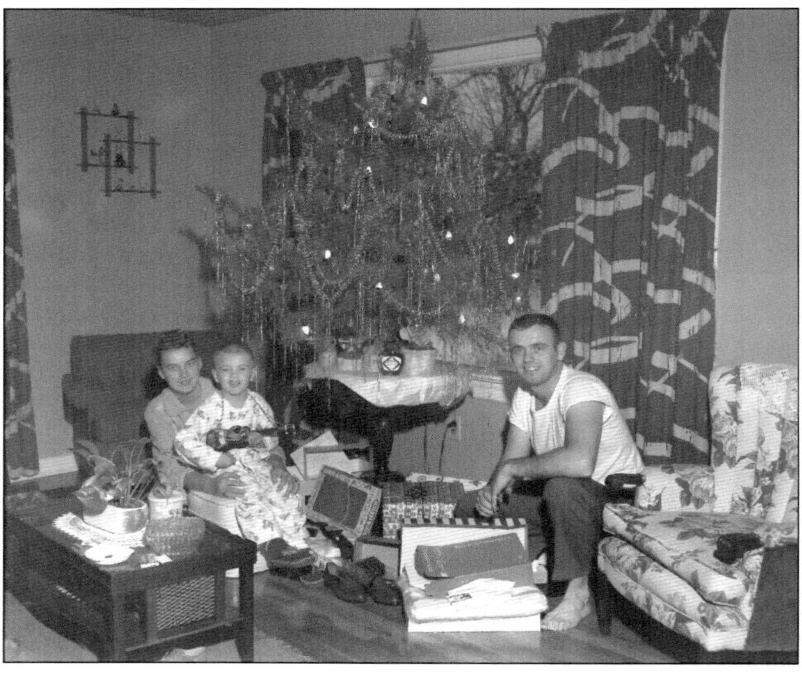

A CHRISTMAS STORY. There may not have been a Red Ryder in sight under this typical 1950s Christmas tree in Bowling Green, but this young lad seemed mighty proud of his Yogi Bear guitar and Etch-a-Sketch, while mom and dad shared his holiday spirit.

HI, HO SILVER, AWAY! Neil Phelps Jr. bravely posed with his shiny new six-shooter in 1959, ready to take on any outlaw who might challenge him to a showdown at his neighborhood corral.

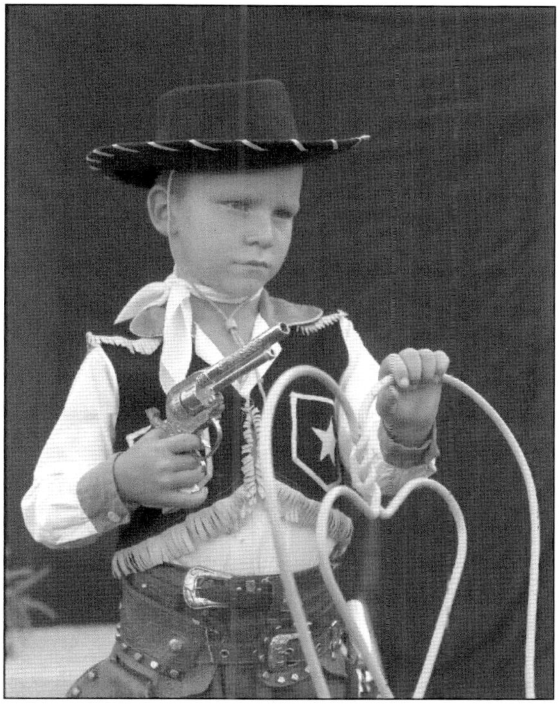

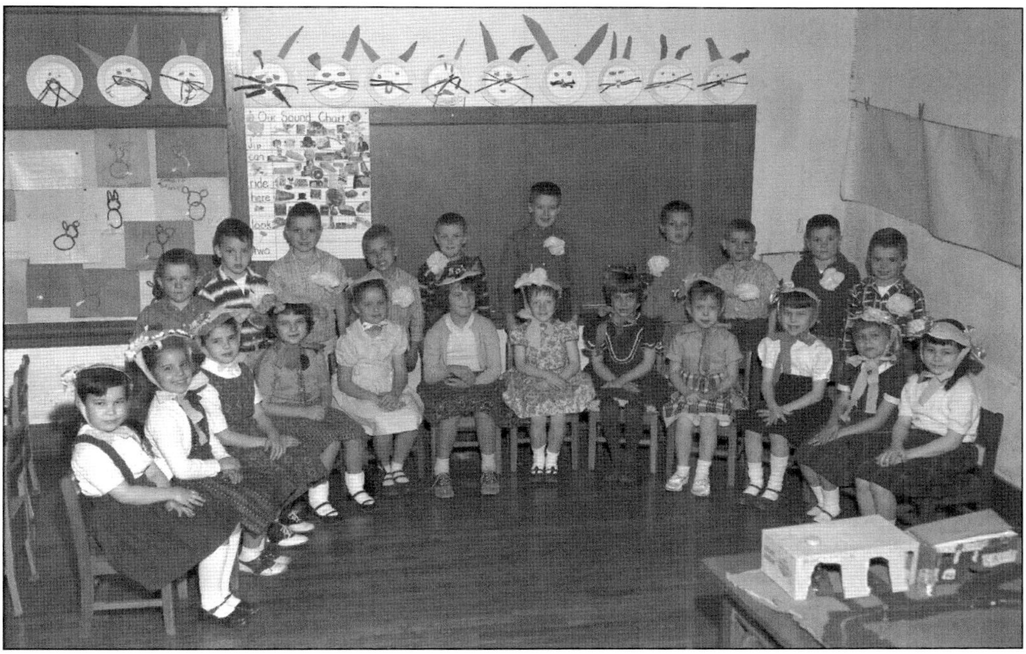

HERE COMES PETER COTTONTAIL. These Warren County School first graders decorated their room with Easter rabbits, and the girls boasted paper plate Easter bonnets, while the young gentlemen sported handmade Easter boutonnieres. The Warren County School stood at Morgantown Road (current site of Warren Central High School) and housed first grade through high school, sometimes in double, back-to-back sessions to accommodate the large number of students.

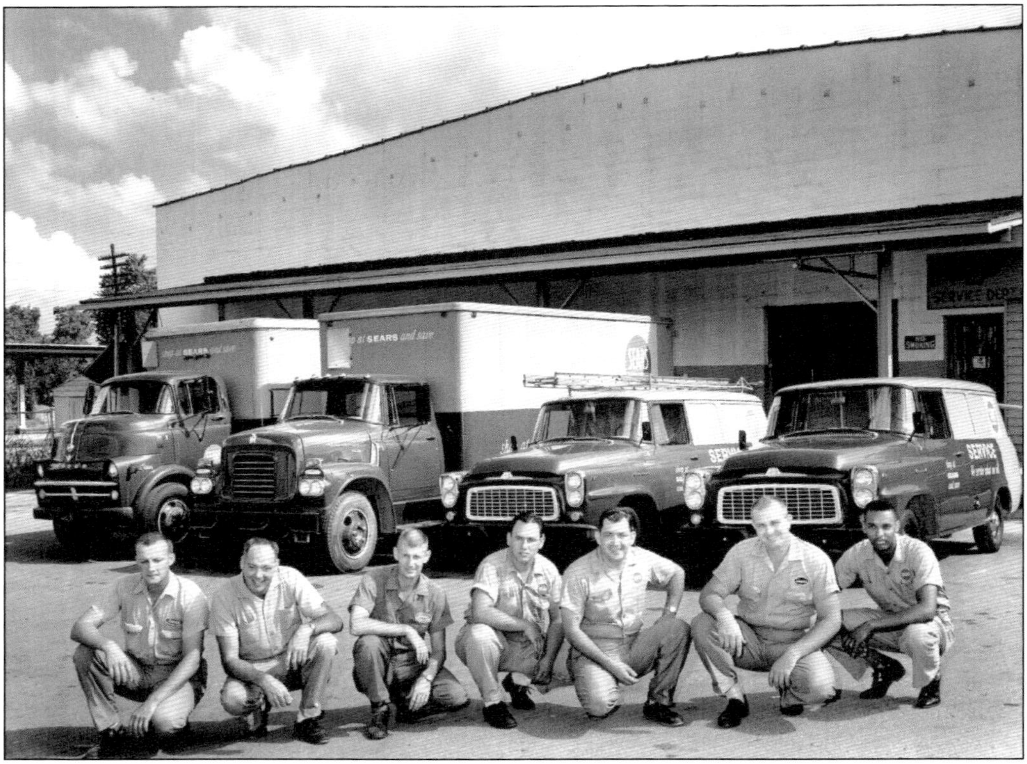

Sears and Roebuck Brigade. With gleaming delivery and repair trucks stocked and ready to hit the streets, from left to right, Bob Hunt, Bob McGown, Ray English, Joe Shanks, Joe Brady, Waymon Hogan, and Oscar Claypool of Sears and Roebuck were poised and ready to serve the citizens of Bowling Green from their downtown location.

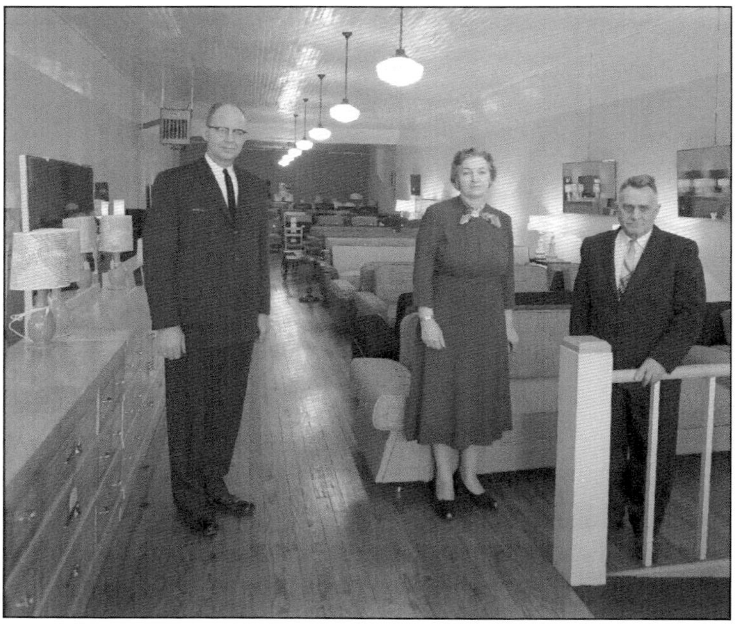

New Furniture for a New Day. Biggs Furniture at 310 Main Street offered the latest in clean, post-modern style for shoppers in Bowling Green. Harry Biggs (left) was proud to welcome shoppers to his immaculate establishment filled with the newest *House Beautiful* fashion, and he generously celebrated every Bowling Green girl's high school graduation with the gift of a cedar jewelry chest, a prized keepsake for many generations of Bowling Green ladies.

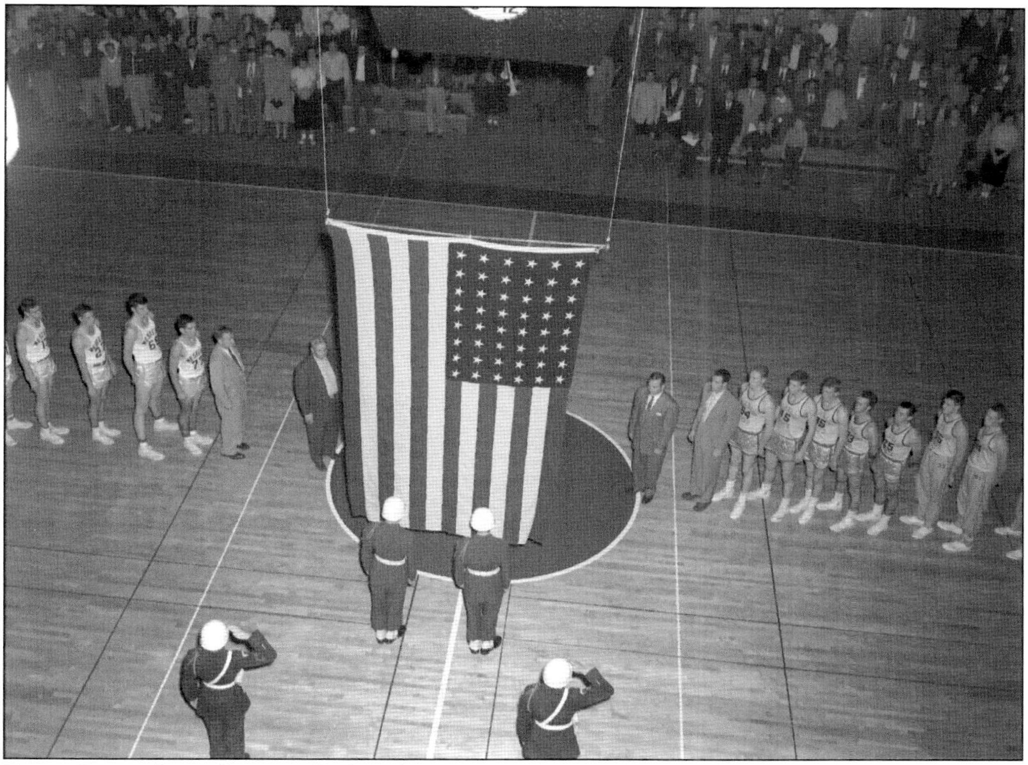

FORTY-EIGHT STAR SALUTE. Before this 1954 Western State College basketball game, athletes, fans, and military representatives paused to salute their nation's then-48-star flag. Coach E. A. Diddle (left of the flag), himself of Red Towel fame, was standing at attention, ready to salute.

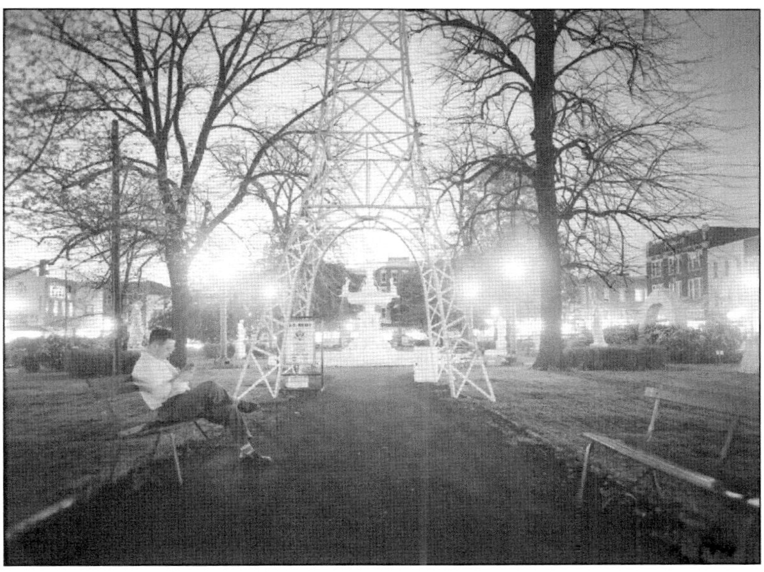

LA VIE FRANÇAIS. After World War I, the children of Bowling Green and Warren County collected $500 to erect a monument to those brave doughboys who had fought and died. Originally in Fountain Square Park, the tower now stands in Fairview Cemetery, a poignant marker for the graves of the fallen military men and women.

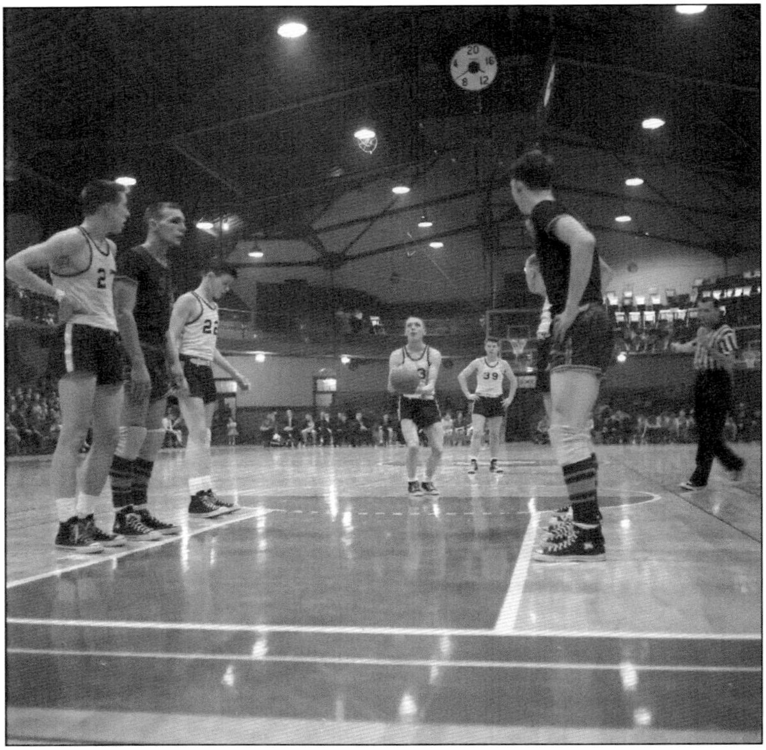

KENTUCKY'S FAVORITE SPORT. The Bowling Green Purples took it to the hoop in this 1954 game held in the Gymnasium and Physical Education Building on the campus of Western State College (current site of Western Kentucky University's Margie Helm Library). Classic high-top Chuck Taylor Converse shoes and striped tube socks were the uniform of the day for these Purple athletes.

FOOTBALL FEVER. Even a cold Kentucky day in 1955 could not keep Nancy Boyd Hammond (left), Mary Lou Taylor (center), and Nona Taylor from enjoying a football game on the hill. A thermos of hot cocoa, a stadium blanket, and ear muffs kept the cold at bay, while Big Red fever kept their hearts racing.

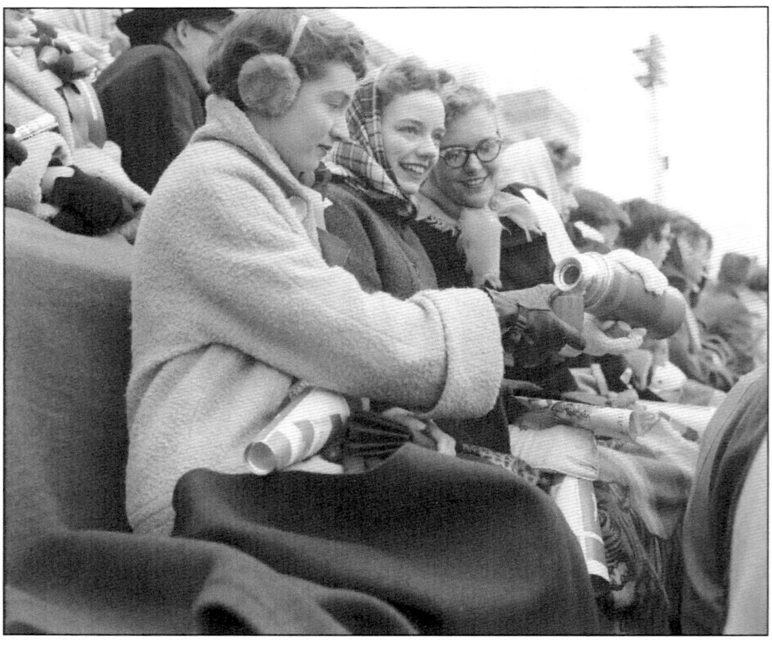

Passion Play. Dorothy Raymer (left) was joyfully airborne and Deloris Tabor Gilliam (right) was bursting with Purple pride as they gave themselves over to the excitement of a Bowling Green High School basketball victory in 1954. Intense, passionate, and epic, Bowling Green High fans continue their school spirit legacy some five decades later.

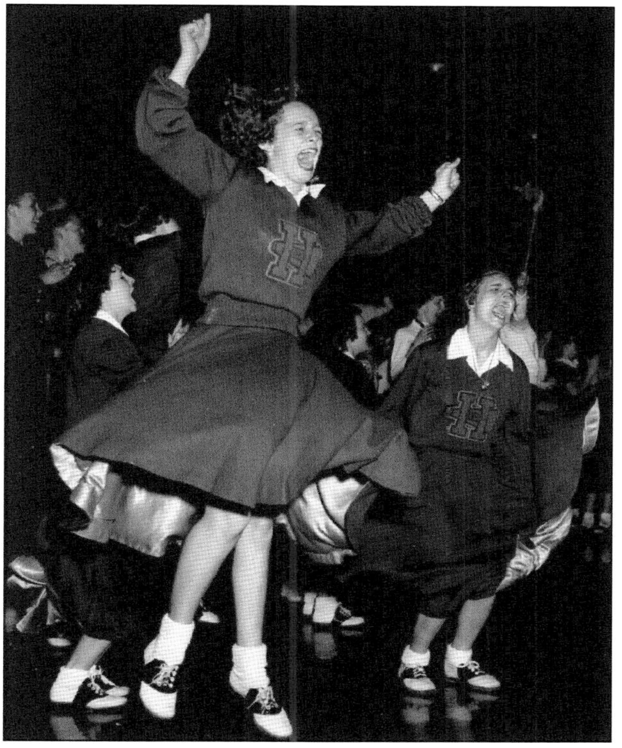

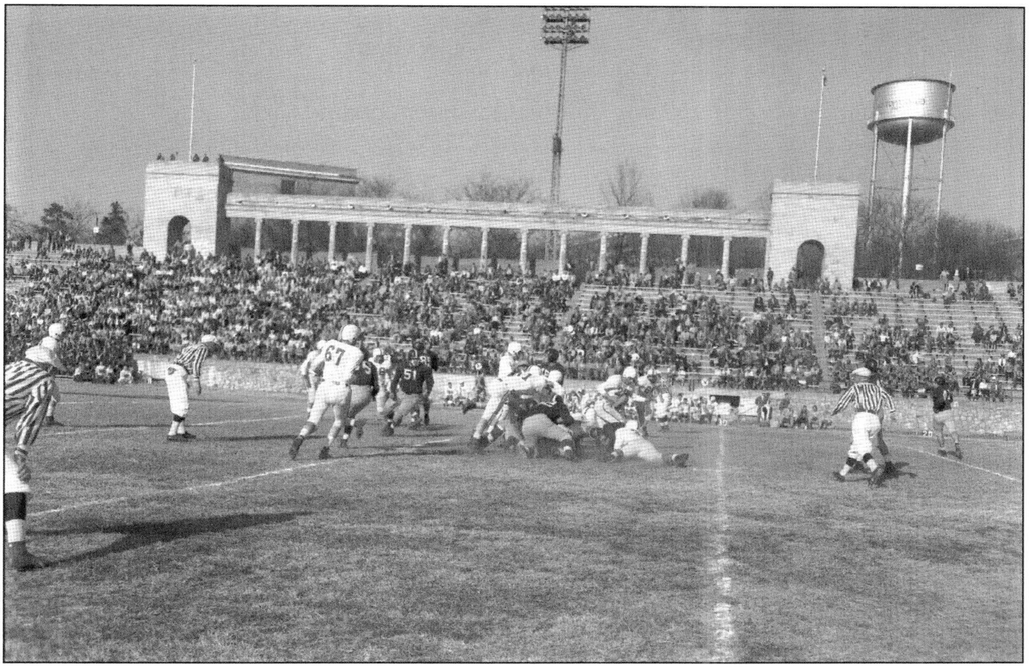

Hilltop Gladiators. These Western State College warriors did battle in the old football stadium at the top of the hill. Fans, like Roman citizens, cheered them on under the classic columns of William "Gander" Terry Colonnade.

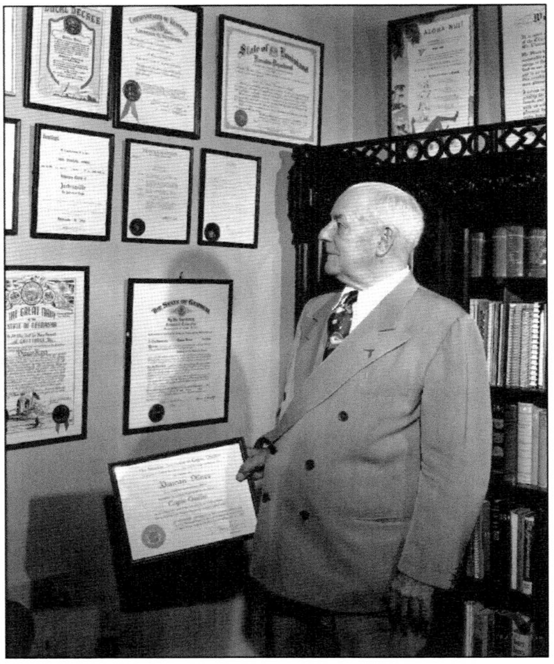

Duncan Hines. World-renowned food connoisseur Duncan Hines surveyed his many awards and proclamations in their place of honor on his office wall. A life dedicated to the culinary arts brought Hines numerous accolades, including that of Cognac Quaffer, bestowed upon him by the American Association of Cognac Quaffers.

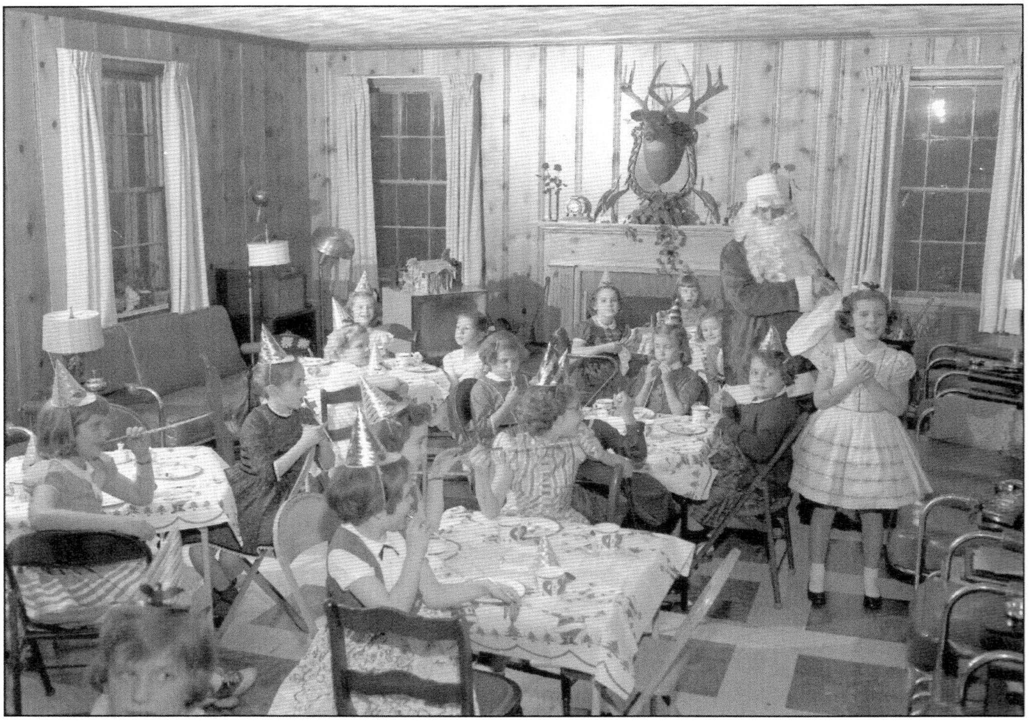

Happy Birthday with a Ho, Ho, Ho. Turning eight was a great day for Cindy Vogler Sims, as her friends gathered at her home on Durrenberger Lane for a storybook party on December 9, 1957. Complete with party hats, noisemakers, and special table settings, Sims's party was made extra special by the appearance of Santa Claus, realistically played by Mr. Emerson, a close family friend.

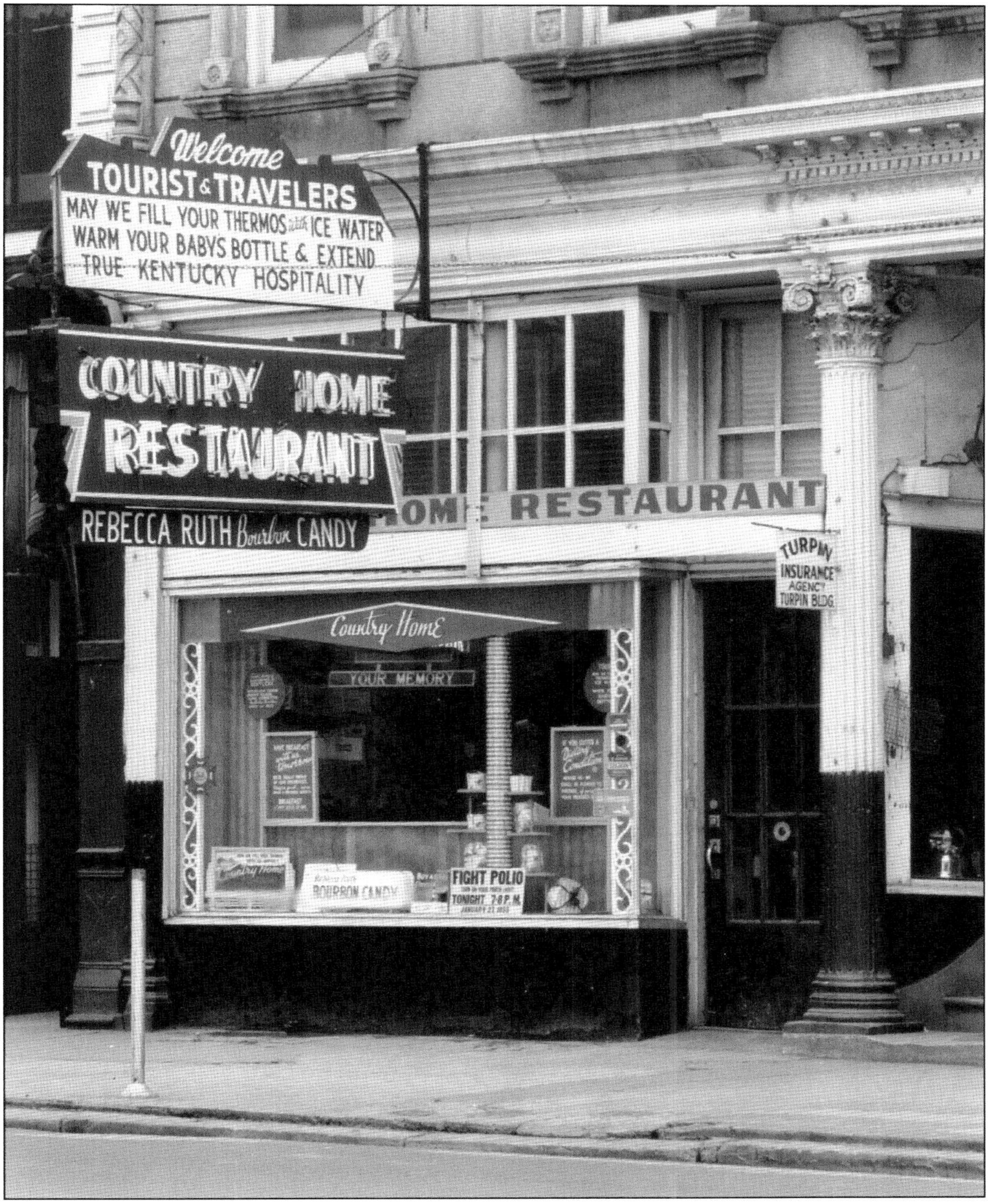

Country Home Hospitality. With a reassuring sign for weary sojourners, the Country Home Restaurant at 914 State Street welcomed all passersby with the promise of home, including a thermos of ice water for the road, a baby's bottle warmed for feeding time, and down home Kentucky hospitality that enticed travelers to stay a while. On a cold January 27, 1955, owners Paul and Maude Schmidt served up hot meals and, in a prominently placed window sign, urged fellow citizens to take a stand against polio by turning on their porch lights from 7:00–8:00 p.m., creating a collective community of light to ward off the darkness of this debilitating disease.

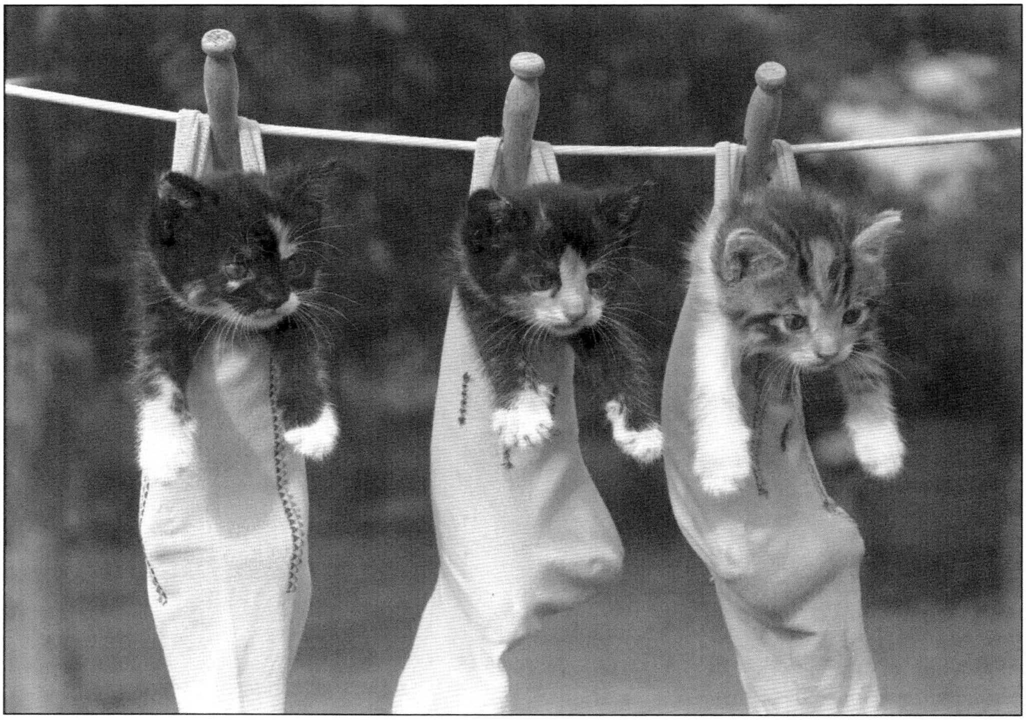

Three Little Kittens. Three little kittens handily hung around in these 1950s cross-stitched stockings. Wooden clothespins and a clothesline were a must-have for most laundresses of the day, but the kittens were an added bonus for this happy homemaker.

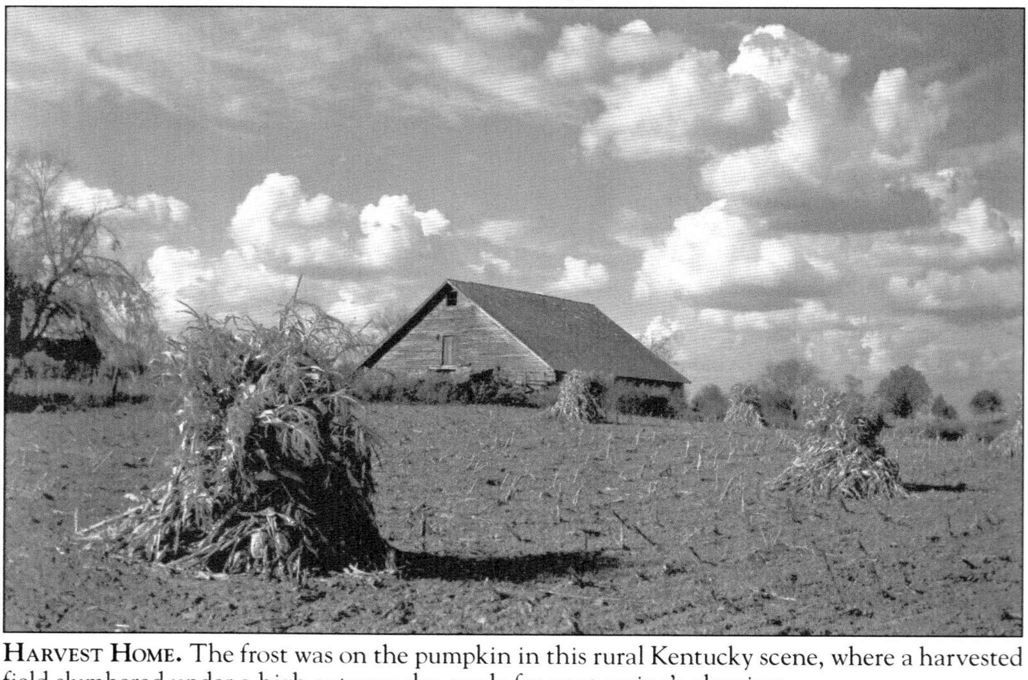

Harvest Home. The frost was on the pumpkin in this rural Kentucky scene, where a harvested field slumbered under a high autumn sky, ready for next spring's planting.

Two

THE 1960S
BLOWING IN THE WIND

The winds of change blew wide and strong across America in the 1960s. The election of Pres. John F. Kennedy heralded a new day, the rise of Martin Luther King Jr. to national prominence and to national influence made real, lasting equality palpable, and the steady movement of American women out of the kitchen and into the workforce forever changed the way the American family functioned.

Bowling Green's response to national shifts was perhaps a step or two behind. The decade began with little fanfare and no overtly noticeable departure from previous years. Women still wore hats and heels to the grocery store, white males continued to make most decisions for the community, and social encounters were conducted with the expected starch of formality.

But even sheltered as it was on the banks of the Barren River in the rolling hills of the Pennyroyal Plateau, Bowling Green began to twitch and tingle with growing pains. Plans were laid and construction begun on Interstate 65, a multilane thoroughfare that put Bowling Green on the interstate map and changed the way America traveled. The city commission reorganized local government in recognition of growing administrative needs, and a section of rural Nashville Road was rezoned for a sleek new shopping mall.

The random calls of a selective service lottery spilled Bowling Green blood in Asian lands, while the needs of the hungry and the violent explosions of the angry consumed local energies. Manufacturing moguls found Bowling Green to be a profitable location with a plentiful and willing workforce, while a hilltop educational mecca continued its transformation into a regionally recognized university.

In many ways, the 1960s were years of preparation for Bowling Green, as the town focused on its own public and private recovery from national and local wounds, the celebration of wedding vows spoken, the mourning of lives lost, the setting of goals, and the laying of plans. In an era that embraced the innocence of *Captain Kangaroo* and the biting sexual satire of *Laugh-In*, the people of Bowling Green held on to each other and to their hope in the future, and photographer Tommy Hughes was there, ever ready to capture their many faces and their many moods.

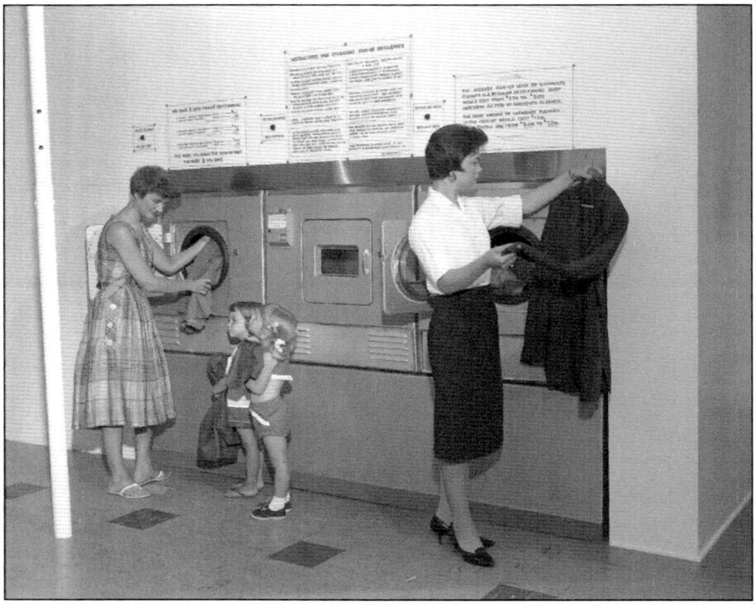

Wash Day. These little girls were happy mother's helpers on wash day at the Edgehill Washette and Diaper Service, a coin-operated laundry, dry cleaner, and diaper service located in the Edgehill Shopping Center at 1615 Russellville Road. Owners Harold Huffman and Erle Duff made the most of every mother's wish for sparkling white cloth diapers and the latest in laundry technology.

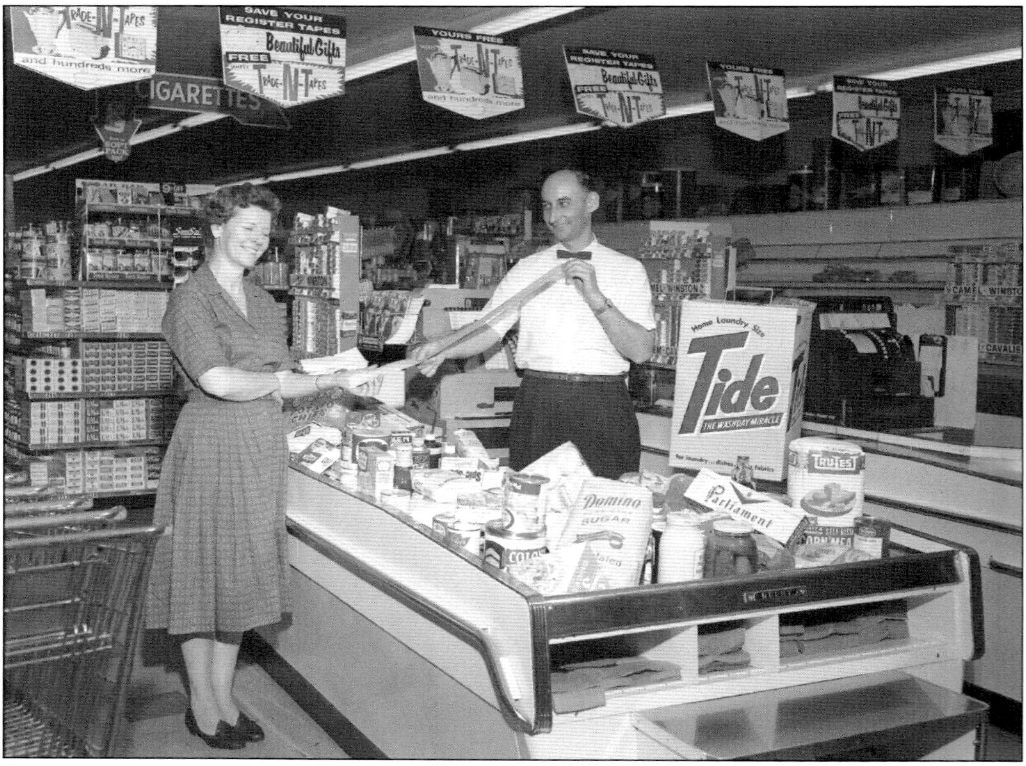

Shoppers' Paradise. Lester Reeves, proprietor of Reeves Food Center at 709 Laurel Avenue, showed the lucky winner of a June 1, 1961, 10-minute shopping spree the value of her prize. A local entrepreneur, Reeves was known to have whatever the discriminating homemaker might need and to allow shoppers "to buy just one if you needed just one," no matter the packaged quantity.

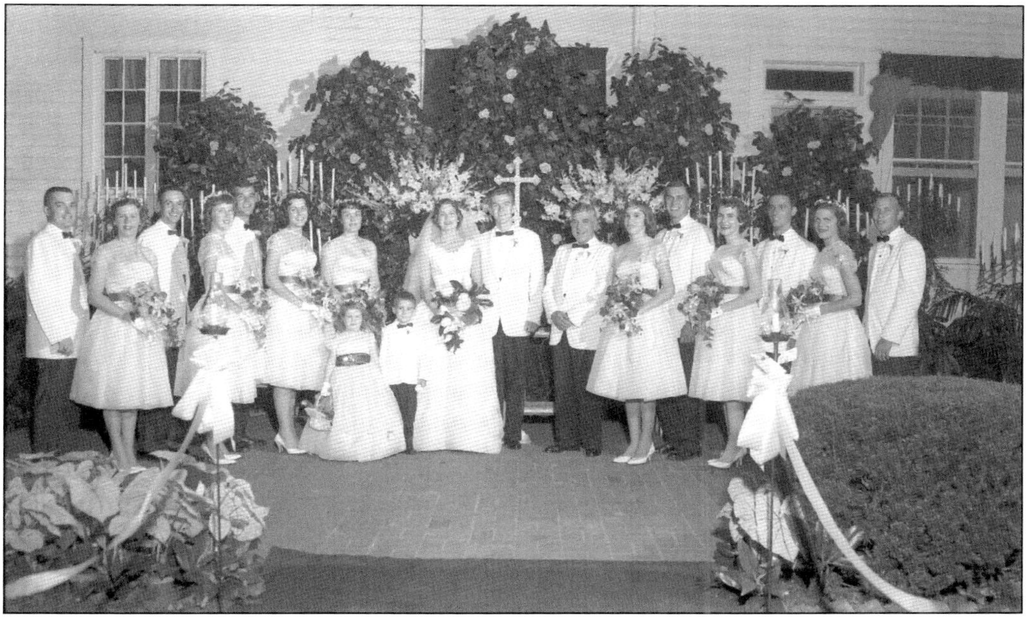

Magnolia Blossom Memories. Ann Whitaker Moore and Lt. Henry Harris Pepper were well attended by friends and family at their July 2, 1960, marriage. Celebrated at 8:30 p.m. at Forty Acres, home of the bride's parents on Cemetery Road, the service was performed by Rev. Henry Howard Surface Jr., rector of Christ Episcopal Church. Candlelight, fresh flowers, a tiered wedding cake, and lovely silver punch service made this a true Southern wedding.

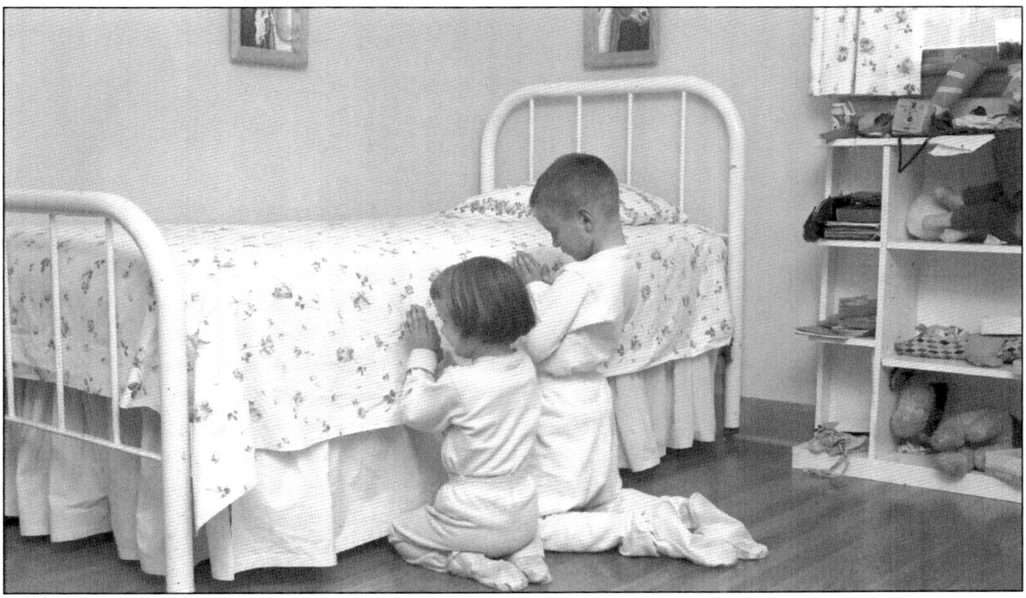

"Now I Lay Me Down to Sleep." Patty (age three) and Chuck (age six) Hanes said a special bedtime prayer in this October 4, 1963, Warren County Tuberculosis Association advertisement photograph. Tuberculosis, a once common and deadly disease known as the "White Plague," was far reaching and debilitating. The Tuberculosis Association was locally active in fund-raising and research efforts and remains active today as the American Lung Association.

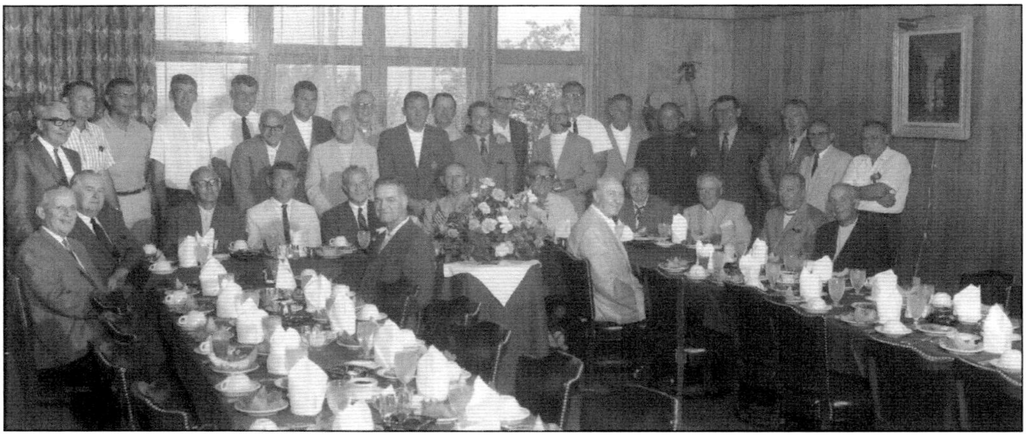

The Liars Club. Although they were formally attired and seriously posed, the walls of the Bowling Green Country Club could certainly tell some tall tales and fascinating yarns shared by this friendly bunch of liars on June 7, 1969. Ready to tell some big ones are, from left to right, (first row) Kelly Thompson, unidentified, Frank Moore, Sam Potter, J. C. "Hoot" Holland, Kenny Wallace, Herschel Webb, J. David Francis, Wally McGinley, Gilbert Biggers, Roy Gaddie, unidentified, and Everett Moore; (second row) Tom Gilbert, Harper Wright, Rich Jackel, Burt Borrone, Houston Griffin, Scott McLean, Monie Beard, Mitchell Leitchardt, unidentified, Murray Hill, Bennie Beach, Jack Moore, unidentified, Chester Hock, unidentified, Roland Fitch, Hillary Carroll, two unidentified, Al "Bro" Dodd, and Jim Hendrix.

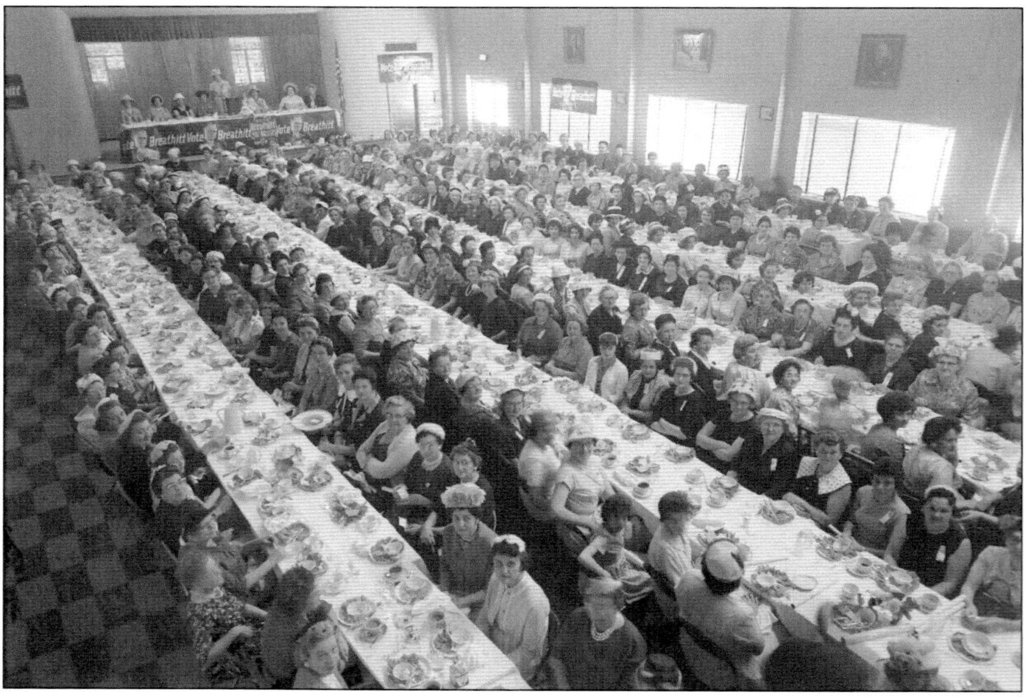

Bonnets for Breathitt. Over 500 ladies lunched and listened at a political rally for gubernatorial candidate Edward T. (Ned) Breathitt on April 19, 1963, at the Moose lodge. Frances Breathitt, keynote speaker and wife of the candidate, addressed the gathering modeling a new spring hat, which was later awarded to lucky winner Dorothy Bartlett.

DEMOCRATIC GRANDE DAMES. Kathryn Bartelt (center) and state Women's Democratic Club officers displayed their donkey pins with dignity at the Women's Democratic Luncheon at Western Hills Restaurant on September 6, 1962. The menu of the day included such fine fare as New Deal tossed salad, buttered Kennedy asparagus, and hot Southern Democratic biscuits, as the ladies of Bowling Green dined in true democratic style.

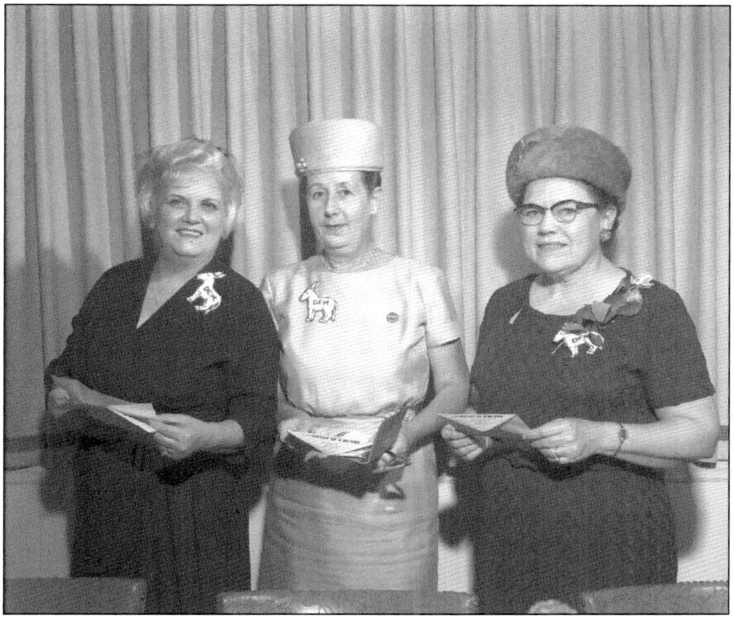

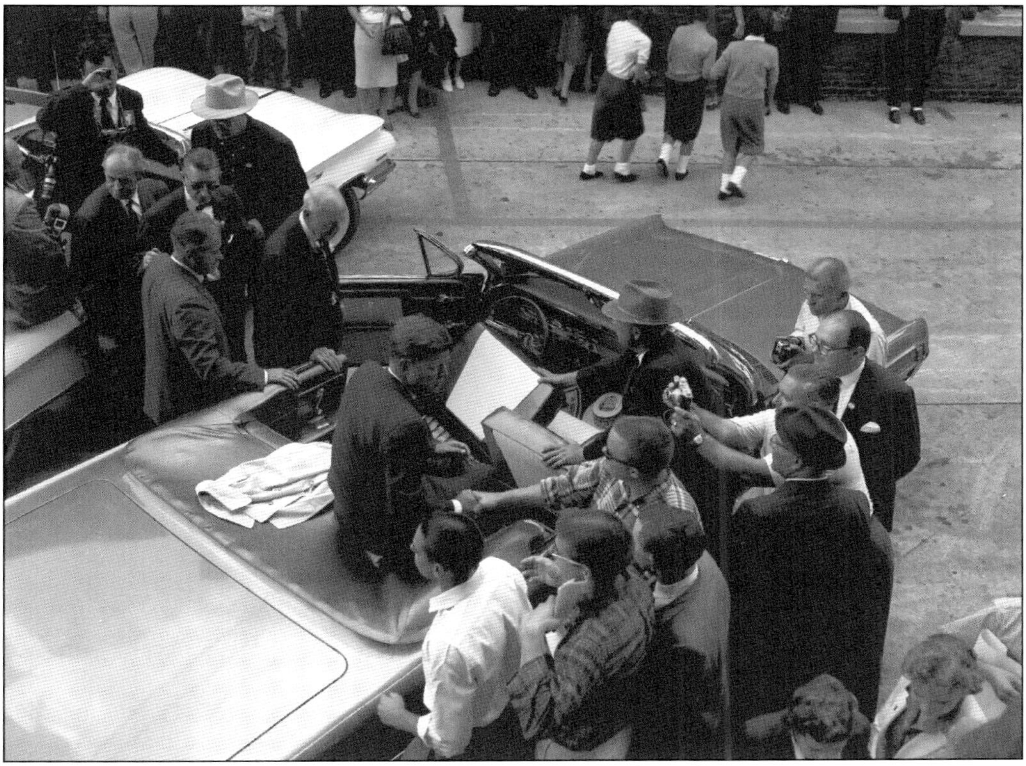

PROFILE IN COURAGE. Presidential candidate John F. Kennedy made an open-air campaign stop in downtown Bowling Green on October 8, 1960. The ever accessible, ever approachable Kennedy shook supporters' hands and chatted with bystanders as he made his way across America in his ultimately successful bid for the White House.

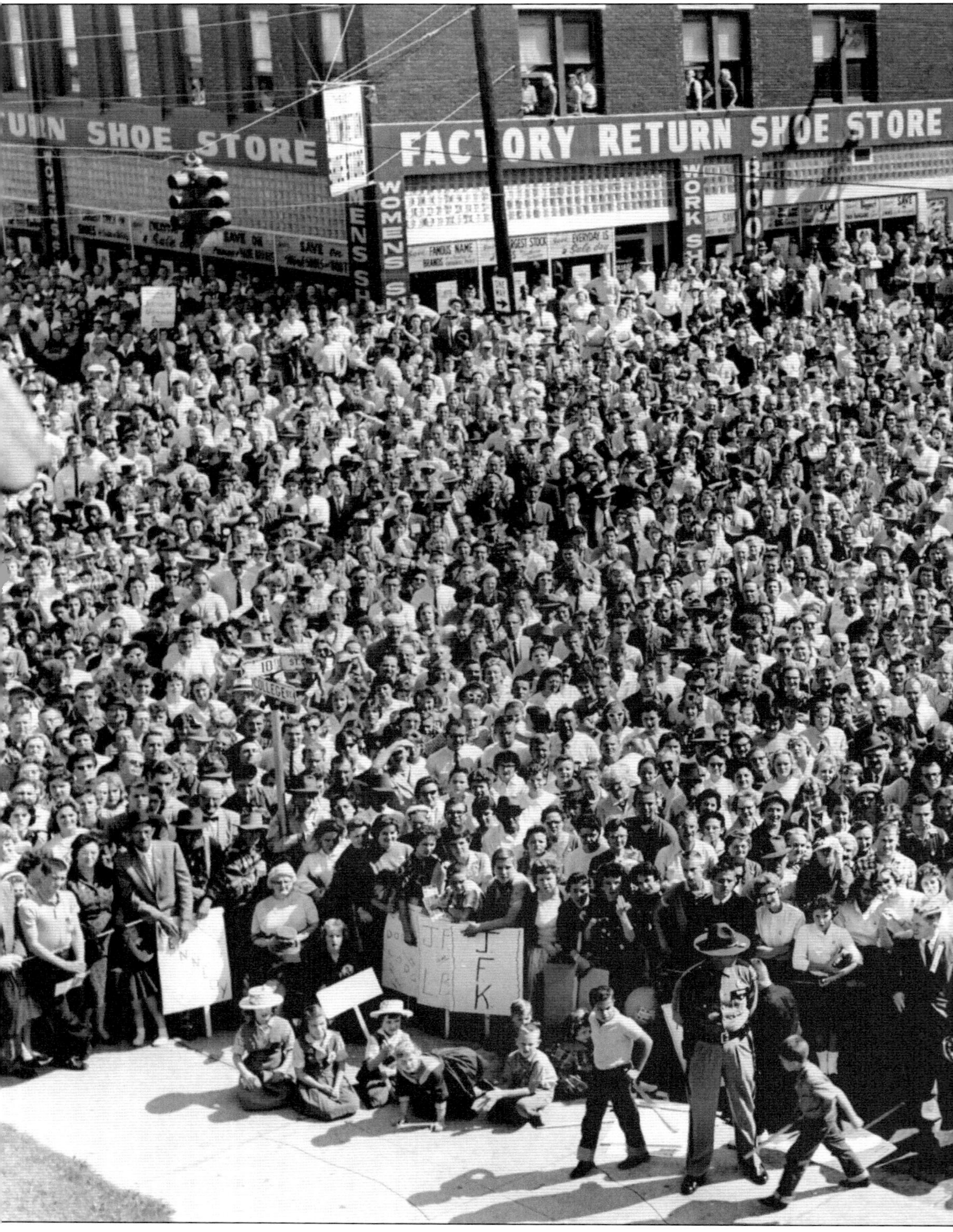
URN SHOE STORE
FACTORY RETURN SHOE STORE
WOMENS SH
WORK SH
FAMOUS NAME BRANDS
EVERYDAY IS a Sale day
10th St
COLLEGE
JFK

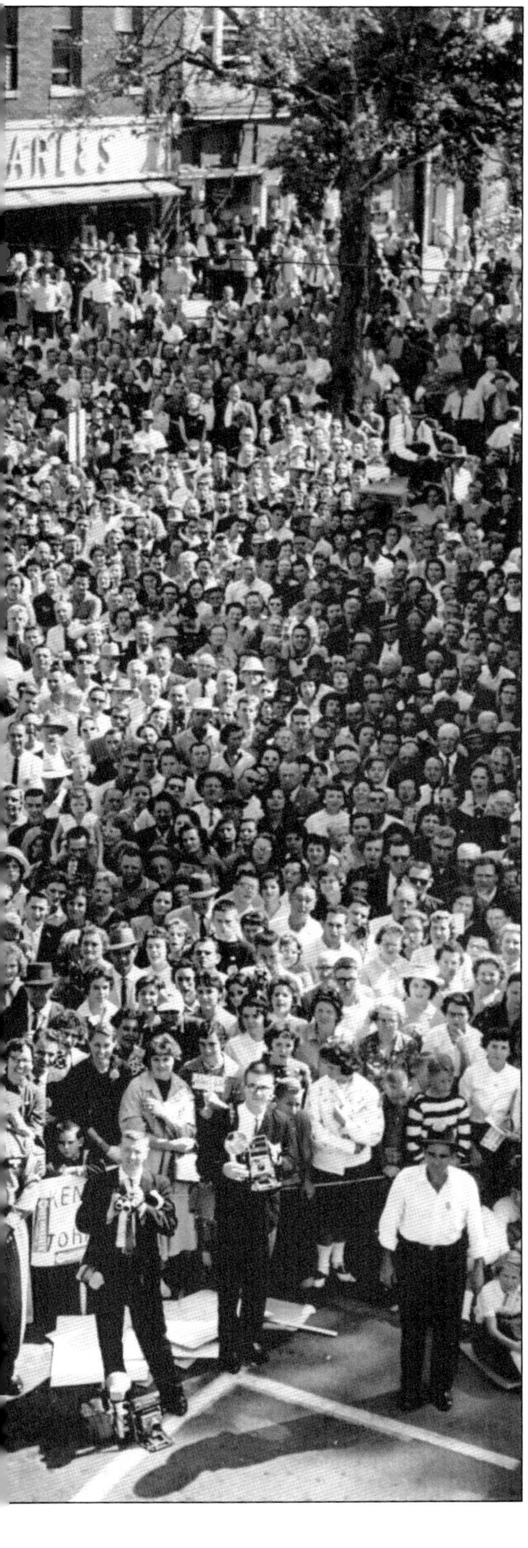

Camelot Came to Town. Thousands of Bowling Green citizens crowded into Fountain Square Park in downtown Bowling Green on a sunny October 8, 1960, to hear presidential candidate John F. Kennedy. They could not have known the historic magnitude of this moment nor of their part in making history. They came in record numbers to hear a striking young man from Massachusetts, a man whose clipped eastern accent may have sounded odd to their southern ears. Hand-lettered signs and a handful of Kentucky state troopers were the only indications that this gathering was political in nature. When Kennedy took the podium on the balcony at Bowling Green City Hall, looking out at the faces of those who would soon become his constituents, photographer Tommy Hughes (far right, front row) was there to capture the moment. (Courtesy of the *Courier-Journal*.)

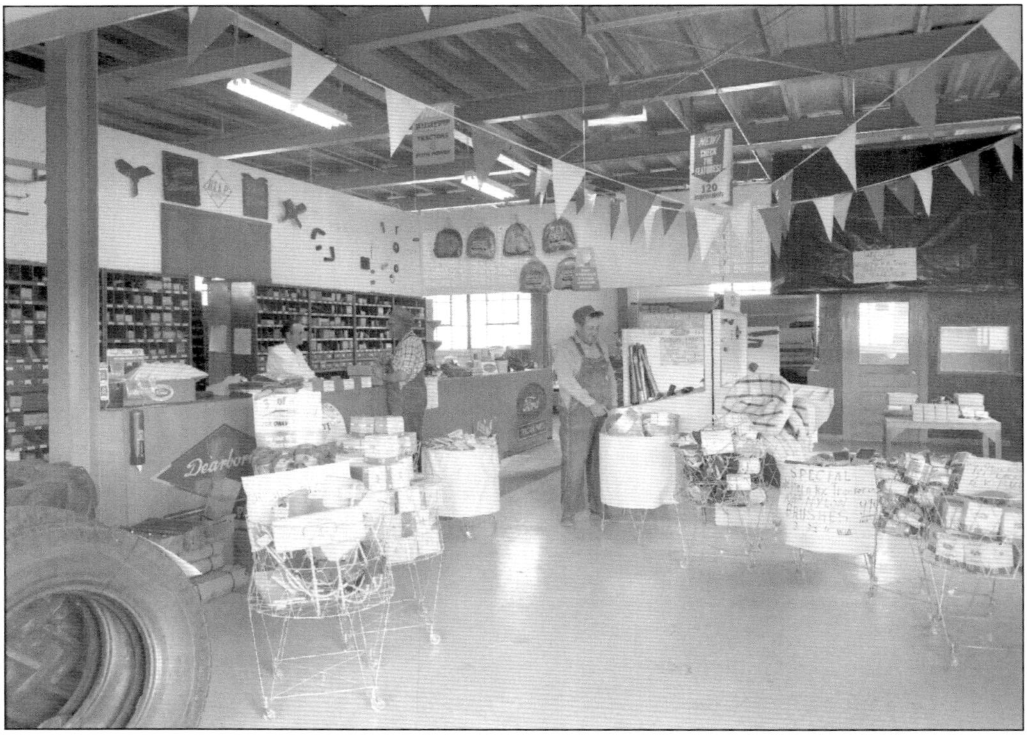

Farmers Market. Western Kentucky Tractor Company on Old Louisville Road supplied area farmers with a variety of parts, tools, and necessary equipment. On April 3, 1963, overall-clad farmers could purchase a 9-by-12 tarpaulin for a bargain price of $4.50 or the latest in Ford tractor parts to maximize "plow power."

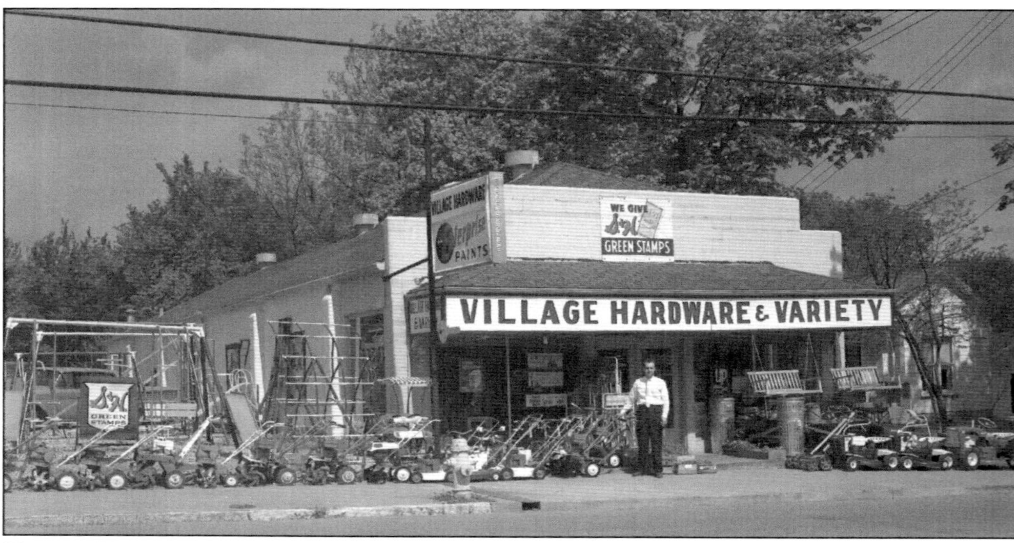

Village Variety. Hargis' Village Hardware and Variety at 840 Broadway was the place to shop for all one's household needs. On May 10, 1961, Kermit Hargis touted his wide inventory of giftware, sporting goods, playground equipment, and paint, as well as porch swings, lawn mowers, and, for enterprising homemakers with books to fill, S&H Green Stamps.

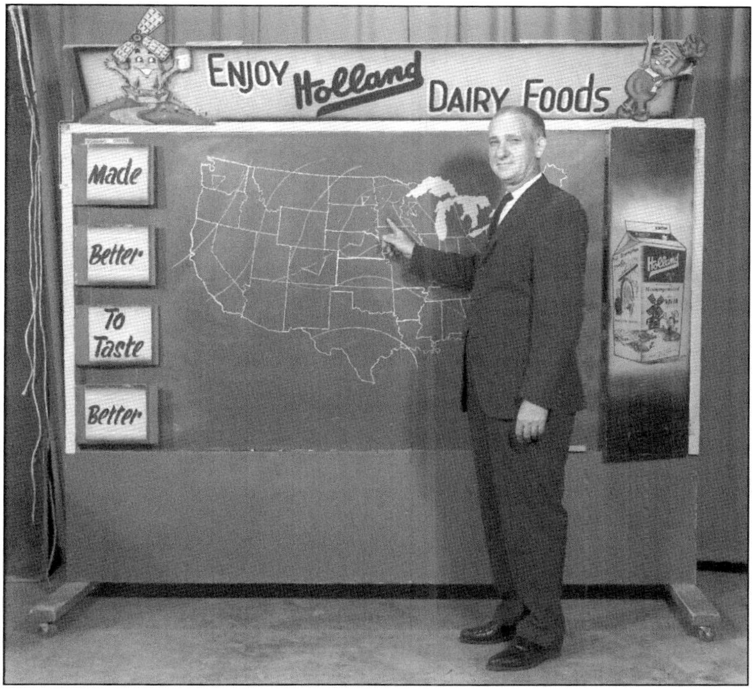

Wise Weatherman. Willard Cockrill, weatherman at WLTV studio on Morgantown Road, kept a sharp eye on ever-changing fronts as he charted the October 16, 1963, forecast on a chalkboard weather map. Far before computers and Doppler radar, Cockrill used chalk and an eraser to keep viewers informed, making a steady hand a must-have requirement for weathermen of the day.

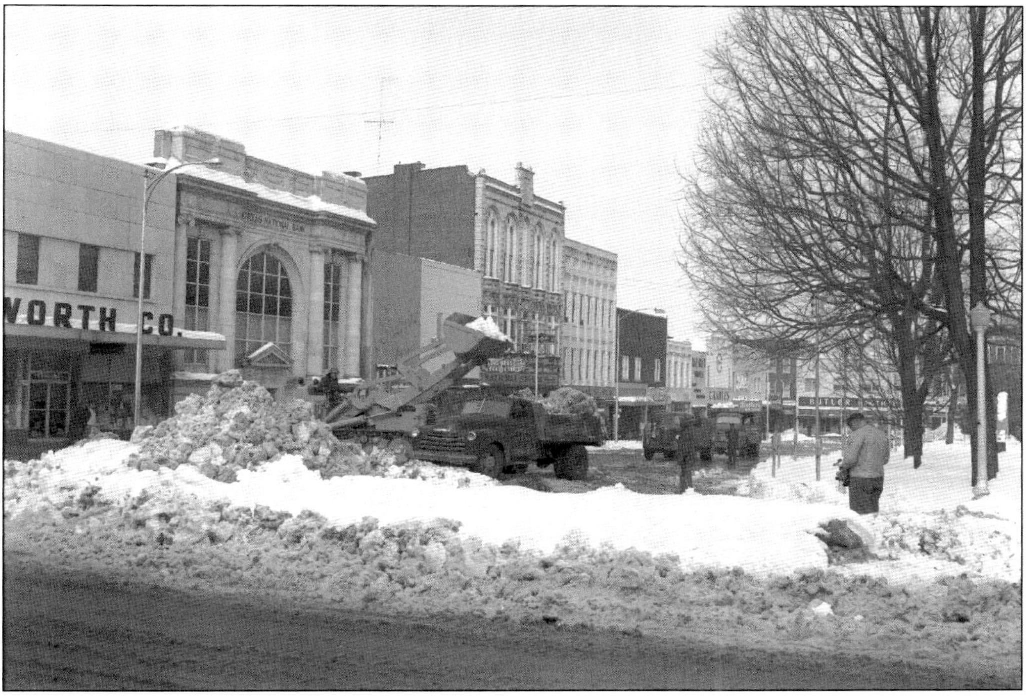

Buttercup Snow. Much of Bowling Green was shut down by the springtime surprise of almost 24 inches of snow on March 10, 1960. Hip boots were a necessity for men forced to walk to work, and jubilant children enjoyed several days of sledding, as the town fathers called out the National Guard with heavy equipment to get city streets moving again.

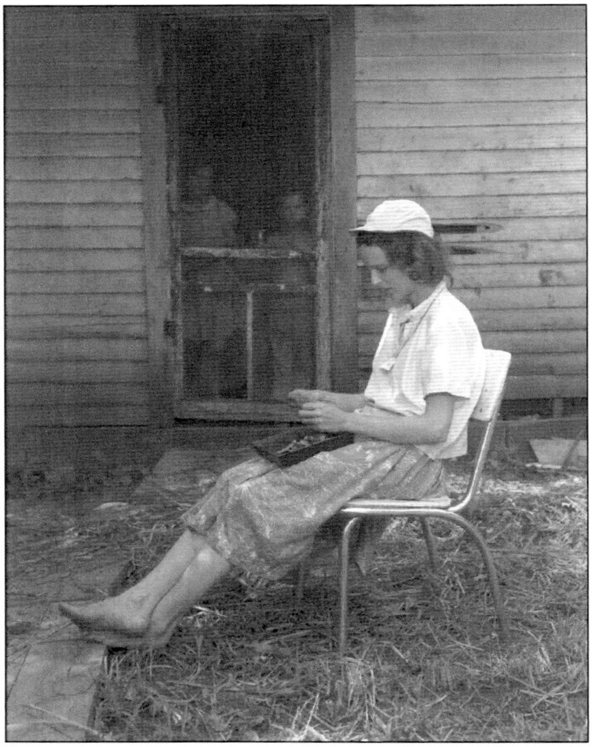

HOMEGROWN GARDEN. The Welfare Center Garden Project, established by the Welfare Center, assisted families in need by providing seeds and, if needed, tools, to plant 100 gardens for fresh summer produce. It also provided valuable vegetables to be canned for the lean winter months of 1962 and 1963. Mrs. Tom Joe Smith, director of the center, and a 26-member board chaired by Thomas L. Diemer managed the project for the center, which had an annual operating budget of $30,000. On August 8, 1962, this hard-working family was reaping the fruits of a summer's labor and looking ahead to homegrown produce for cold winter days.

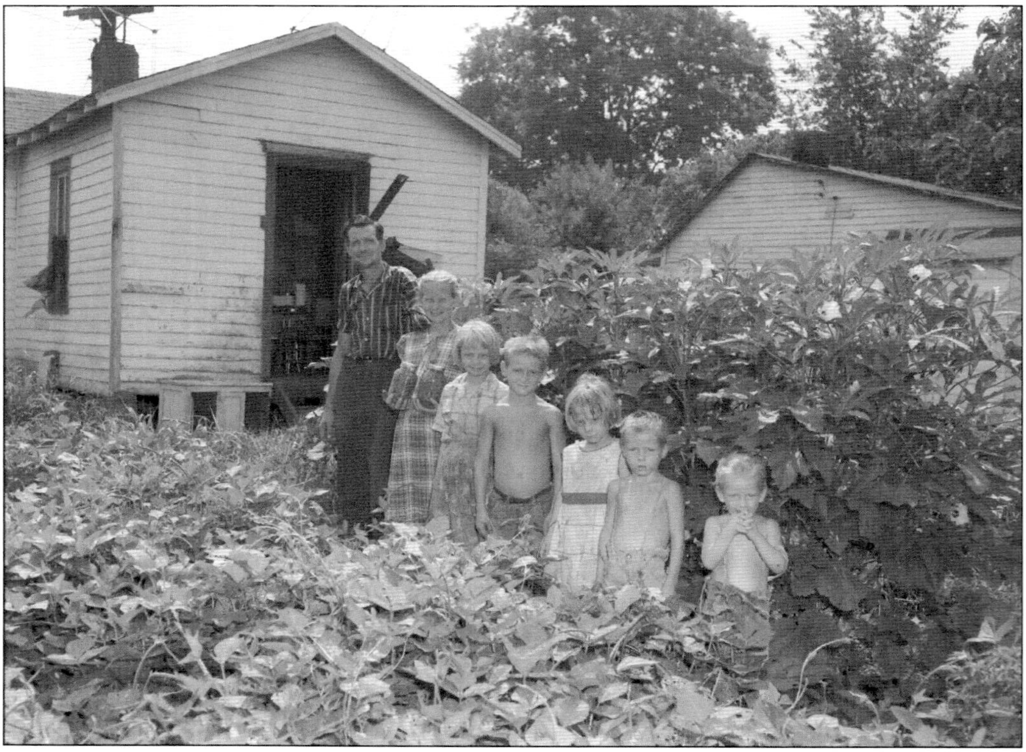

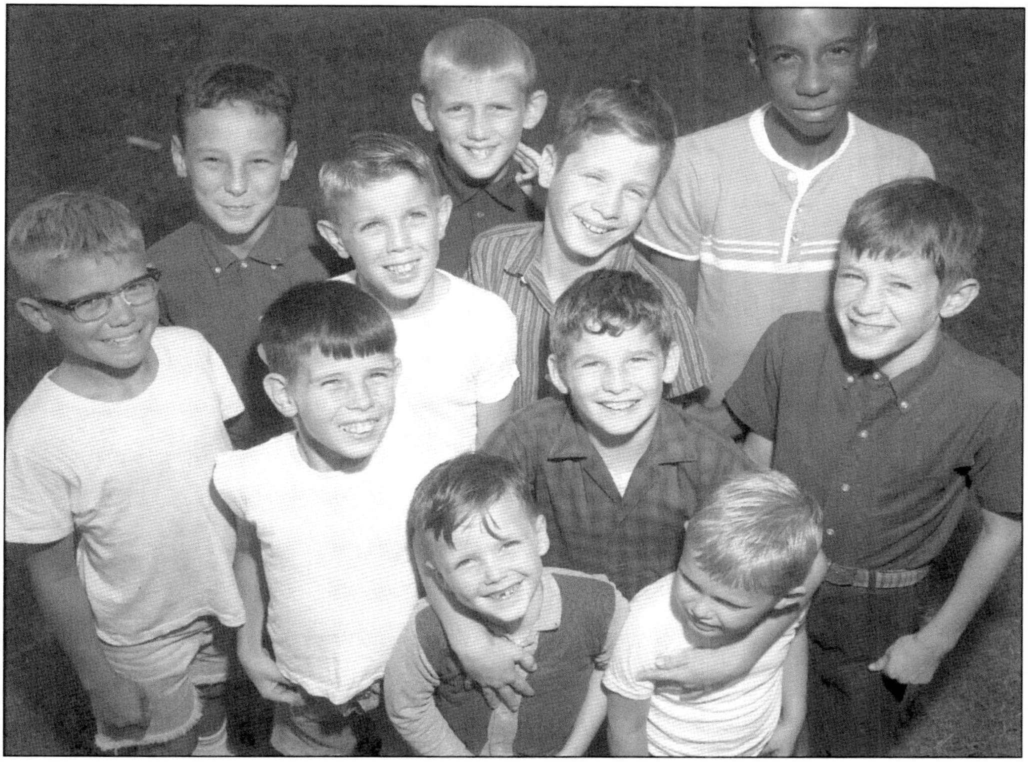

Boys' Club Buddies. The Boys' Club, under the able direction of Charles Collins and located at the end of West Eleventh Street, had a yearly attendance of over 35,000 visits from area youth and an annual budget of $13,000. On September 14, 1966, these good buddies assembled at the club for sports, games, and friendship.

Community Pride. On August 26, 1960, these ladies and children gathered together on the tidy porch of the George Washington Carver Community Center, located at Second and Center Streets. Over 200 children and adults annually engaged in educational and leisure activities, many advancing their education while creating a community of learning and of fun at the center.

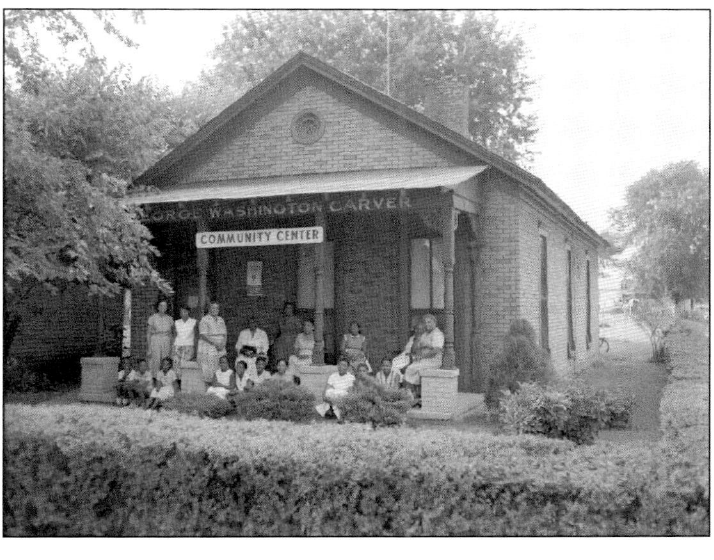

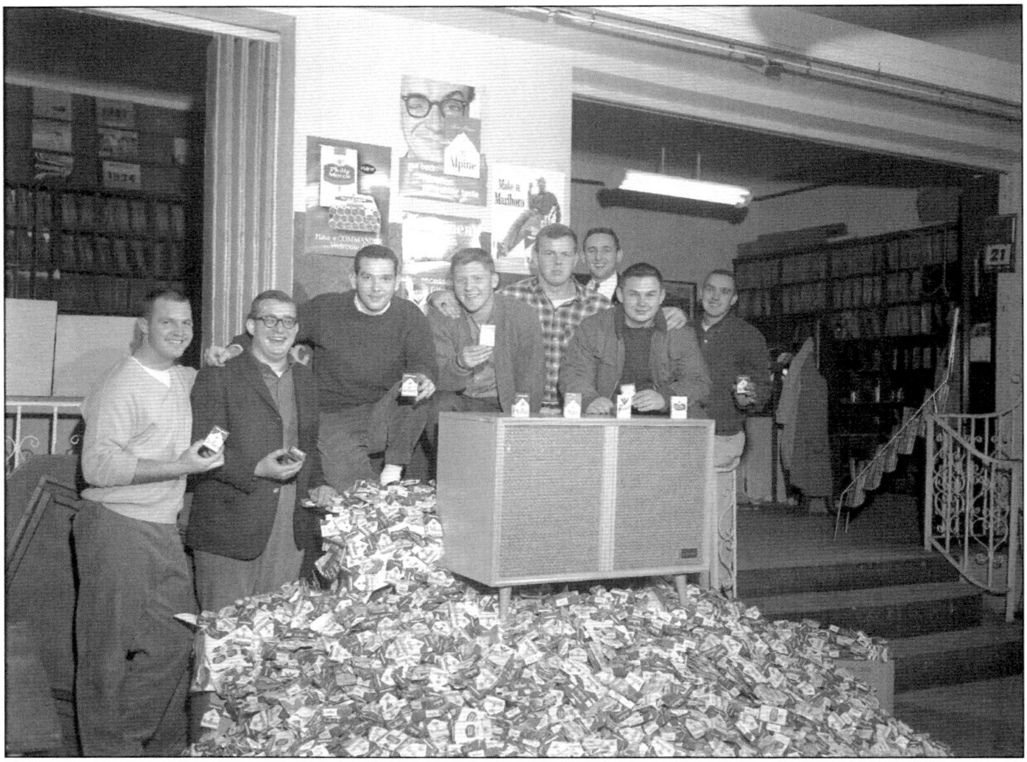

FRAT PACK. These enterprising members of Sigma Phi Alpha fraternity were the lucky winners of a January 19, 1961, giveaway sponsored by Kirby Brothers Radio and Record Shop at 1148 Center Street. From left to right, Fred Fish, Karl Weiss, Sid Parrish, Dickie Thomas, Jerry Wilder, Dickie Roberts, and Jerry Borders collected enough cigarette packs to earn the cabinet stereo given away by Kirby's for their fraternity house. (Strangely enough, the same group won a television the very next year, with a faintly familiar collection of cigarette packs.)

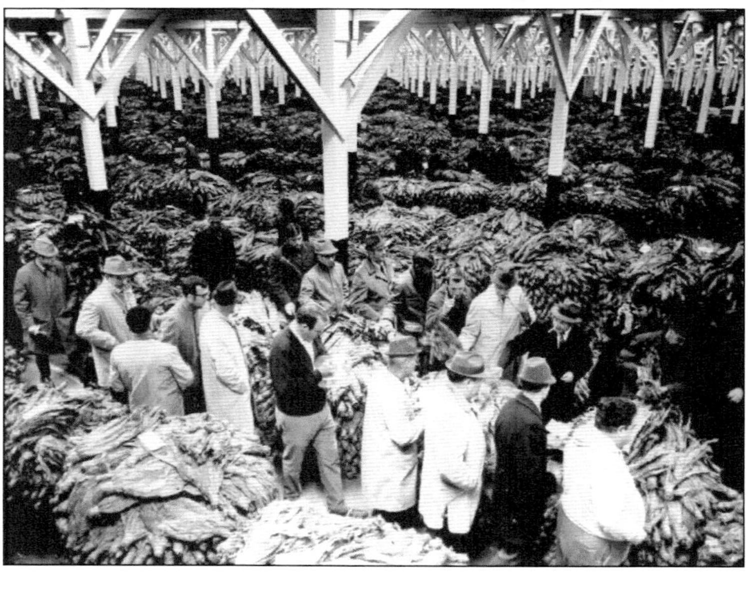

BIDDING ON BURLEY. November 29, 1966, was the middle of peak tobacco-buying season at the Bowling Green Burley Tobacco Market, where farmers came to sell and buyers came to bid on this valuable cash crop. Warren County farms produced over six million pounds of burley each year, and auction houses were hubs of financial activity with far-reaching impact.

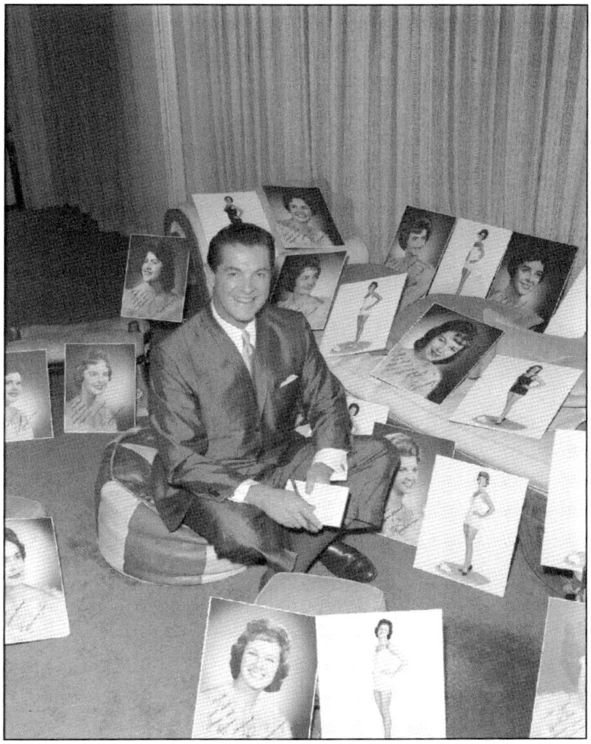

QUEEN FOR A DAY. Hollywood television star Bob Cummings was happy to serve as a judge for the Southern Kentucky Tobacco Festival queen. He selected from among these portraits of 23 southern Kentucky beauties representing 14 counties, all of whom were vying for the coveted crown, which was awarded on November 3, 1961, to Sherry Depp of Glasgow.

HOLIDAY HAPPENING. Downtown Bowling Green ushered in the holiday season with its annual Christmas parade in December 1961, when on-lookers packed the square for a glimpse of fantastic floats and feminine finery. Ladies wearing scarves securely knotted under their chins to keep out the winter chill was a sure sign of the times.

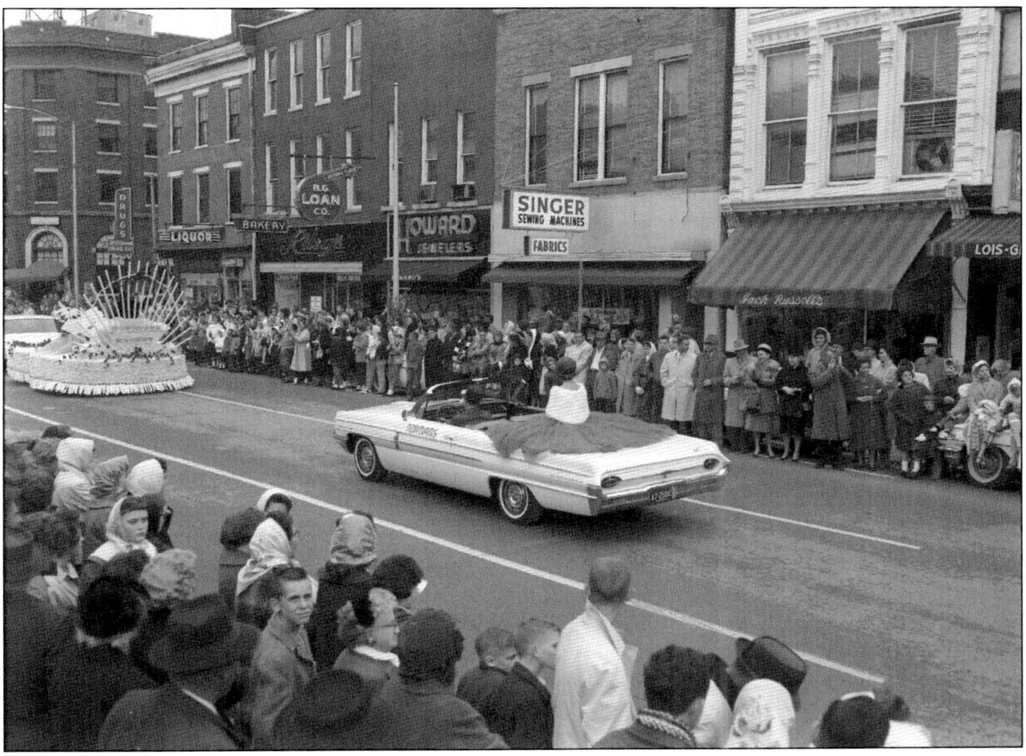

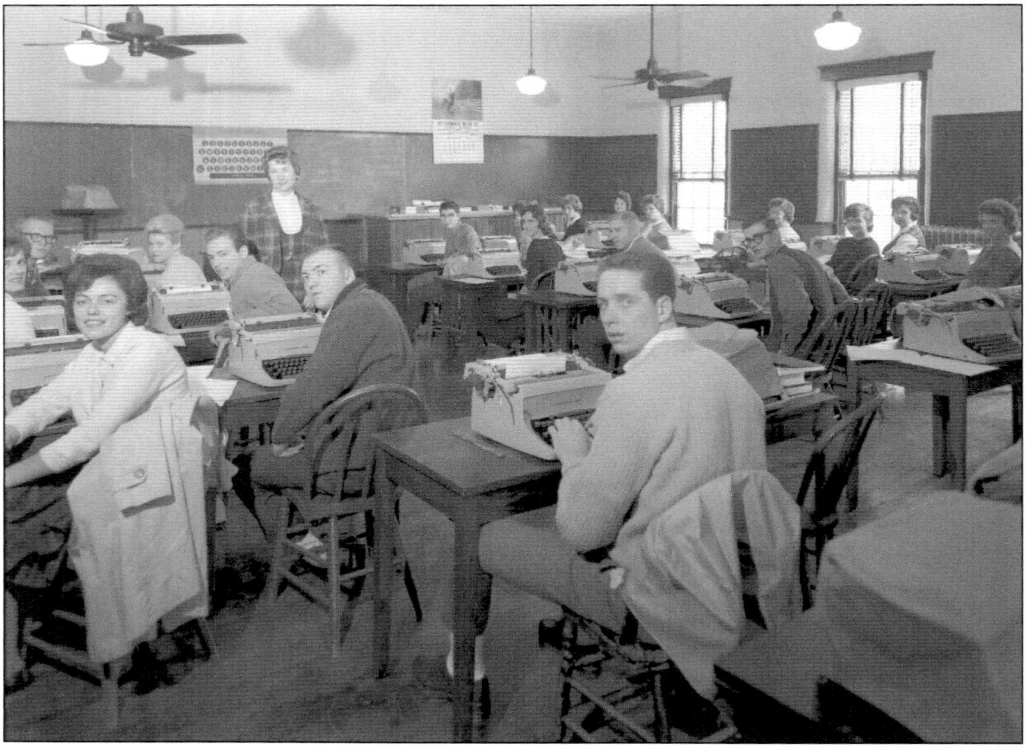

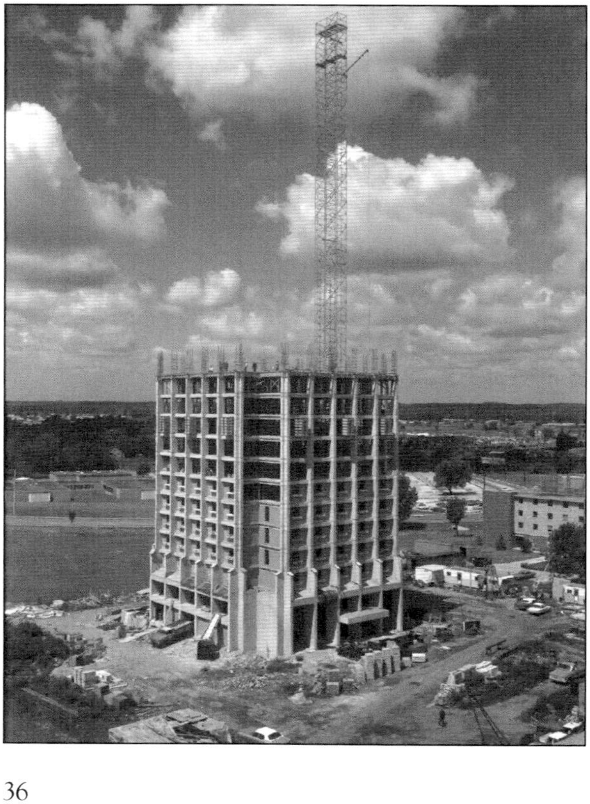

Typing 102. These industrious students had fingertips at the ready as they mastered the manual typewriter under the careful tutelage of instructor Gloria M. Young at the Bowling Green College of Commerce on October 26, 1962.

Rising High. A symbol of a new era on the hill, this October 24, 1969, photograph illustrates one of many stages in the ongoing evolution of Western Kentucky University, the construction of a new men's dormitory. Originally called Dorm No. 10, it was renamed Pearce Ford Tower. Housing hundreds of coeds each semester, Pearce Ford Tower, or "PFT," as it is locally known, remains the tallest building in Bowling Green, with a more-than-memorable Kentucky view.

Splendor in the Grass. Bowling Green College of Commerce students, with their skirts like summer flower petals, enjoyed fresh-cut watermelon slices on the lawn at this July 6, 1961, watermelon feast.

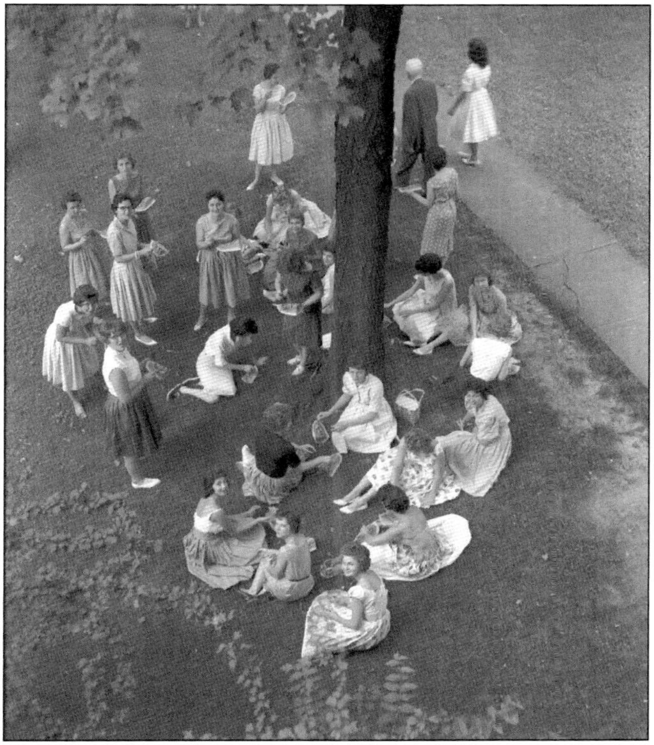

Tea and Crumpets. Afternoon tea and punch was a formal affair for these ladies. From left to right are Ann Barnes, Barbara Sowards Grider, Linda Yarberry, Rachel Allen, and two unidentified, all Bowling Green College of Commerce students. Hosted by Ruth Hill, wife of the Pres. J. Murray Hill, at their home at 1320 Park Street on September 24, 1961, the tea was an annual back-to-school event for ladies of the college.

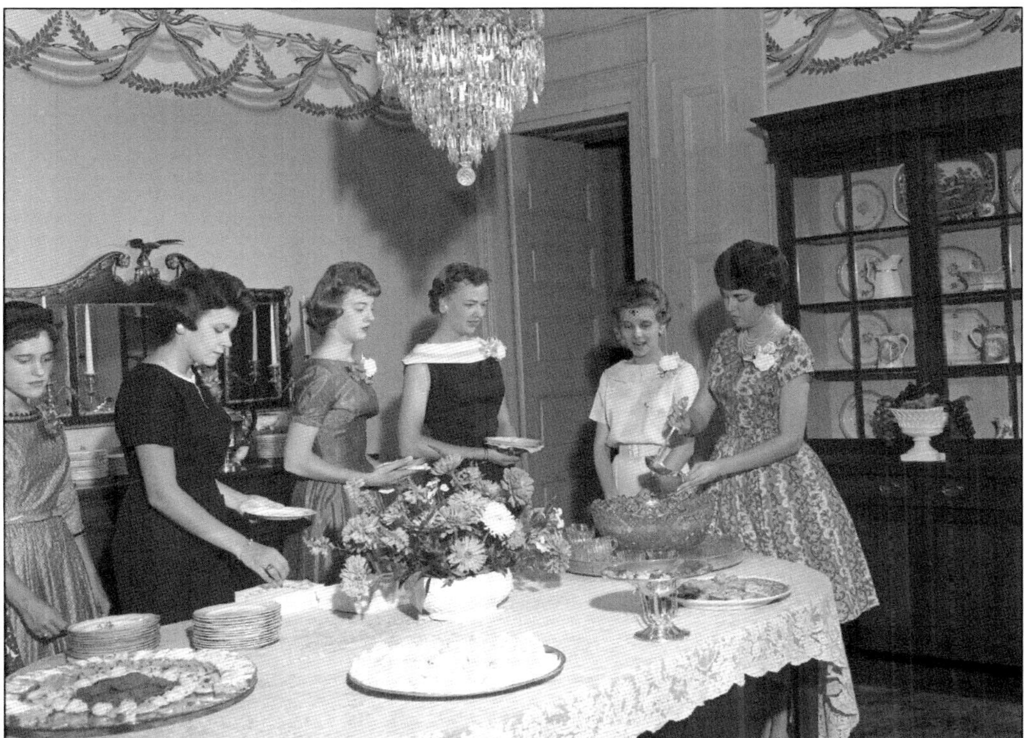

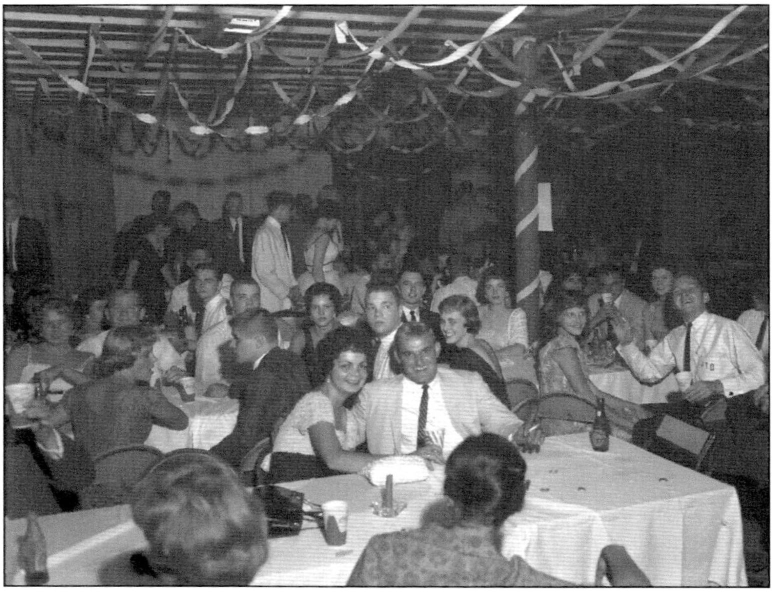

Belles of the Ball. Young men and women enjoyed a festive night at this September 24, 1960, Bowling Green Business University Hospitality Ball, held at the Moose lodge on Louisville Road. With music provided by Upton's Orchestra, the Moose lodge was "the students' place to visit" for a night of fun and, perhaps, romance.

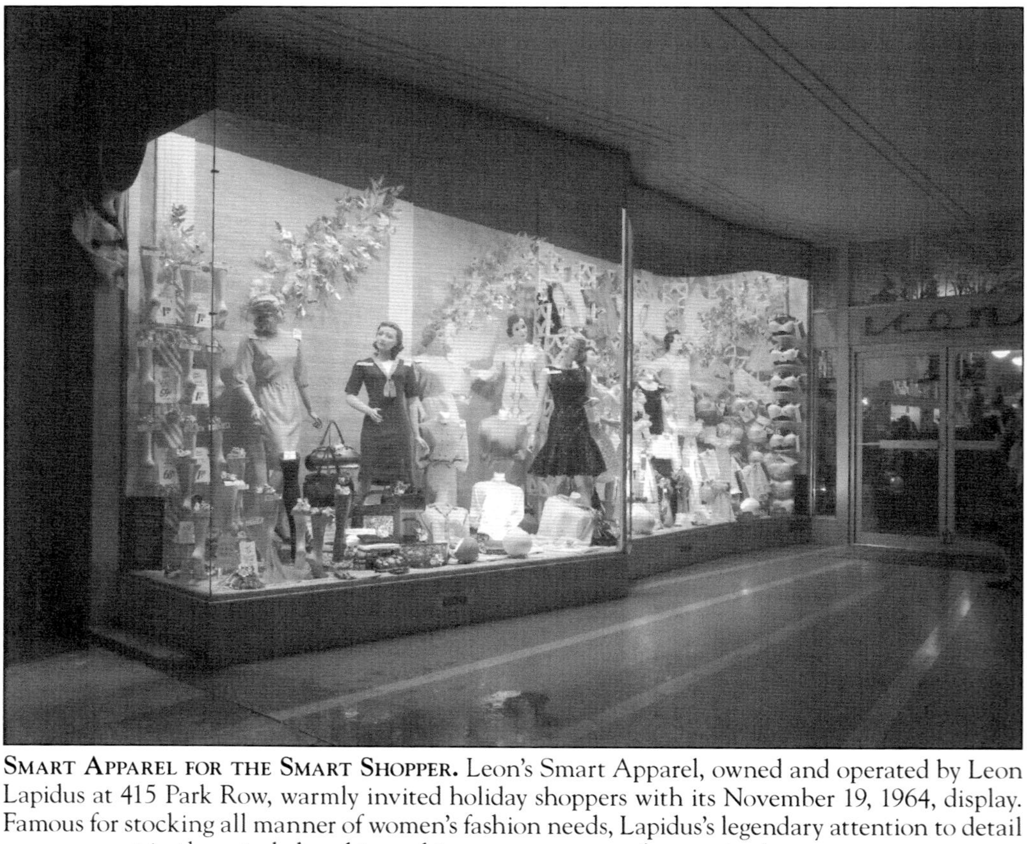

Smart Apparel for the Smart Shopper. Leon's Smart Apparel, owned and operated by Leon Lapidus at 415 Park Row, warmly invited holiday shoppers with its November 19, 1964, display. Famous for stocking all manner of women's fashion needs, Lapidus's legendary attention to detail was apparent in the crisply hand-ironed inventory on every hanger in the store.

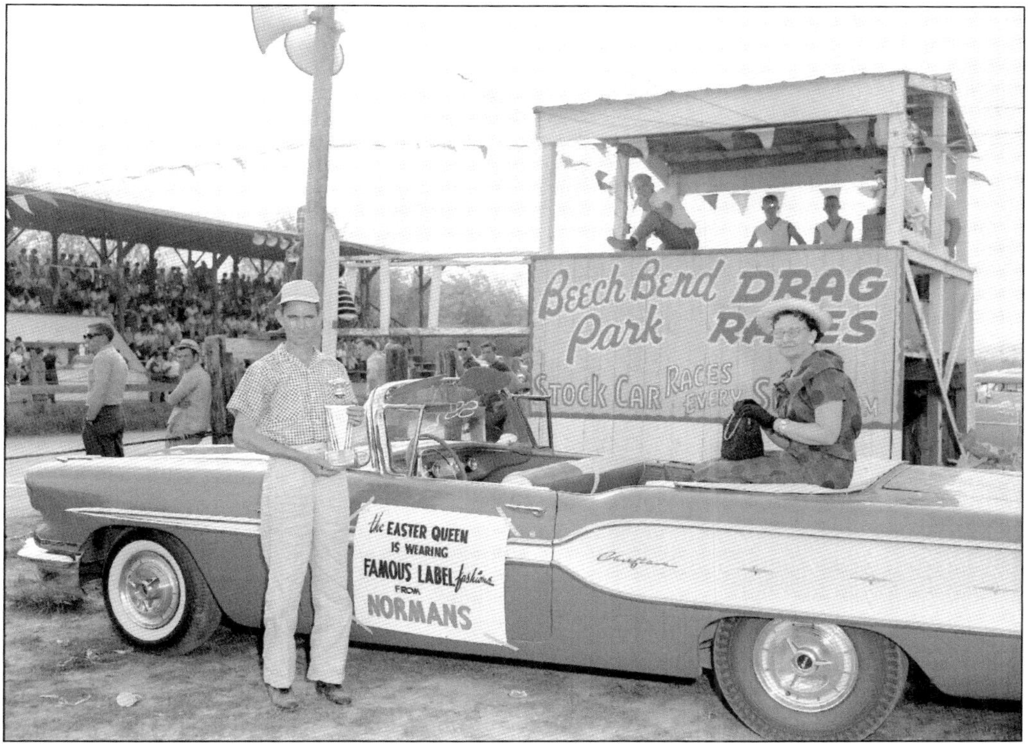

Beech Bend Beauty. On April 24, 1960, Beech Bend Park celebrated the naming of the Easter queen, presented in an open-air 1957 Pontiac convertible wearing famous-label fashions from Norman's, a ladies' shopping mecca in downtown Bowling Green. From his bird's-eye view in the press box, entrepreneur Charlie Garvin oversaw operations at the track, where Sundays were "bumper to bumper" stock car days.

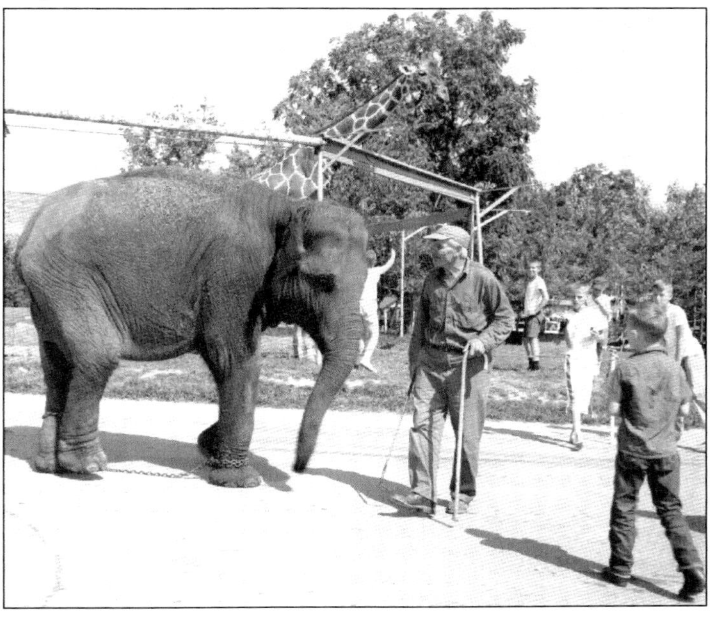

Wild Kingdom. A surprising and unusual sight in the 1960s-era rural Kentucky landscape, Beech Bend Park boasted an array of exotic animals, including demurely silent giraffes and the familiar favorite Jewel the elephant. Expertly wrangled by Ringling Brothers alumnus Sleepy Gray (center, with cane), the pleasant pachyderm seemed to relish her place as the jewel in the Beech Bend crown.

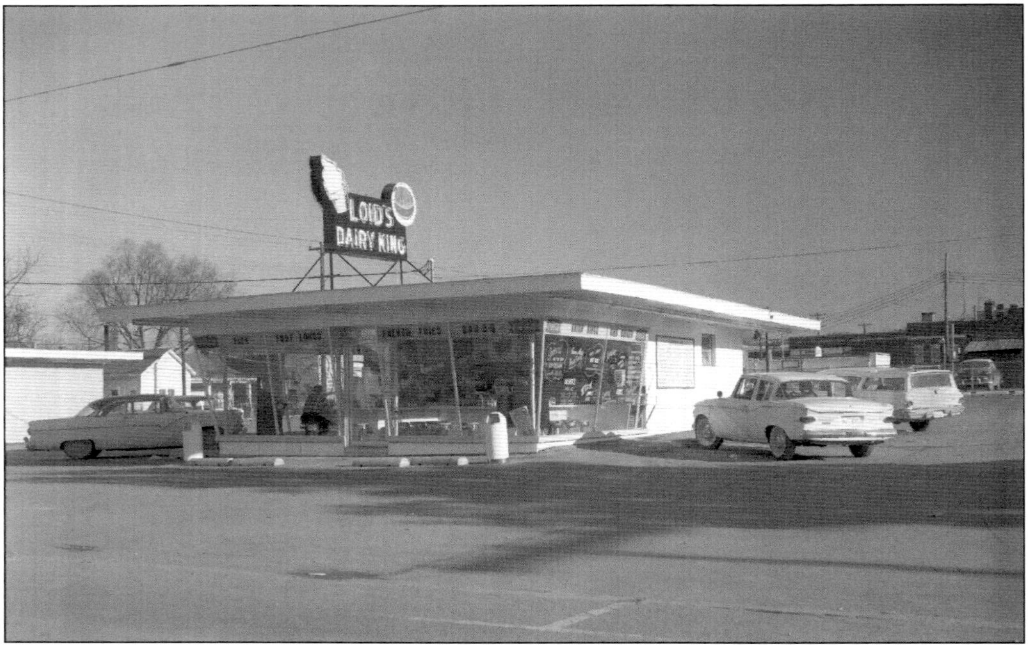

Cruising the King. After cruising the strip, a stop at Loid's Dairy King at 1601 Laurel Avenue (now U.S. 31-W Bypass) was a must. Owners John and Edna Loid served up foot-longs and fries, king burgers, and shakes to customers of all ages.

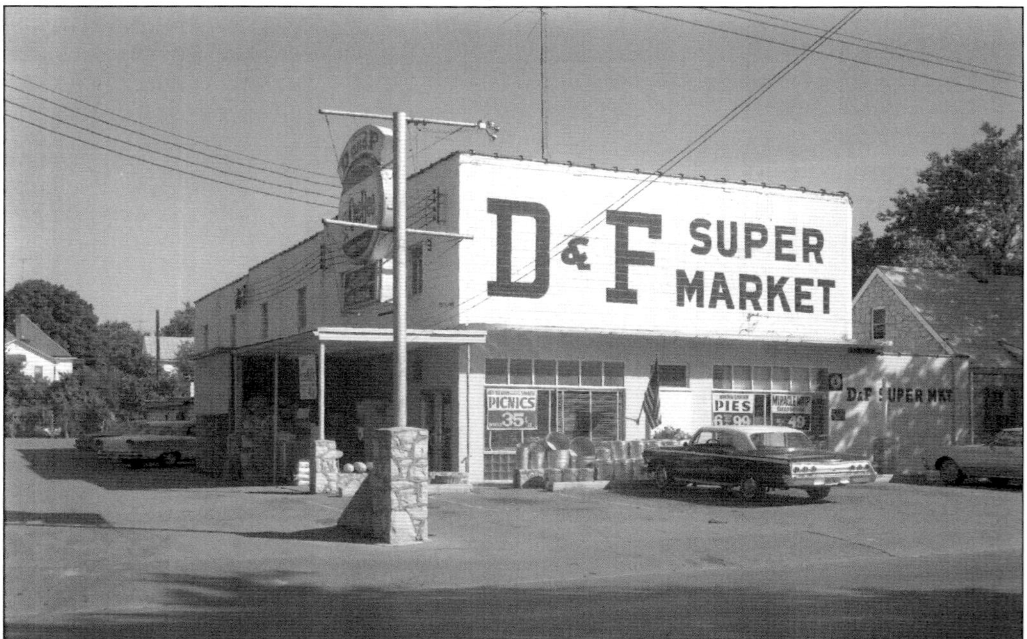

Supermarket Spirit. Owner Thomas L. Diemer proudly displayed the stars and stripes on June 15, 1966, at his 1232 Adams Street store, D&F Super Market. Known for "Groceries, Meats, and Ample Free Parking," the store continues to operate at the same location today.

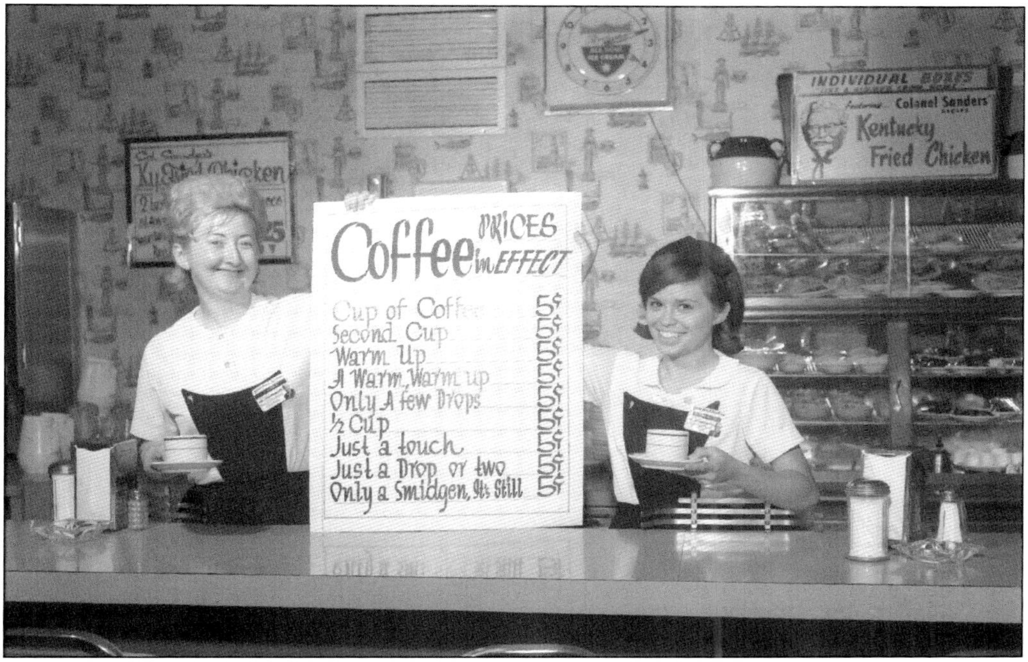

HAVE A CUP? Owner Charles Ray Woosley knew how to build his business by offering an affordable cup of steaming hot coffee, as advertised on June 8, 1966, by Carolyn Rice (left) and Cathy Herman. From "only a smidgen" to a brimful cup, 5¢ was a bargain at Ray's Drive-In on the U.S. 31-W Bypass.

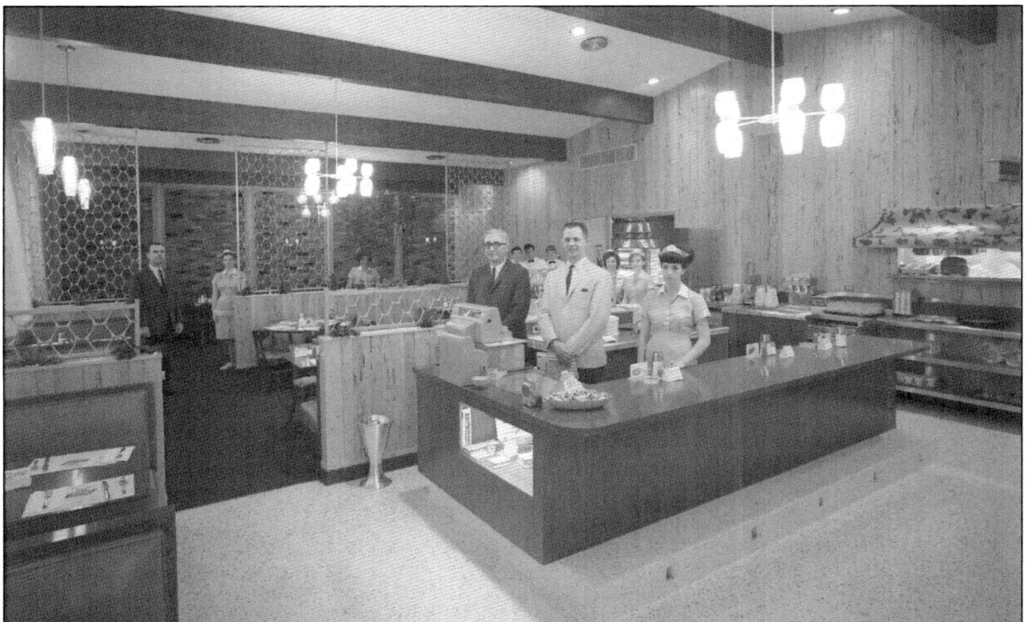

HOME OF THE CHAMP. Jerry's Restaurant opened its second Bowling Green location on March 15, 1967, at 1818 Russellville Road. One of the first chain restaurants to arrive in Bowling Green, Jerry's heralded a new era in dining out for the city's residents.

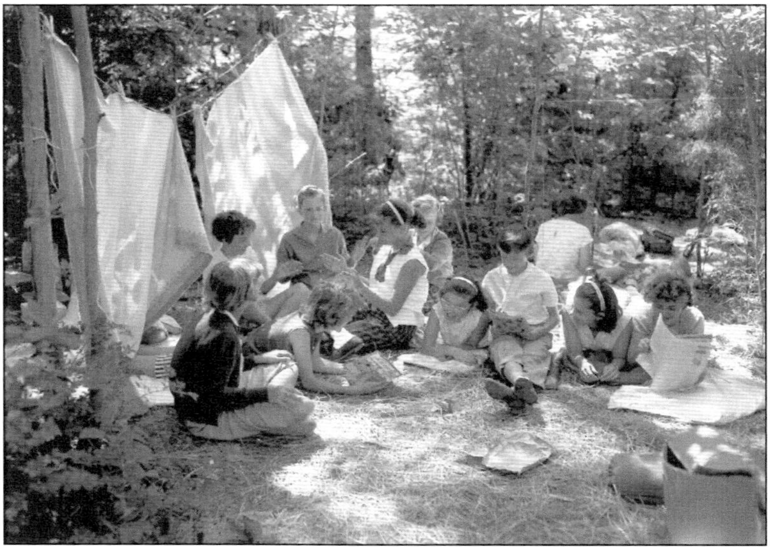

CAMPFIRE GIRLS. Summer days were lazy days in the great outdoors at this June 4, 1960, camp out. The Girl Scouts of America provided a variety of outdoor learning experiences for young girls, such as building a tent with simple sticks, a trusty tarp, and some twine, as well as basic outdoor survival skills.

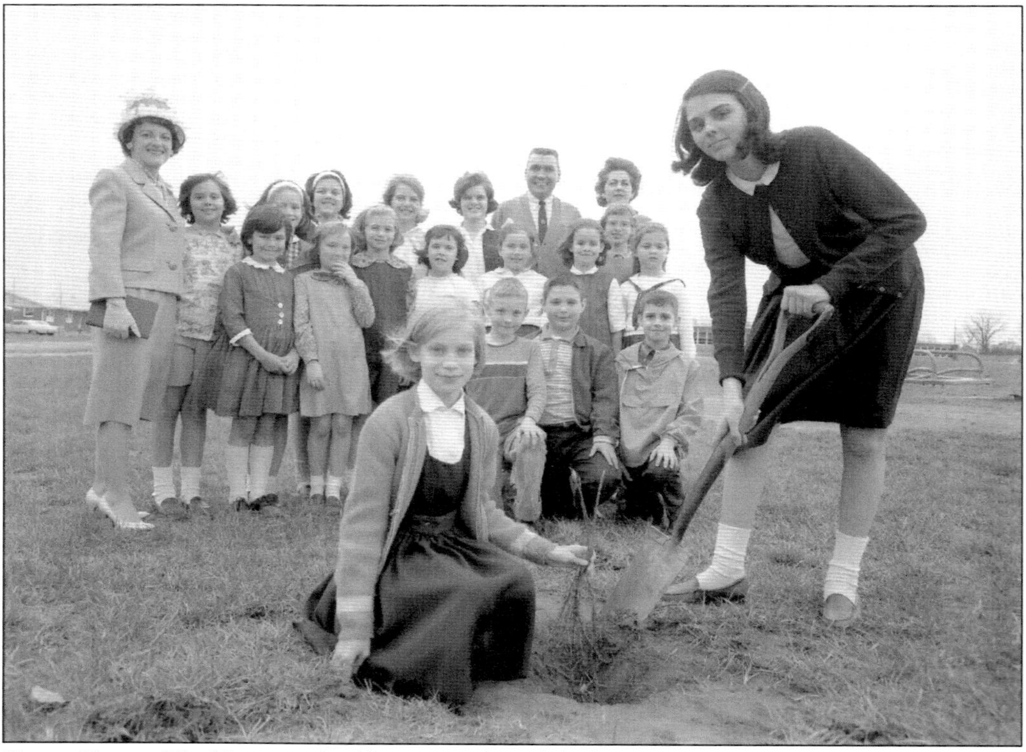

GOING GREEN. The Hummingbird Junior Garden Club planned for the future at this April 3, 1964, Arbor Day ceremony at Potter Gray Elementary School. Vice Pres. Ann Durbin lent a hand while Pres. Mary Hawkins plied the shovel. Supporters from left to right are (first row) Brent Mason, Pat Reynolds, and Kevin Karl; (second row) Marion Lee Allen, Carol Lee Bryant, Rebecca Parrott, Donna Todd, Connie Howard, Carolyn Smith, Carla Utley, and Melinda Palmore; (third row) Mrs. David Cooksey (club sponsor), Debbie Anderson, Elaine Smith, Mary Jo Hayden, Linda Gray, Janice Hayden, Ellis Maggard (school principal), and Mrs. Rodney Parrott (club sponsor).

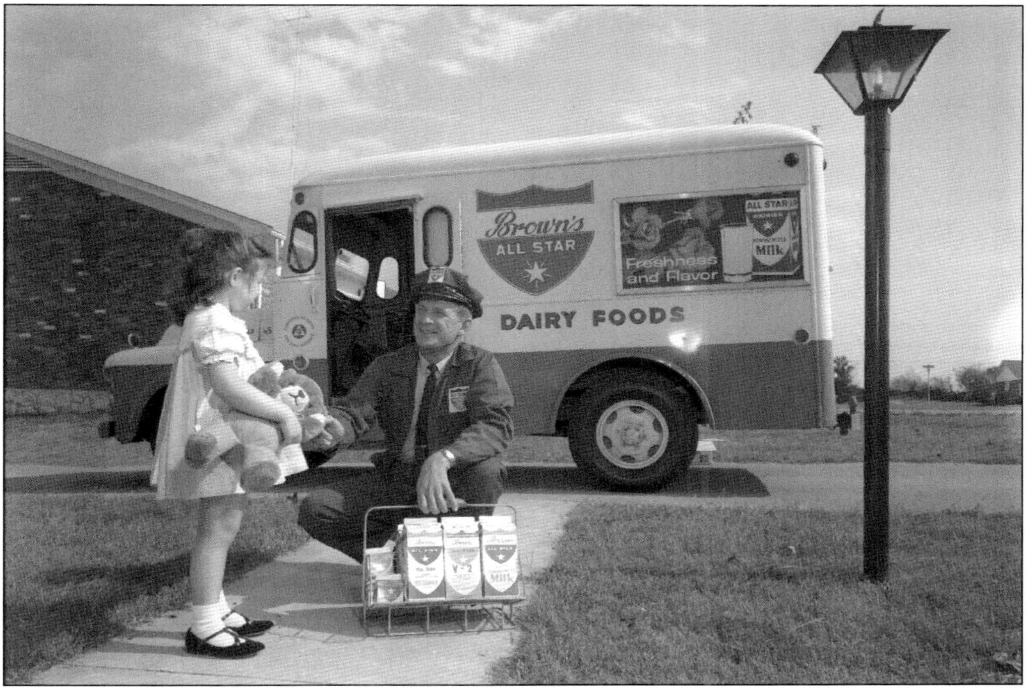

DAIRY DELIVERY. Brown's All Star Dairy Foods, located at 331 College Street in 1963, delivered milk, buttermilk, eggs, and butter on Monday, Wednesday, Friday, and Saturday. Thrifty Bowling Green homemakers left their orders inside an insulated box on the front porch, which then yielded fresh dairy foods right at their doorstep.

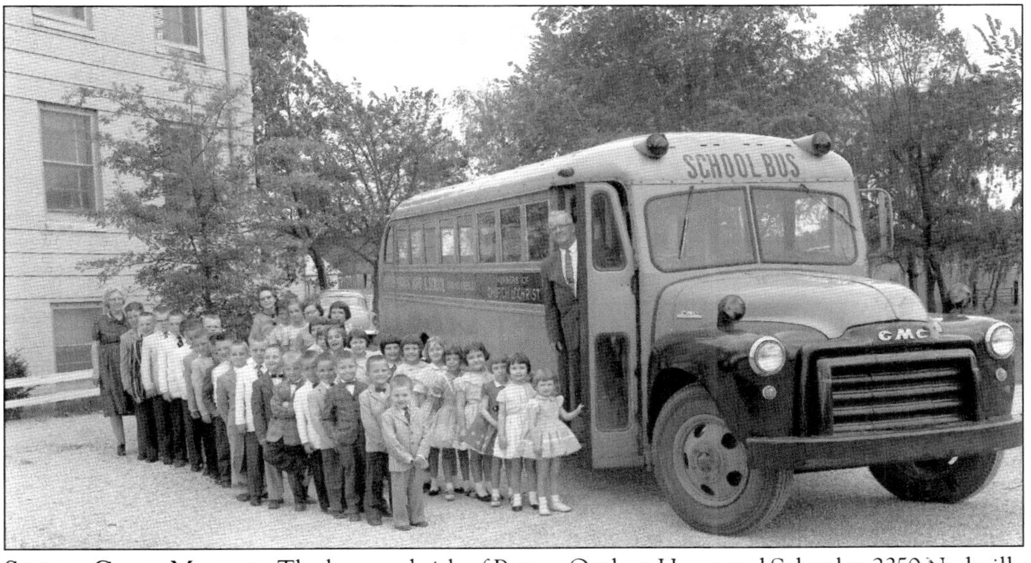

SUNDAY GO-TO-MEETING. The boys and girls of Potters Orphan Home and School at 2350 Nashville Road boasted their Sunday best with smiles all the way down the line as they boarded the bus with the help of Herman Taylor to head to church in March 1962. Potters Orphan Home, affiliated with the Church of Christ, received its first young resident in 1915 and has since provided a safe, nurturing home for more than 5,500 children and young adults.

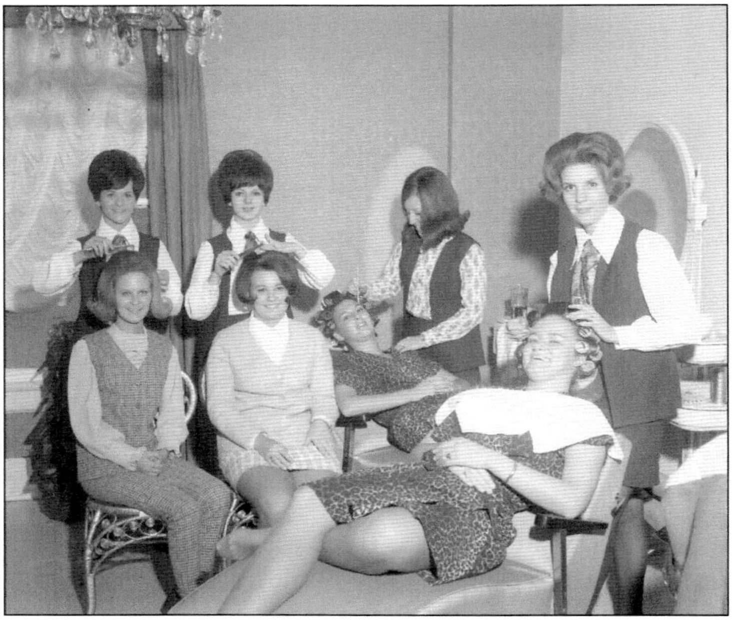

Need a New Do? Staff at Bette Barrett Coiffures at 1022 Laurel Avenue employed the latest techniques and styles for their patrons, many of whom made weekly visits to the salon for the very best "hair in action." On October 25, 1969, a tease out and flip were popular trendsetting styles of the day, provided with precision by, from left to right, Gracie Crandall Hunt, Lana Vincent VanMeter, Joyce Smith Woods, and Sharon Vertrees Dahle.

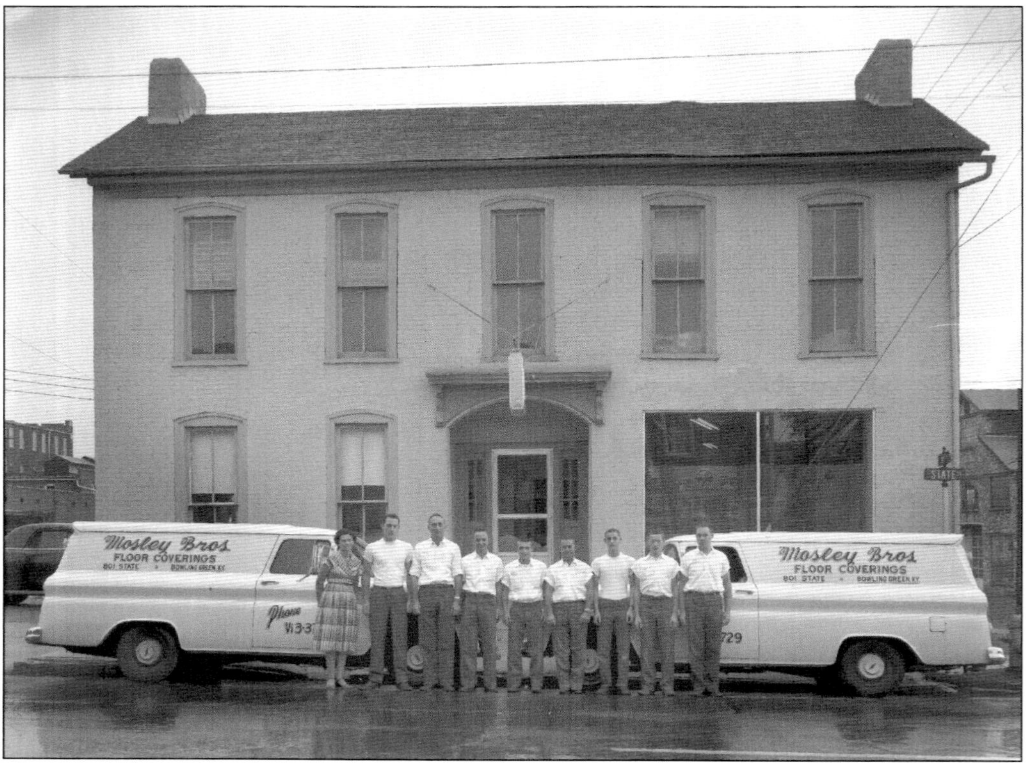

Floors Galore. Mosley Brothers Floor Covering, located at 801 State Street on July 5, 1962, covered many Bowling Green floors and provided rubber, asphalt, and linoleum products. Located in the Mariah Moore house, considered the oldest brick building in Bowling Green, Mosley Brothers urged homeowners to "See Us for Your Floor Covering Problem."

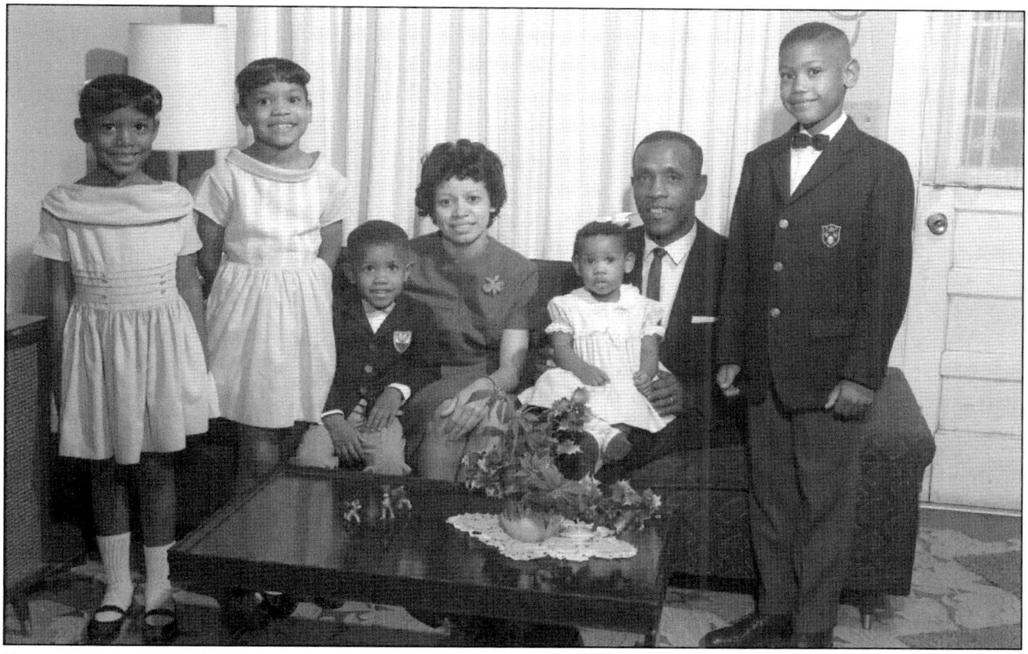

Proud Family. Welmon and Liz Britt celebrated their fine family with a spit-and-polish portrait in 1964. Dressed for the occasion from left to right are Marcia, Felicia, Kevin, Liz (family matriarch), Carmen, Welmon (family patriarch), and Michael.

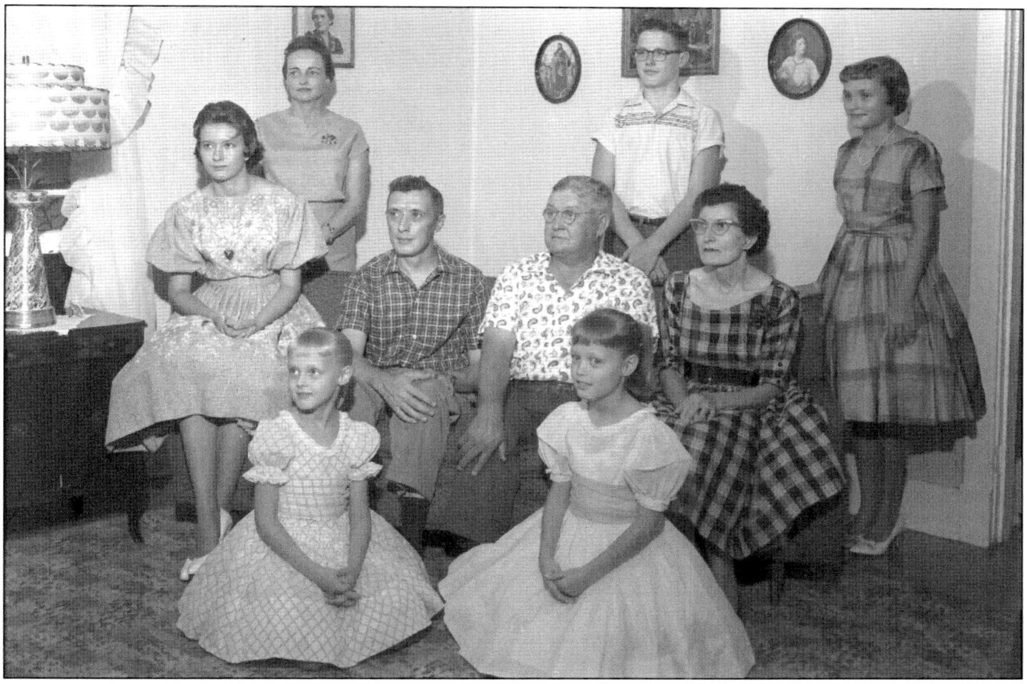

Gunnels Gathering. Ray and Pearl Gunnels gathered several generations of their family together on August 10, 1960, at the family home on 1346 Kenton Street for a pressed and starched portrait.

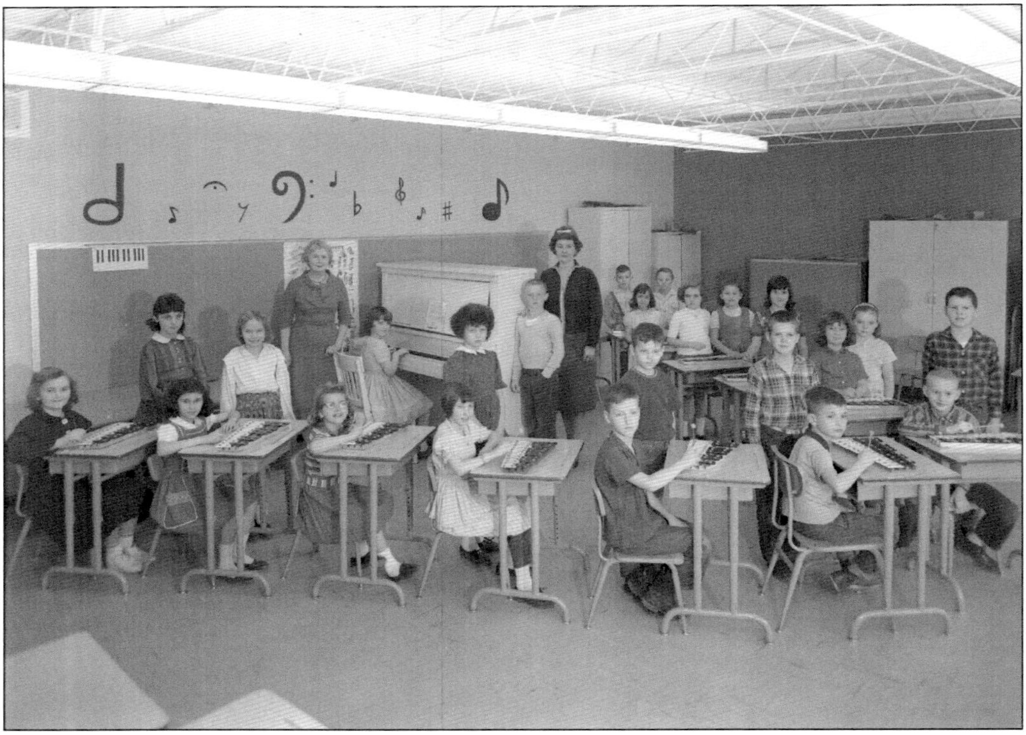

MAKING MUSIC. The students in Kathryn Duncan's 1962 music class at Parker Bennett Elementary School were poised and ready to make beautiful music together, with xylophones, a piano, and their own childlike voices raised in harmonious song.

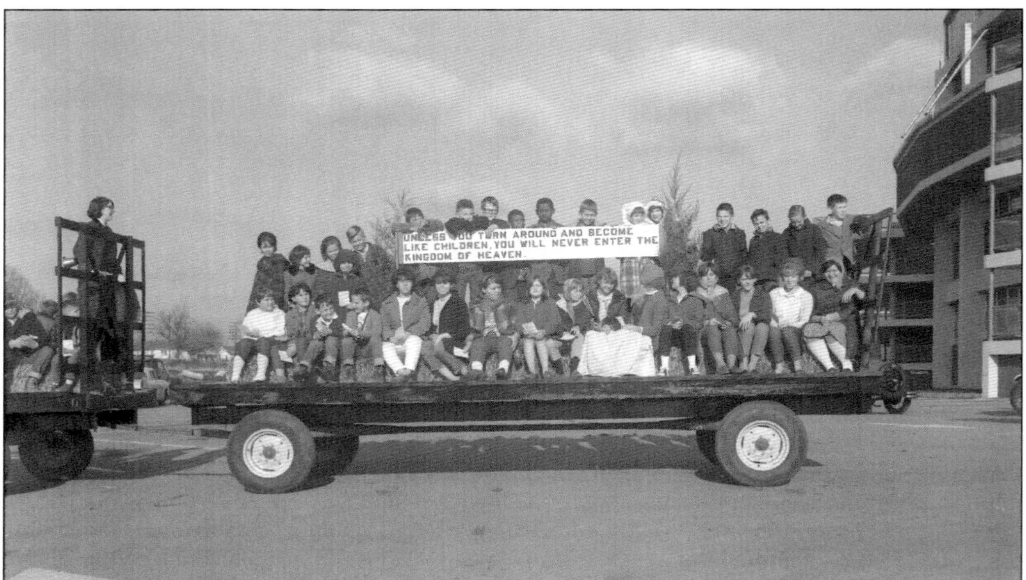

MOBILE MESSAGE. The Delafield Little Rock Presbyterian Sunday School took their evangelical message to the streets on this float in the sunny but cold December 3, 1967, Christmas parade.

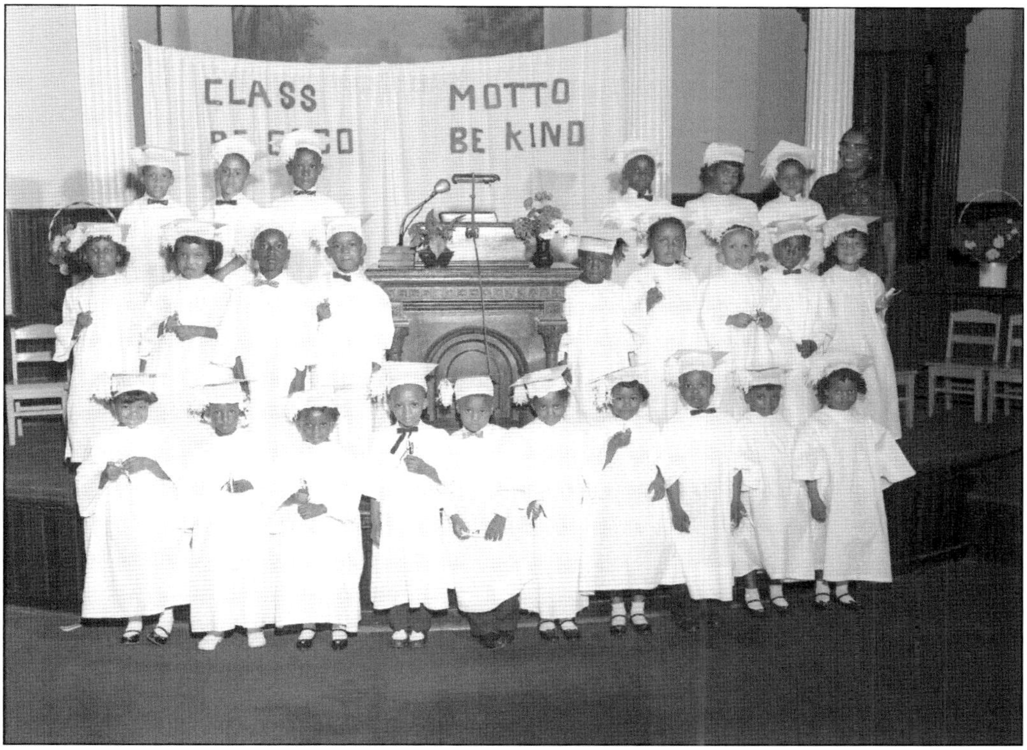

Graduation Day. Under the oversight of Rev. J. E. Jones, State Street Baptist Church, located at 338 State Street, graduated a large class of solemn students in a dignified June 2, 1961, ceremony. With a class motto of "Be Good, Be Kind," these graduates of Bessie Jones's class were sure to be stellar citizens.

Cherries Jubilee. Ruth Donaldson's kindergarten class posed for a 1965 holiday portrait at T. C. Cherry Elementary School. The large kindergarten classroom boasted a memorable circular window of glass bricks, and students took daily siestas on nap mats. The original T. C. Cherry Elementary School has been razed to make way for a new building to serve the students of Bowling Green.

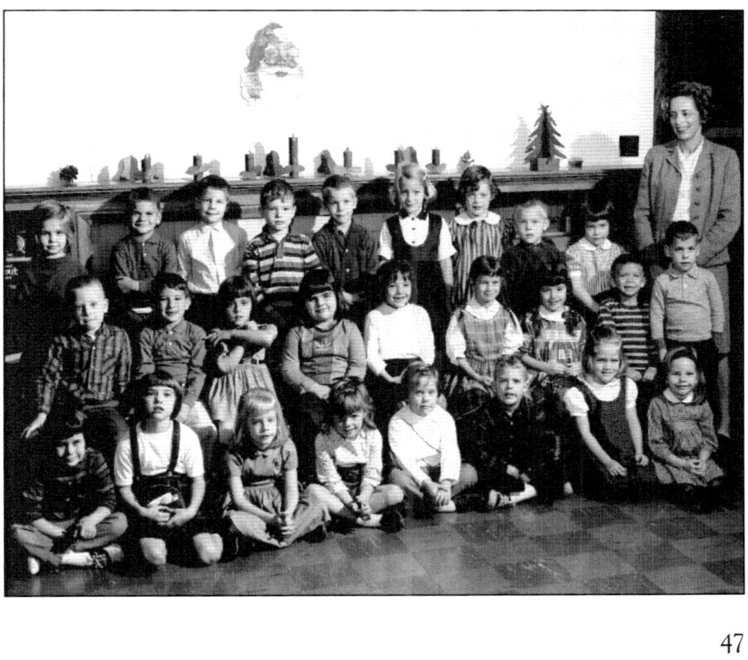

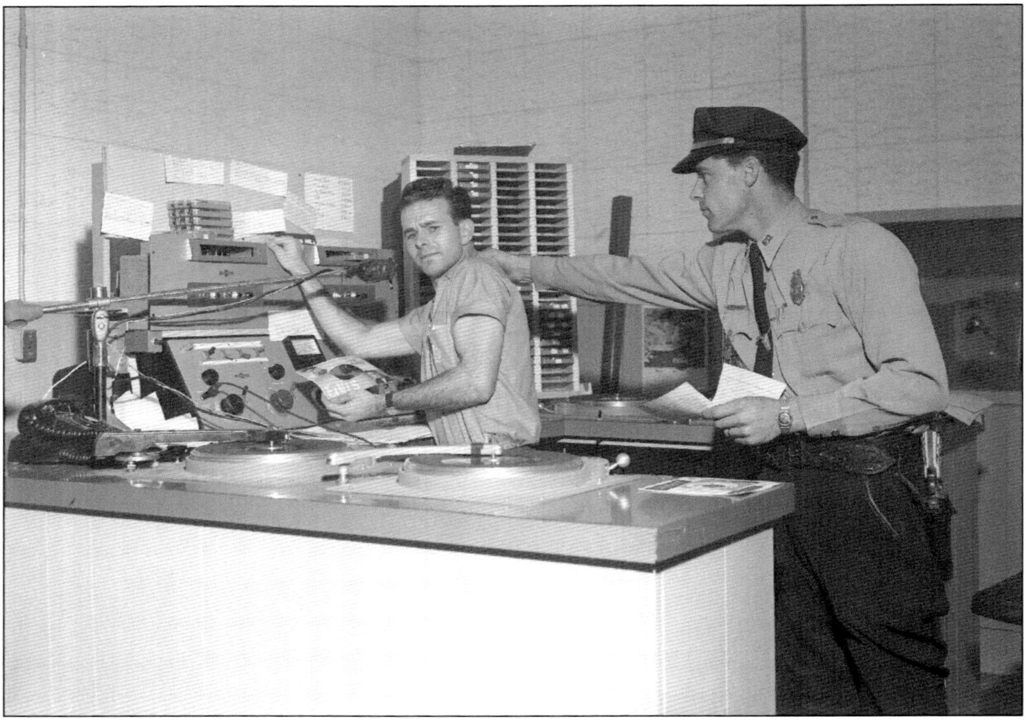

Jailhouse Rock. Wayne Morse, the voice of WBGN, was "under arrest" by officer William (Bill) Dawkins on April 1, 1960, perhaps for playing up-and-coming rock and roller Elvis Presley on "1340—the Happy Sound Radio."

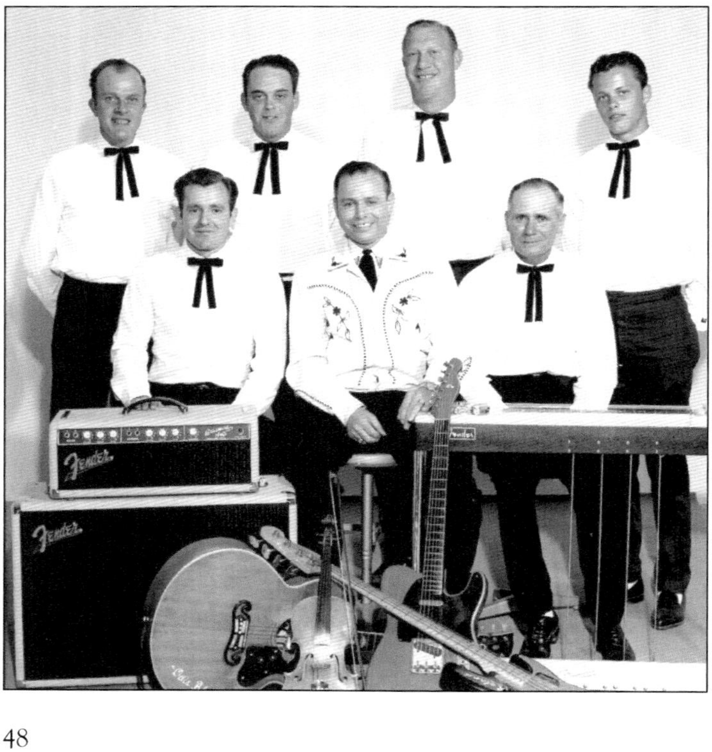

Picking and Grinning. An entertainment scene staple for many years, Odis Blanton and the Blue Star Rangers were loved for their blend of classic country and twangy bluegrass music. Regulars at the Beech Bend Dance Hall for 16 years, the Rangers, from left to right, are (first row) Roland Logsdon, Odis Blanton, and John Blanton; (second row) Hugh Poteet, Carroll Pemberton, Jim Vaughn, and Phillip Rigsby. They were the first band to appear live on WBKO and regularly served as back-up musicians for classic stars of country on the stage of the *Grand Ole Opry*.

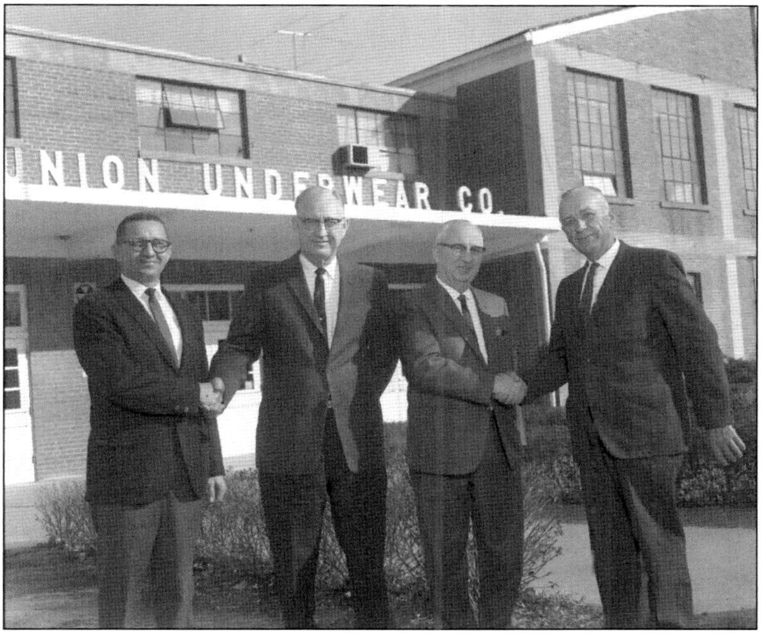

SILVER DOLLAR HANDSHAKE. Union Underwear Company officials celebrated the silver 25th anniversary of the plant's location on Church Street on January 17, 1966. Marking the special occasion from left to right are longtime Warren County judge executive Basil Griffin, chief product designer Earl Musgrave, Bowling Green mayor Walter Weis, and president of Union Underwear Company Everett J. Moore.

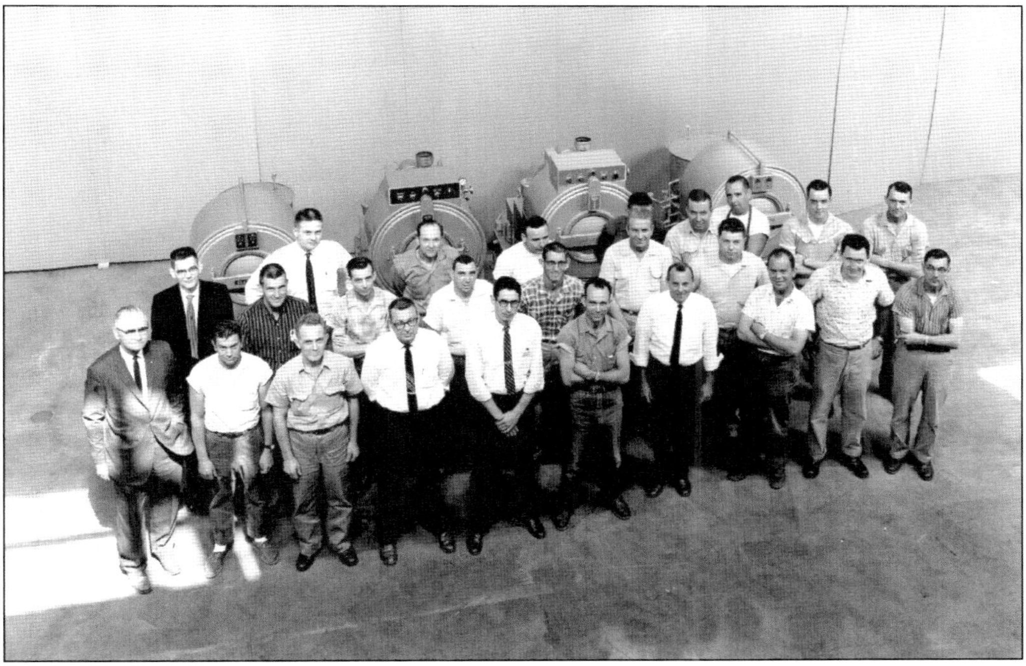

HOLDING THE LINE. The $1.5-million Detrex plant provided welcome jobs for Bowling Green and the region. These men of Detrex were serious about their business of manufacturing dry-cleaning and laundry equipment. From left to right are (first row) Elvis Campbell, Felix Davidson, Mack Madison, Vernon Rudd, Pete Vaught, Johnny Sturdivant, two unidentified, Merle Stewart, and unidentified; (second row) Ed Etterman, two unidentified, Bill Lockhardt, unidentified, Wilson Carver, Joe Morgan, unidentified, and Bob Sadler; (third row) Adolf Habic, Bob Carver, and three unidentified.

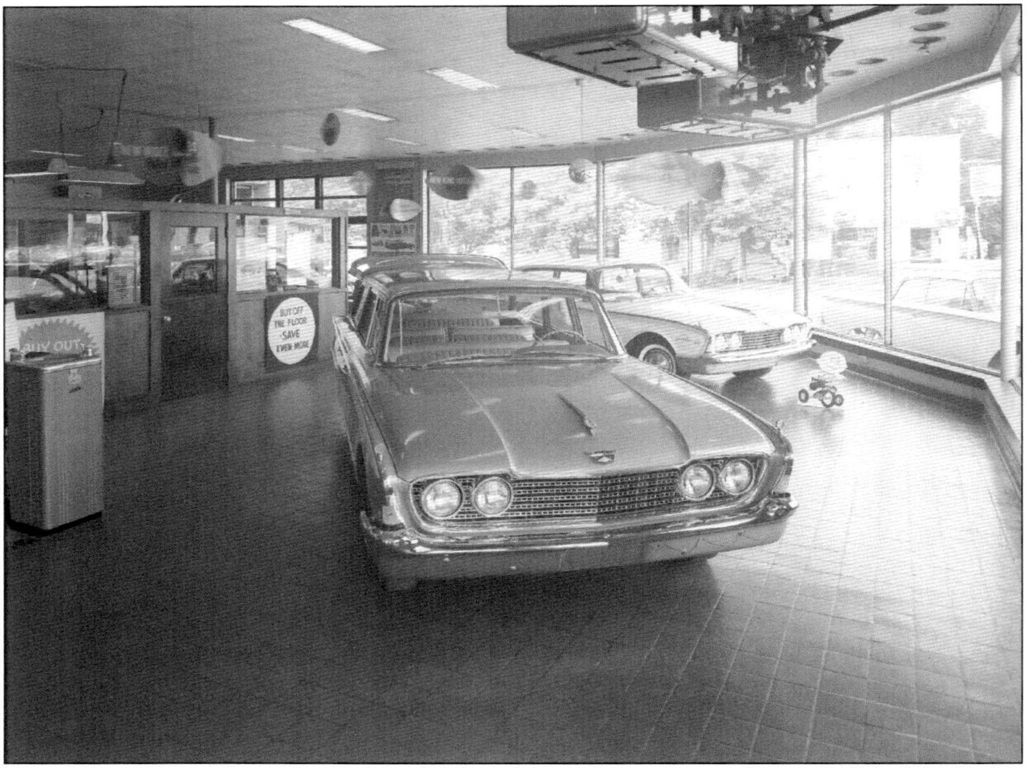

Buy off the Floor, Save Even More. Wallace Motor Company, a well-regarded Ford dealership located at 601 State Street (now Circus Square), was operated by O. H. Wallace, president. On August 10, 1960, the open, sunlit showroom was the perfect place for the latest models, with room to spare for junior salesman Charlie Brown.

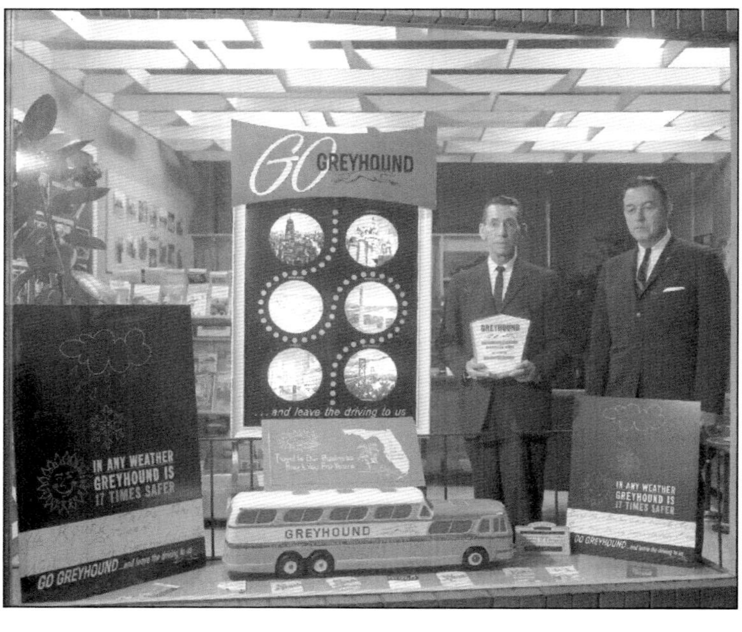

Go Greyhound. This April 1, 1963, display window was at the chamber of commerce office, located at 438 East Tenth Street. A Greyhound representative is shown with Harold Huffman, executive vice president of the chamber. A popular and vital form of travel, Greyhound offered 14 round-trips between Nashville, Bowling Green, and Louisville at the affordable price of $6.60.

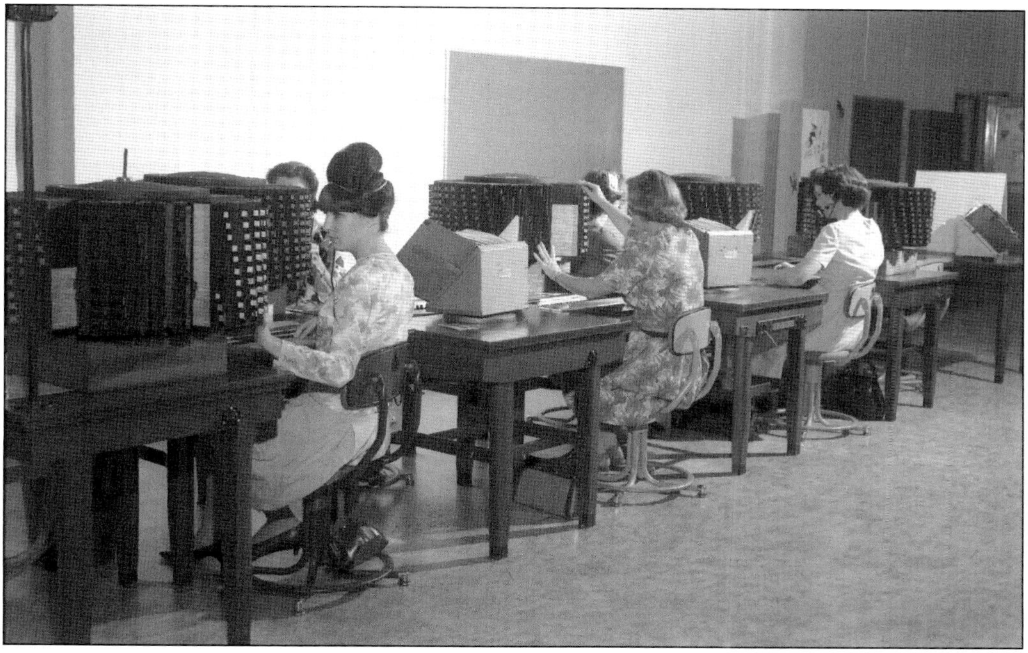

NUMBER, PLEASE? Southern Bell Telephone and Telegraph Company at 1150 State Street operated 20,000 telephone exchanges throughout the Bowling Green area in 1965. Ethel Hatler (right) and Algea Young performed the vital, pre-computer-era service of directory assistance, utilizing rotary handwritten files and headsets to provide telephone help for callers.

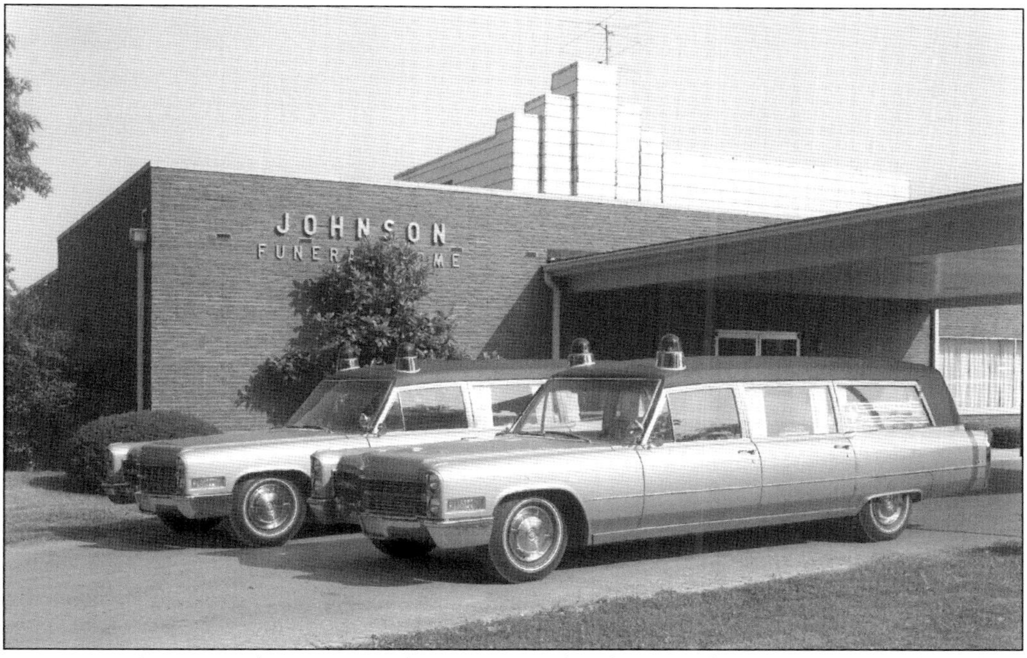

EMERGENCY SERVICE. Johnson Funeral Home, owned and operated on June 24, 1966, by Aubrey and Elaine Johnson, provided 24-hour air-conditioned ambulance service from its location at 901 Fairview Avenue.

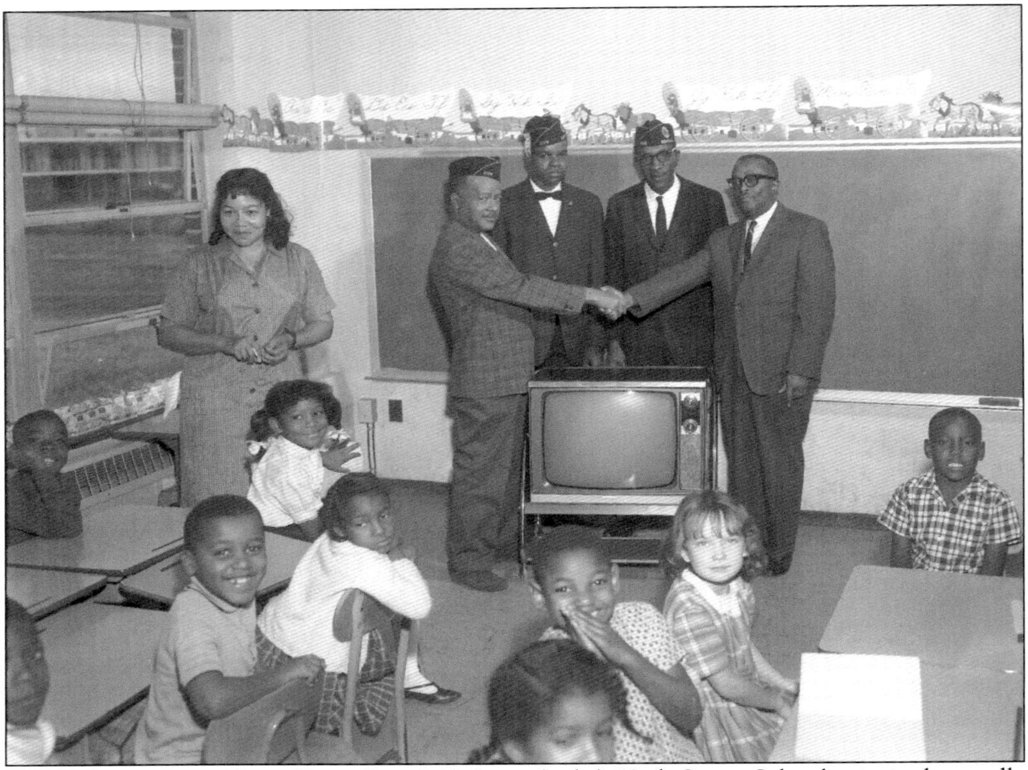

HIGH STREET GOES HIGH TECH. Rev. J. E. Jones (right), High Street School principal, proudly accepted the gift of a new television for Cornelia Ballinger's fourth-grade class on November 24, 1965, from American Legion Post No. 209. From left to right, vice commander George Luvall (shaking hands with Jones), adjutant Ken Saunders, and child welfare officer Walter L. Ray assisted in the presentation.

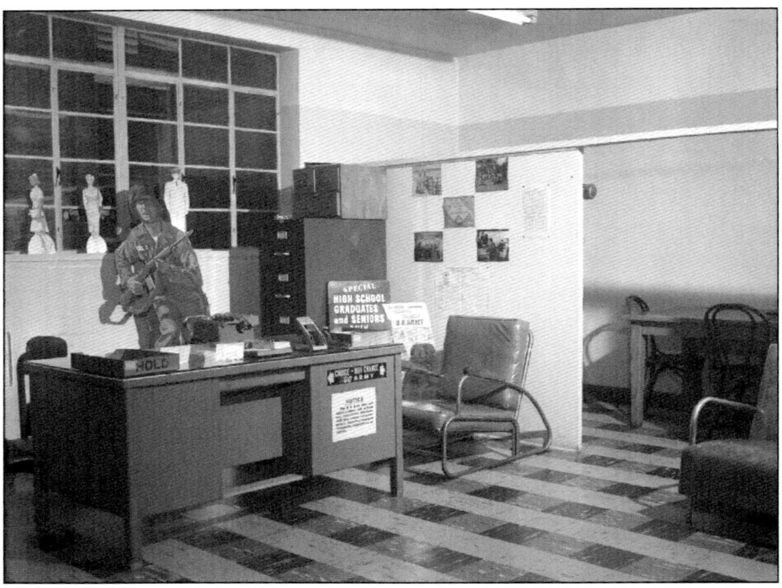

GO ARMY. A small office with a large task, the U.S. Army Recruiting Office, located at 814 State Street, was established to encourage young men and women to "go army." On December 1, 1965, the official army adage of "choice, not chance," was ever more powerful against the backdrop of the Vietnam War.

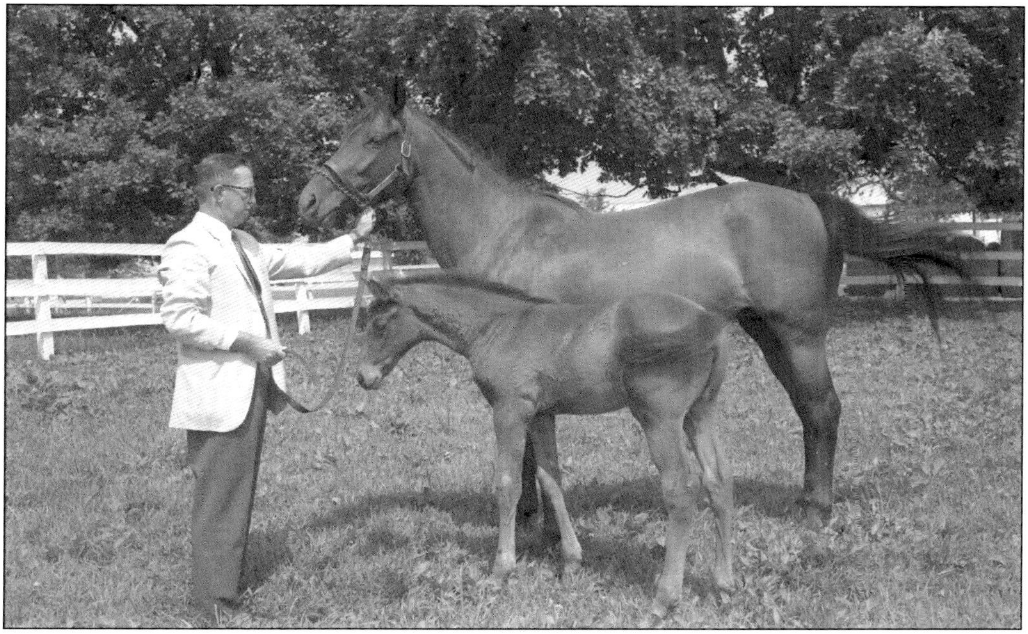

Bluegrass Born and Bred. Attorney Joe Orr at 900 Smith Lane proudly displayed mother and foal, two Thoroughbred beauties, on June 17, 1963. Too young to run for the roses but not too young to pose for a picture, mother was pleased and baby was off to a good start in their Kentucky bluegrass home.

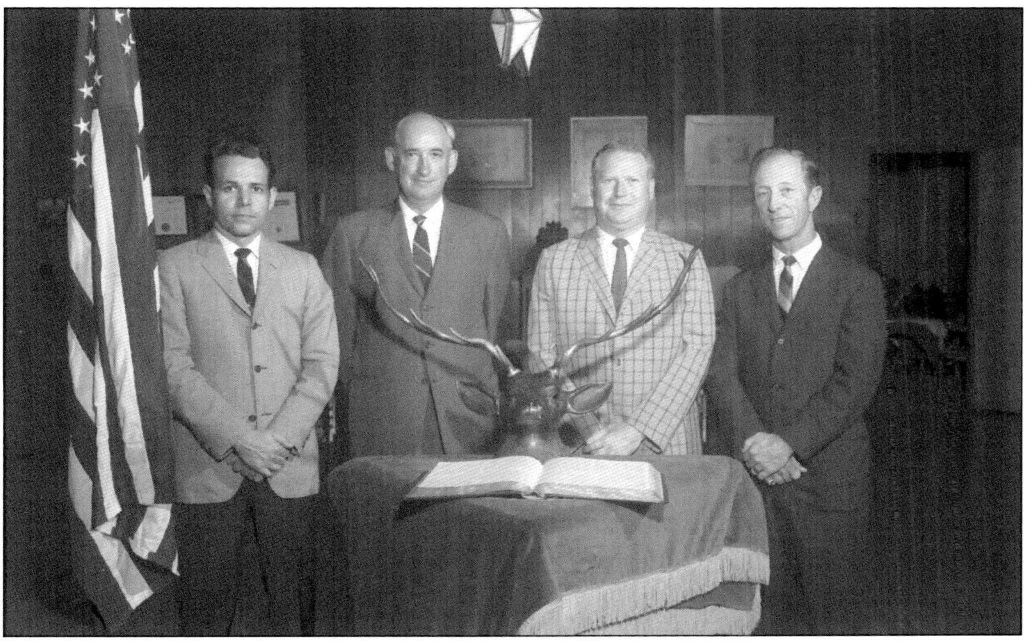

Exalted Elks. From left to right, J. C. Janes, Bill Stamps, Joe Lones, and Bob Preston gathered for an auspicious October 1, 1969, meeting. The esteemed Elks, whose motto was "the faults of our brothers we write upon the sand, their virtues on tablets of love and memory," were a vital part of Bowling Green civic life.

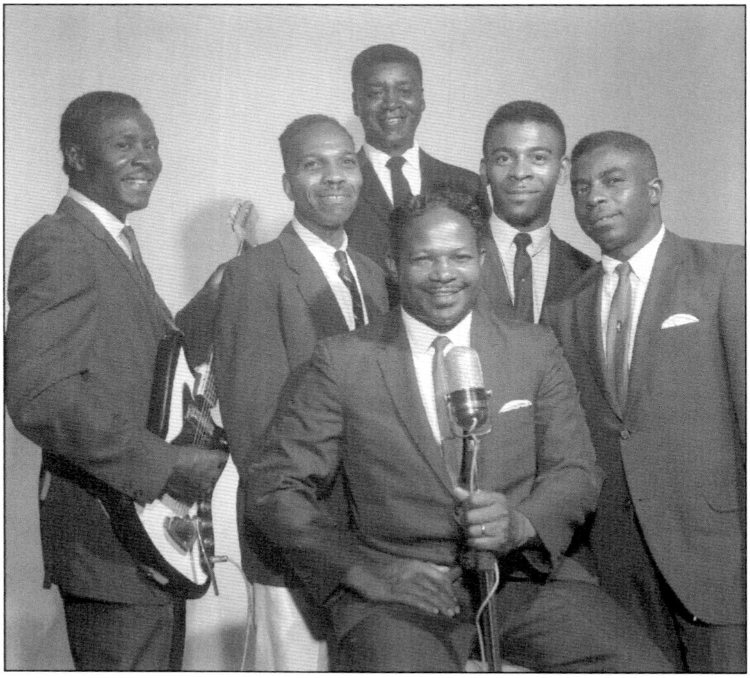

Singing with Soul. The Gospel Soul Burners, under the direction of George Rountree in 1968 (center, with microphone), sang together for a number of years. Their sole aim was sharing the news of Jesus. Burning up the microphone with Rountree from left to right are Charles Johnson, Ralfa Williams, William Alexander, Ivan Campbell, and James Murrell.

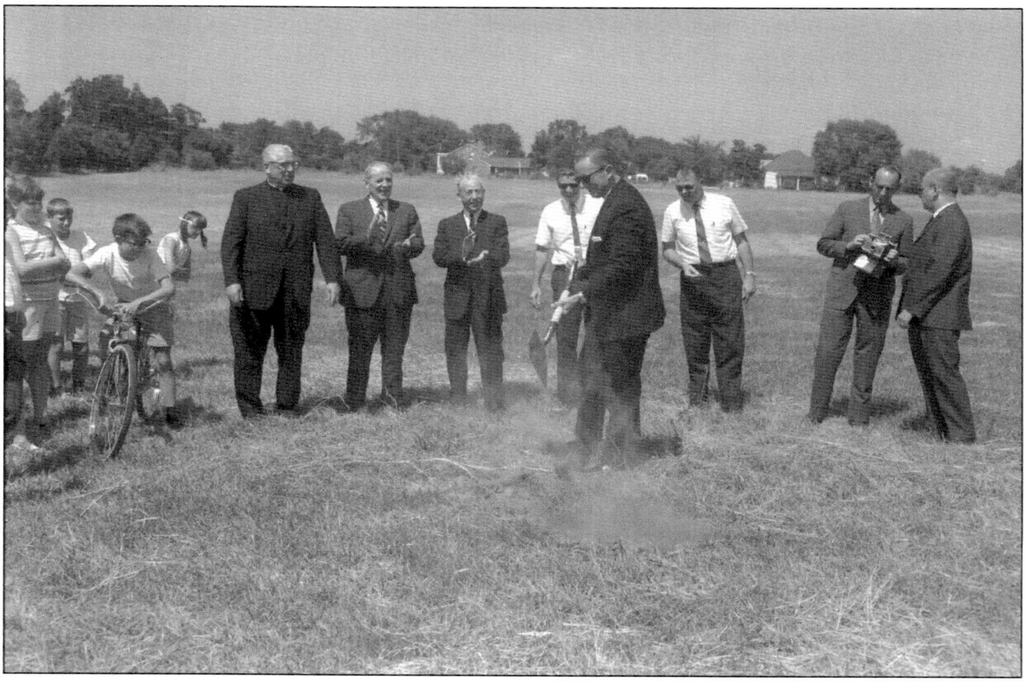

Holy Ground. A group of youngsters leaned in for a better look as Fr. Henry Willett blessed the first shovelful of ground being turned for the new Holy Spirit Catholic Church at 2232 Smallhouse Road in Bowling Green on August 10, 1969. This memorable day was shared by Father Spaulding (far left), Kelly Thompson (second from left), and Mayor Bob Graham (third from left), while a careful photographer checked his equipment as he also hoped to capture the special moment.

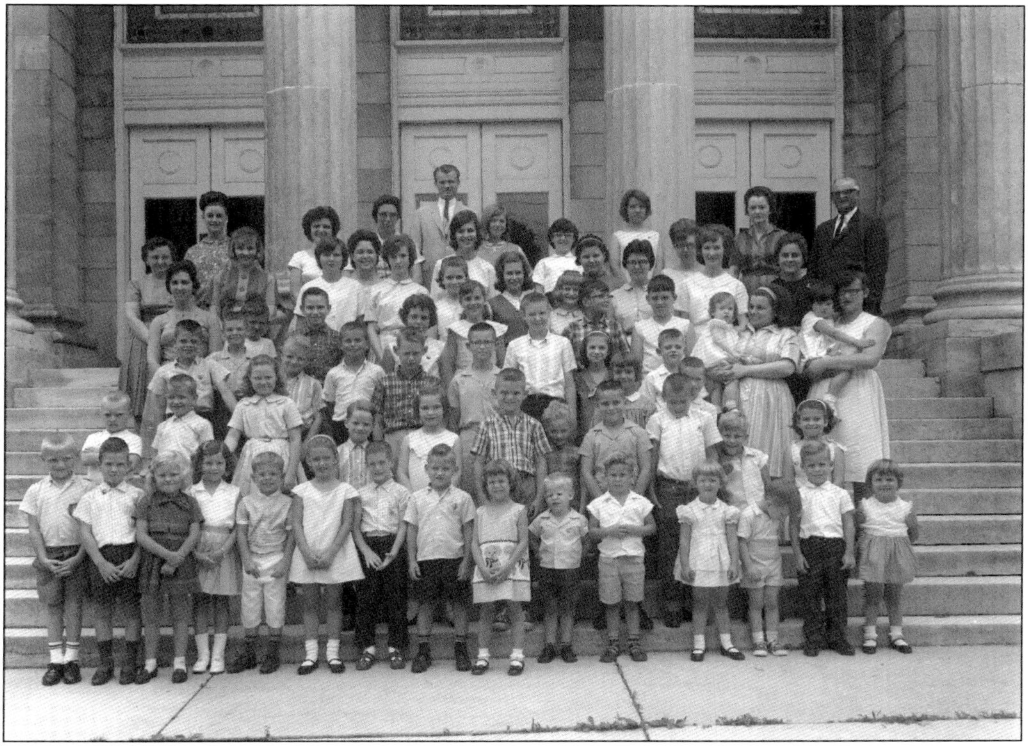

Happy Bible Scholars. A much-anticipated event of summer in 1965 was vacation Bible school at State Street General Baptist Church, located at 1202 State Street. Under the leadership of Rev. Irvin V. Jaggers, the program drew children and young people from across Warren County for a week of cookies, Koolaid, and Bible coloring sheets.

Amazing Grace. The choir of Taylor's Chapel African Methodist Episcopal Church at 314 East Seventh Street gathered under the guidance of Rufus Stokes (seated) on May 18, 1966, to sing with spirit for their congregation, filling their hearts and their church with the love of song. From left to right are (first row) Maezell Hines, Margaret Morrow, Allie Jewell, Mary Roseangel, and Emma Whitney; (second row) Everett Halsell, William Jenkins, Raven P. Taylor, and James Hockersmith.

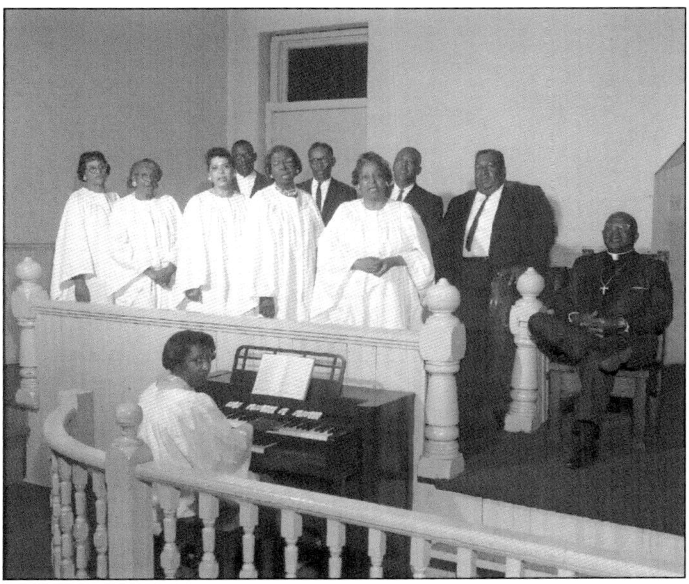

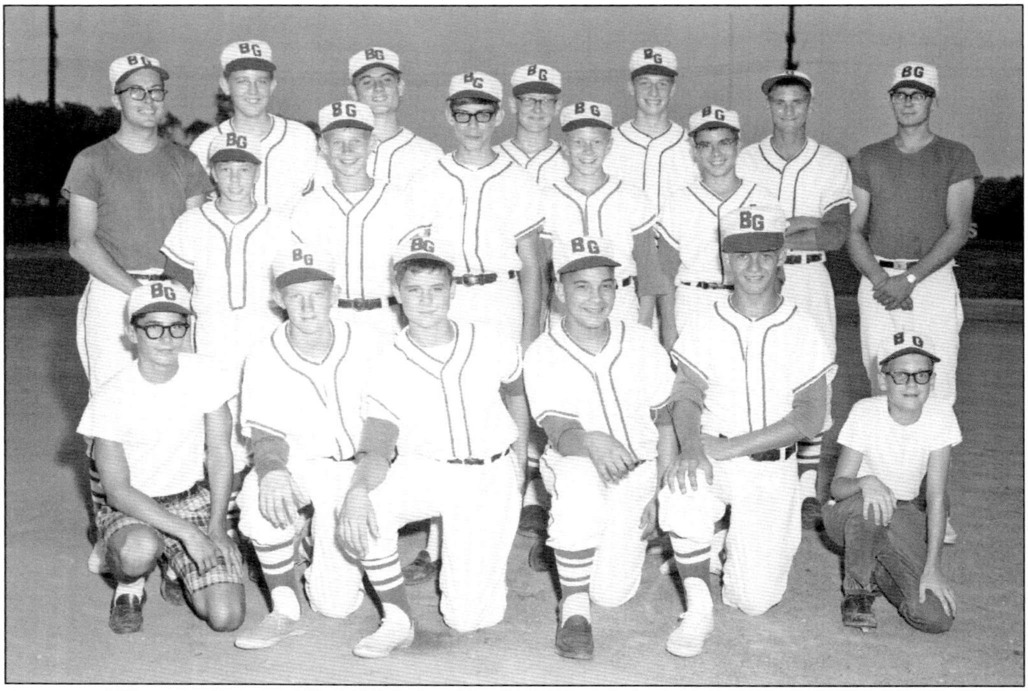

All the Way to State. The Babe Ruth League 13-year-old all-stars prepared for the state tournament at Elkhorn City on July 27, 1965. Representing Bowling Green from left to right are (first row) Billy Vaught, Sid King, Bobby Hulen, David Masters, Tommy Davis, and Phil Creek; (second row) Steve Henderson, William Morris, Wade Markham, Tommy Freeman, and Billy Everly; (third row) manager Malcolm Ray, Mark Cummins, Holly Sharp, Wayne Oliver, Mark Faxon, Tom G. Kitchens, and assistant manager Tommy Gentry.

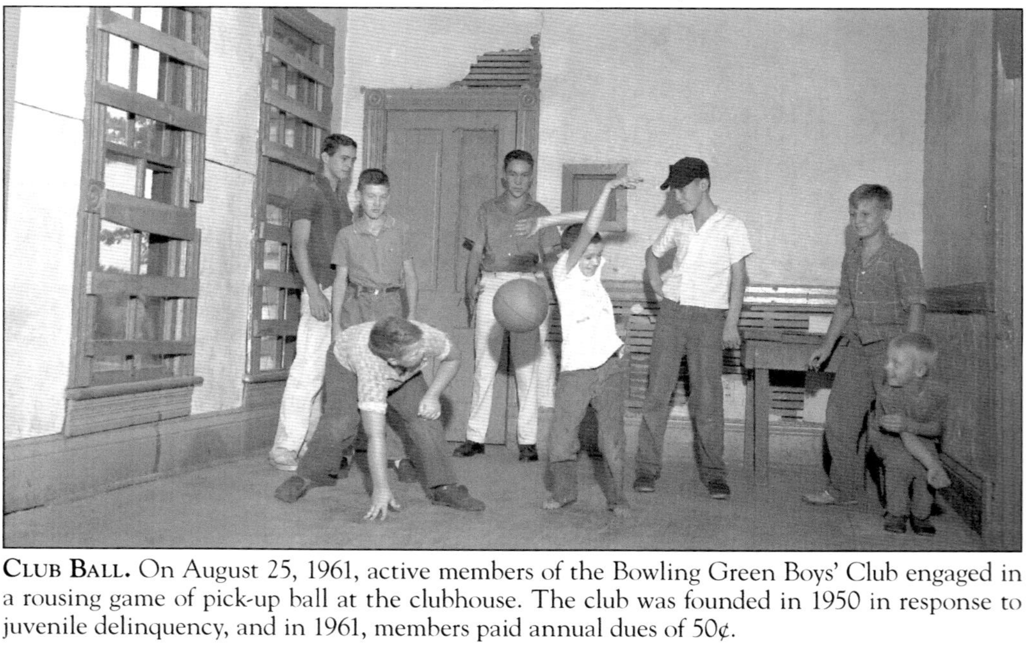

Club Ball. On August 25, 1961, active members of the Bowling Green Boys' Club engaged in a rousing game of pick-up ball at the clubhouse. The club was founded in 1950 in response to juvenile delinquency, and in 1961, members paid annual dues of 50¢.

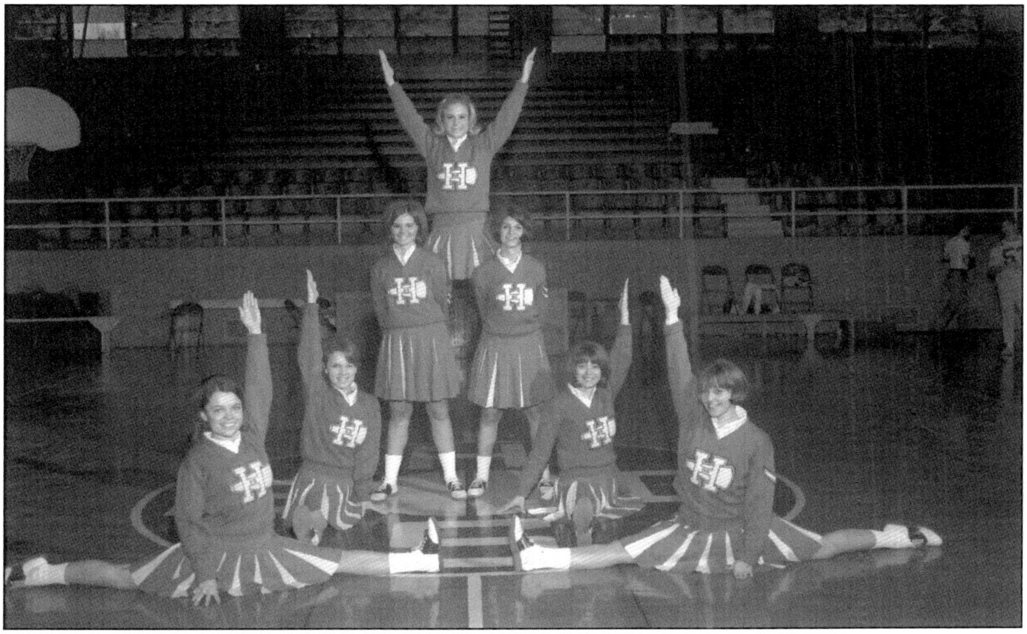

Purple Pride. Bowling Green High School cheerleaders posed with pride in the gymnasium at the high school on January 30, 1969. In the era of pin curls and flips, saddle oxfords, and pleated skirts, these ladies had Purple spirit to spare. From left to right are Barbara Magee, Debbie Phelps, Sylvia Butler, Sally Shreve, Jeannie Gour, Debbie Bradford, and Donna Porter.

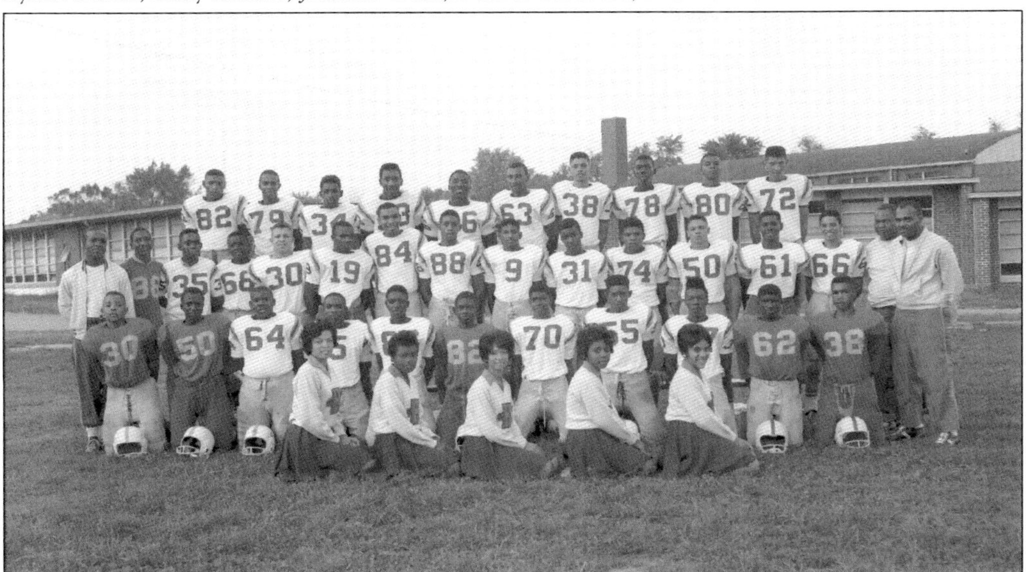

High Street, High Street, High Street High. Coach Joseph S. Owmby (far left) and assistant coaches Charles Bradshaw and Herbert Oldham (far right) prepared to lead the High Street School Mustangs to battle on October 11, 1962. Located at 200 High Street, the students were integrated into the Bowling Green school system, and the building was eventually razed. Accomplished athletes, committed coaches, and spirited cheerleaders were fine representatives of the school and its programs.

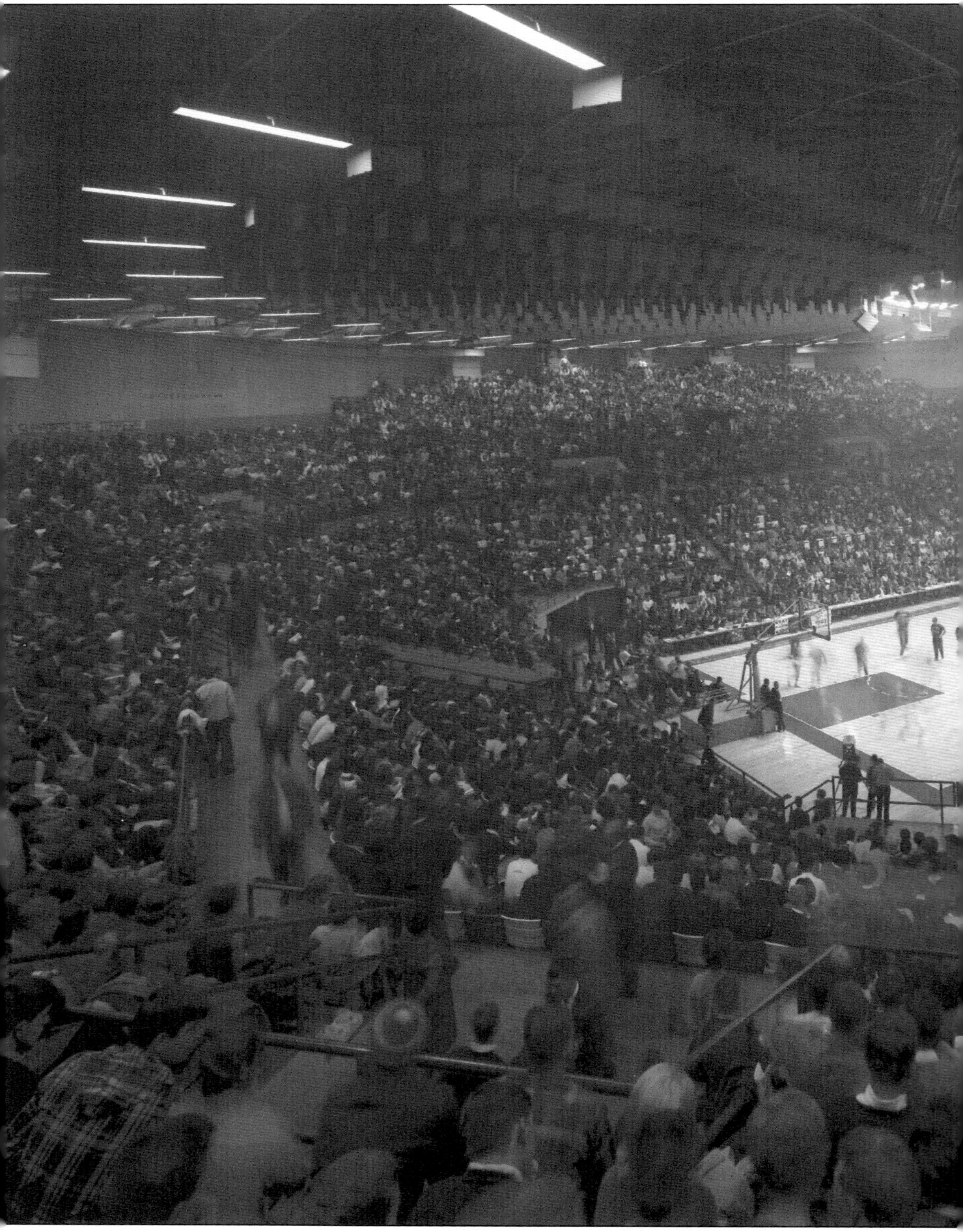

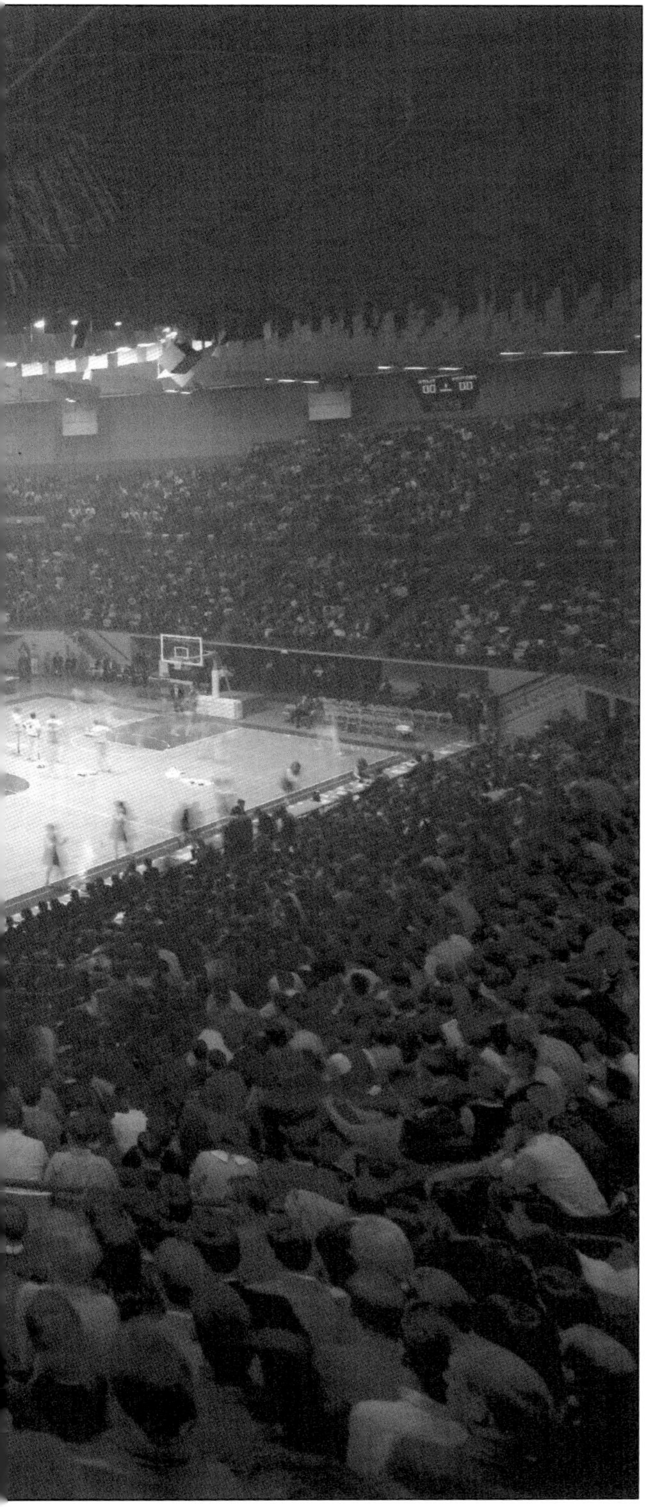

FULL HOUSE AT DIDDLE. Opening night of the 1966–1967 Hilltopper season at Diddle Arena on December 2, 1966, saw a record crowd of 13,720 for Western Kentucky University's game against Vanderbilt University. A complete sell out, with added chair seats on the top concourse to make even more room for Hilltopper fans, Diddle Arena was a sea of fluttering red towels. Under the leadership of coach and Hilltopper veteran Johnny Oldham and with 24 points scored by Clem "the Gem" Haskins, the nationally ranked Hilltoppers gave the Commodores a tough battle but fell at the buzzer with a final score of 76-70.

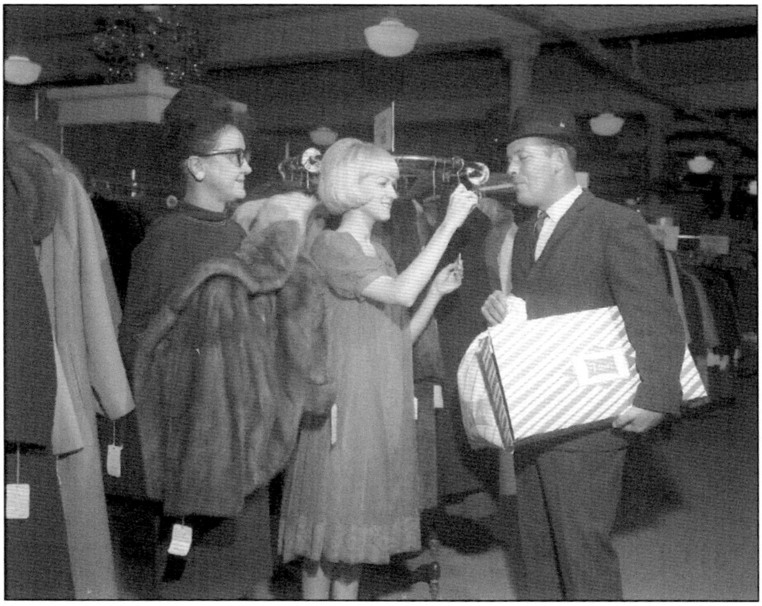

PUSHIN'S PATRONAGE. Lovely ladies catered to Henry (Hank) Brosche, a popular WKCT announcer, at a November 18, 1966, men's night held at Pushin's Department Store. Heralded as the largest department store in southern Kentucky, Pushin's, located at the corner of Main and College Streets, stood behind its motto, "Quality Tells, Price Sells."

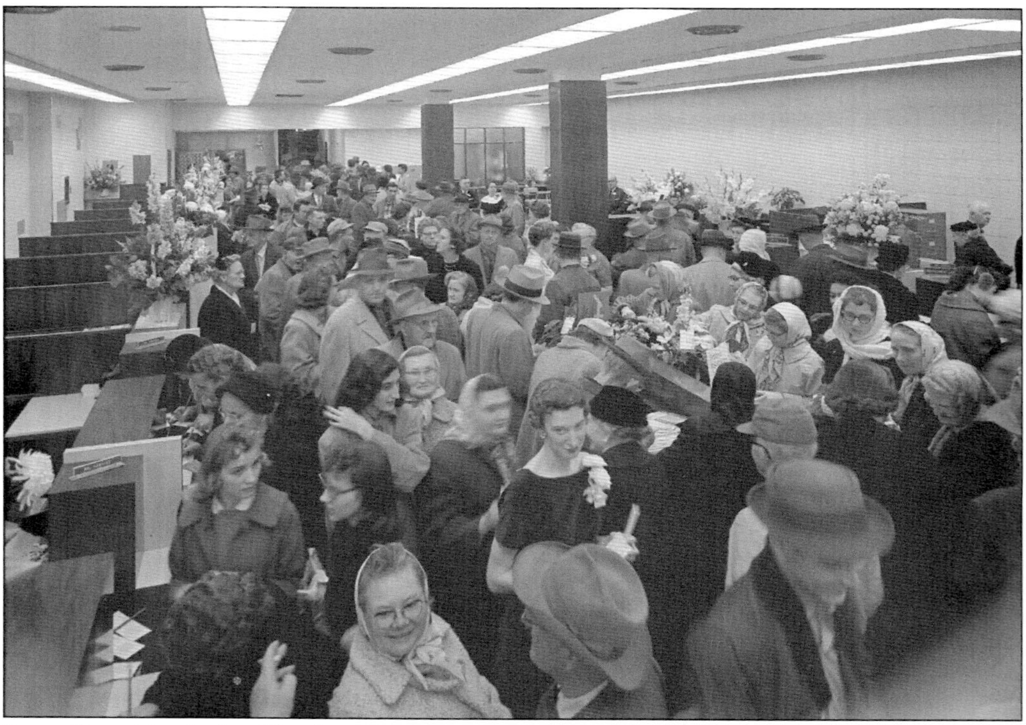

BANK RUN. Hundreds of Bowling Green citizens thronged the lobby of American National Bank in celebration of its January 27, 1960, grand opening at 922 State Street. Crowds were enticed by $1,000 in free prizes and a glimpse of this new, modern building throughout the day-long event.

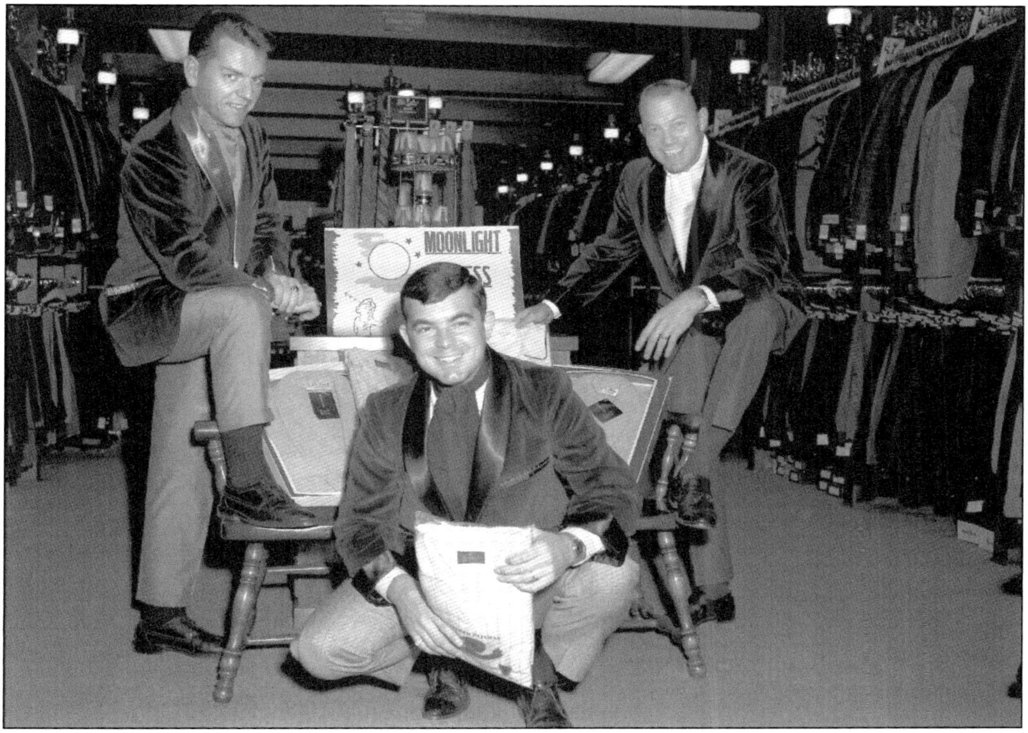

MOONLIGHT MADNESS. Golden Farley Men and Boys Shop at 436 Main Street celebrated October 4, 1966, moonlight madness in high style, as, from left to right, Jim King, Sam Hall, and Ron Raymer modeled daringly debonair smoking jackets. A staple of the square since 1958, Golden Farley continues to provide "the look of distinction" for discriminating Bowling Green shoppers.

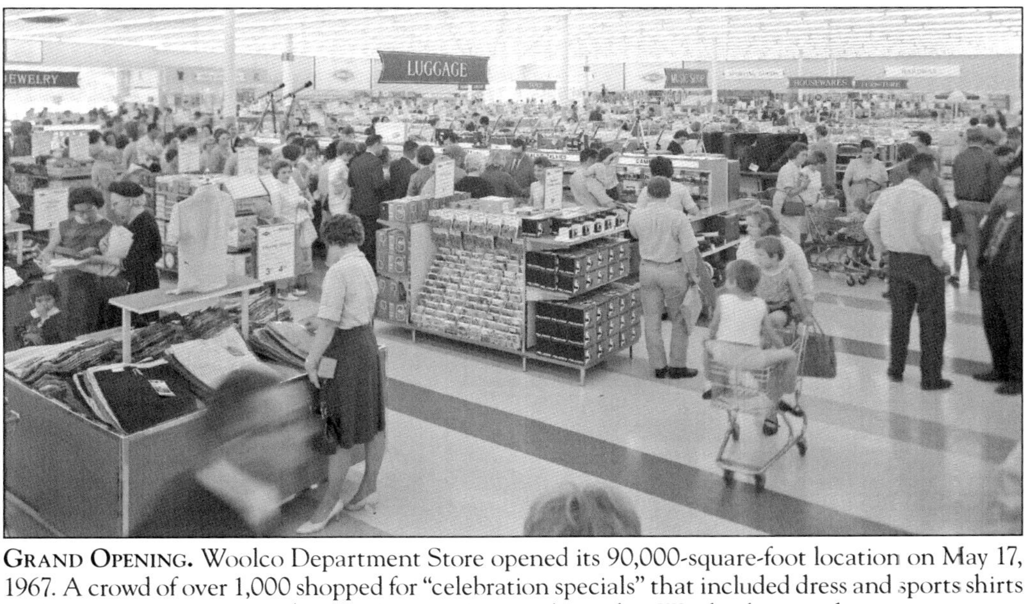

GRAND OPENING. Woolco Department Store opened its 90,000-square-foot location on May 17, 1967. A crowd of over 1,000 shopped for "celebration specials" that included dress and sports shirts for $1.99 and stereo LPs for $2.38. The crowd was so large that Woolco later took out a newspaper advertisement apologizing for the chaotic confusion created by enthusiastic shoppers.

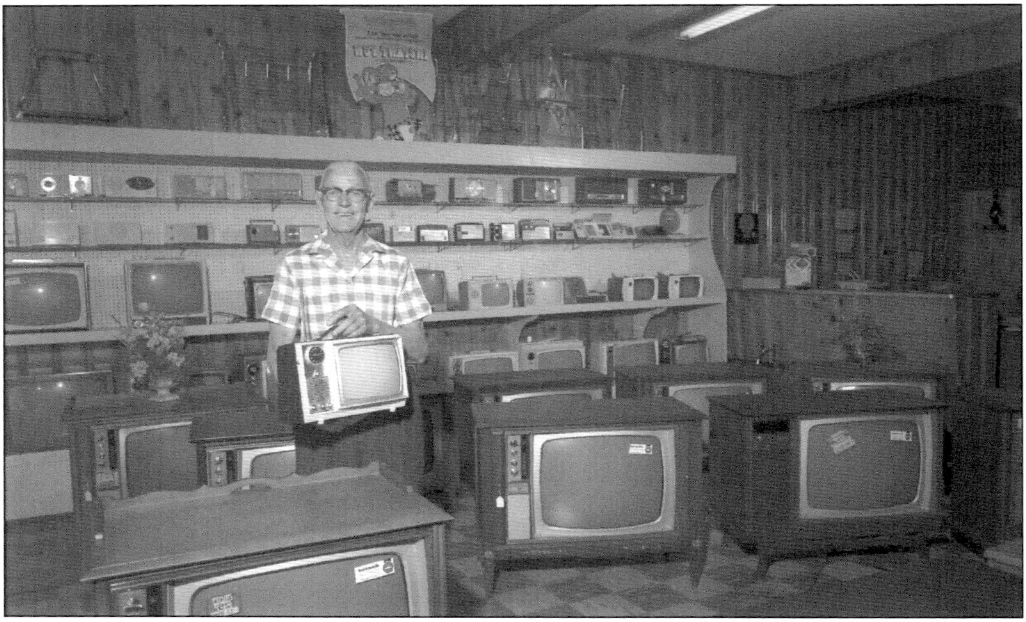

Television Time. Televisions, large and small, and transistor radios (some pocket-sized) were rapidly becoming staples of American life on September 8, 1966. E. C. "Pop" Wiltshire, owner of Wiltshire Television at 354 Laurel Avenue, was an enthusiastic purveyor of the latest in new technology.

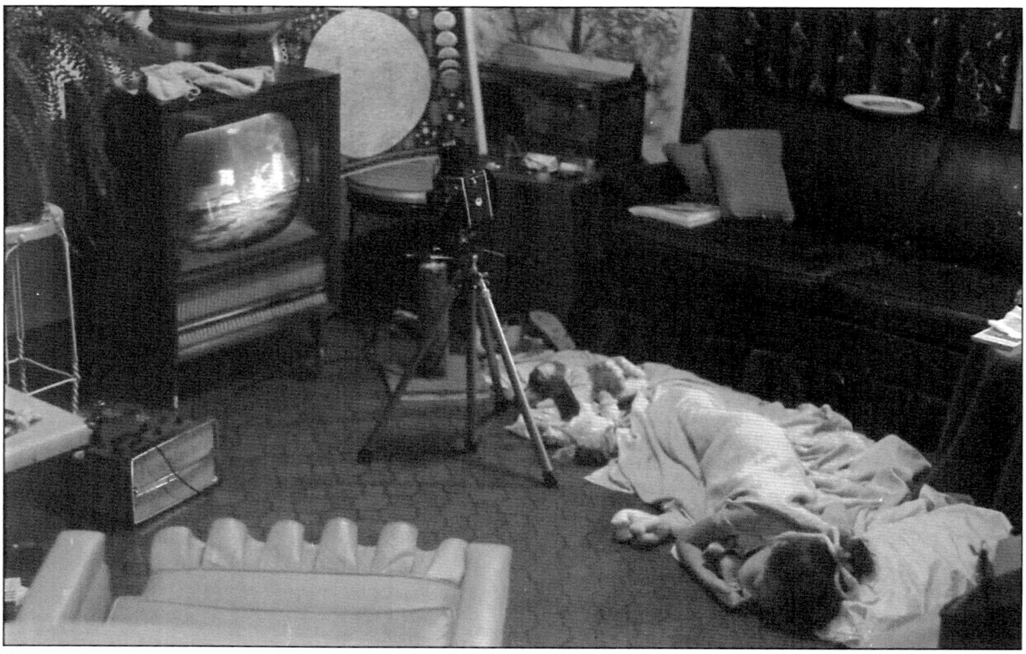

One Small Step. In the late hours of July 20, 1969, the United States made a great leap forward in the space race when Neil Armstrong first placed his booted foot on the surface of the moon. A sleepy little girl slumbered through the moment, but it was documented in this charming tableau, capturing the television image of the lunar-planted American flag and interplanetary charts and graphs amid the comforts of a typical 20th-century American home.

Three

THE 1970S
ALL IN THE FAMILY

The pain of Watergate and the disillusionment of a nation stoked the fires of 1970s discontent smoldering in an increasingly self-absorbed populace. The synthesized beat of disco and the synthetic wash-and-wear of polyester were 1970s symbols of change in pop culture, in women's roles, in a new politics of sexual equality that had permanent implications for life in the country, and in Bowling Green.

Increasing tensions between past and present created new forms of communication, or illuminated the lack thereof, between the generations, the sexes, and the races, as sit-ins, marches, protests, and riots became the norm. The Iran hostage crisis brought home the reality of an ever-shrinking world, while Kent State University, the killing fields of Cambodia, and the Jonestown massacre were unavoidable reminders of mortality.

The streets of Bowling Green, while perhaps greener and more sedate, bore telltale scars of growth. Sit-ins were held on the campus at Western Kentucky University, snowstorms and tornados rocked the countryside, and a growing police force dealt with increasing teenage drug and alcohol abuse. Cigarette companies remained major advertisers in local newspapers, and Kentuckians mourned the death of the king of rock and roll. The 1970s were new, strange, and difficult, yet oddly familiar.

Bowling Green families found more to watch and less time to watch it, as cable television entered their homes for the first time. Nostalgic recreations of *Happy Days* shared air time with a first on television: the acerbic wit of a black family living through *Good Times* together. Sexual mores and values were challenged and envelopes consistently pushed by shows such as *Saturday Night Live*, while televised fashions were ever more accessible with the opening of another multi-retail shopping mall on Scottsville Road.

The completion of Green River Parkway provided another high-speed point of access into and out of the city, and the hospitality industry flourished as travelers found their way to area restaurants and hotels. Traffic, an ever-changing problem for Bowling Green's leaders, required the expansion of Campbell Lane, while October 1979 saw the last passenger train make its final stop at the Louisville and Nashville Railroad depot.

The people of Bowling Green weathered the storms of the 1970s, and they did so with their classic philosophy of hard work, commitment to the future, and innovation. There were growing pains, but they were assuaged by common bonds, and photographer Tommy Hughes remained a constant, steady link in the chain of change.

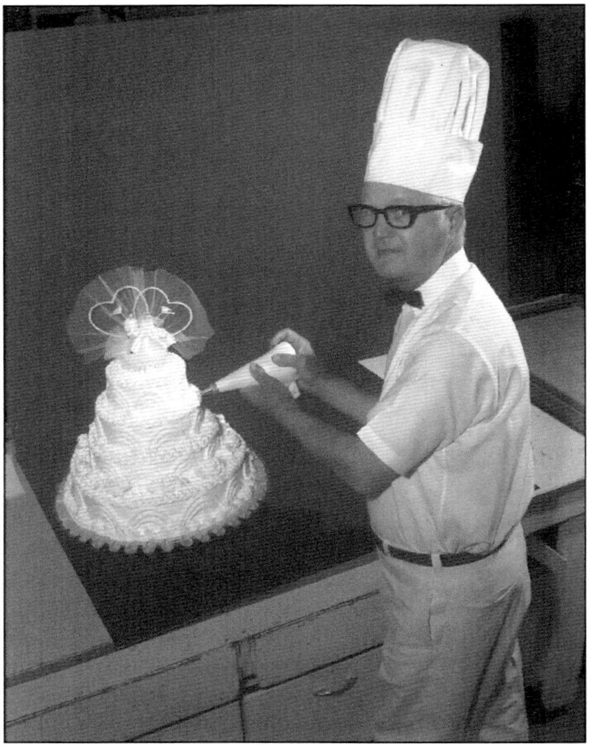

SWEET TREATS. William Riley took his first delicious cake out of a Bowling Green oven in 1943. Thousands of cakes later, Riley put his personal finishing touch on a wedding creation for a lucky bride and groom in this May 25, 1970, photograph. Active in civic life throughout his years in Bowling Green, Riley ran for mayor in 1967 and served as president of the chamber of commerce and of the Kentucky Retail Baker's Association. Lucky for Bowling Green, Riley's Bakery is still satisfying the sweet tooth of its residents at the store's U.S. 31-W Bypass location.

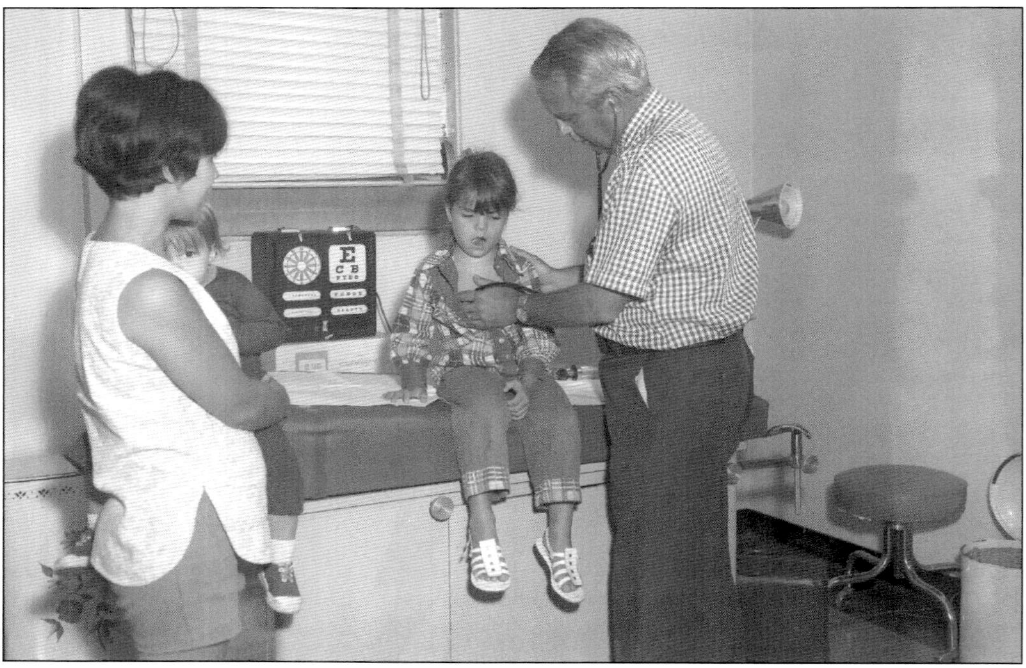

THE DOCTOR IS IN. Dr. Earl Williams treated hundreds of Bowling Green patients during his years of dedicated service. In 1973, this young patient dutifully held a big breath, while a nervous sibling peeked around mother.

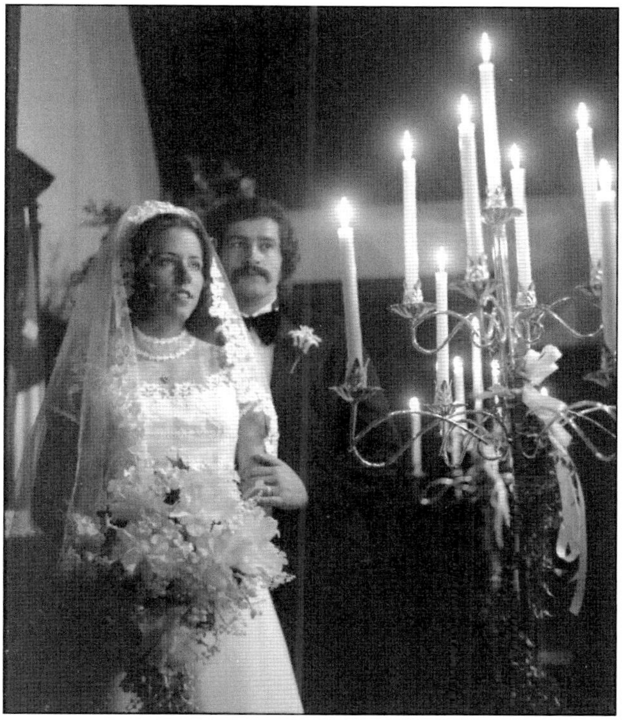

CANDLELIGHT AND ROSES. Ellen Deemer and Mike Buchanon celebrated their marriage at 8:00 p.m. on June 8, 1973. Officiated by Rev. H. Howard Surface at Christ Episcopal Church, the candlelit service was a study in lovely Southern ceremony, filled with the fresh scent of gardenias and orchids, pink roses, and lily of the valley. Beautiful bridesmaids in scalloped-brim pink-ribboned straw hats and handsomely suited groomsmen completed the elegant and memorable gathering.

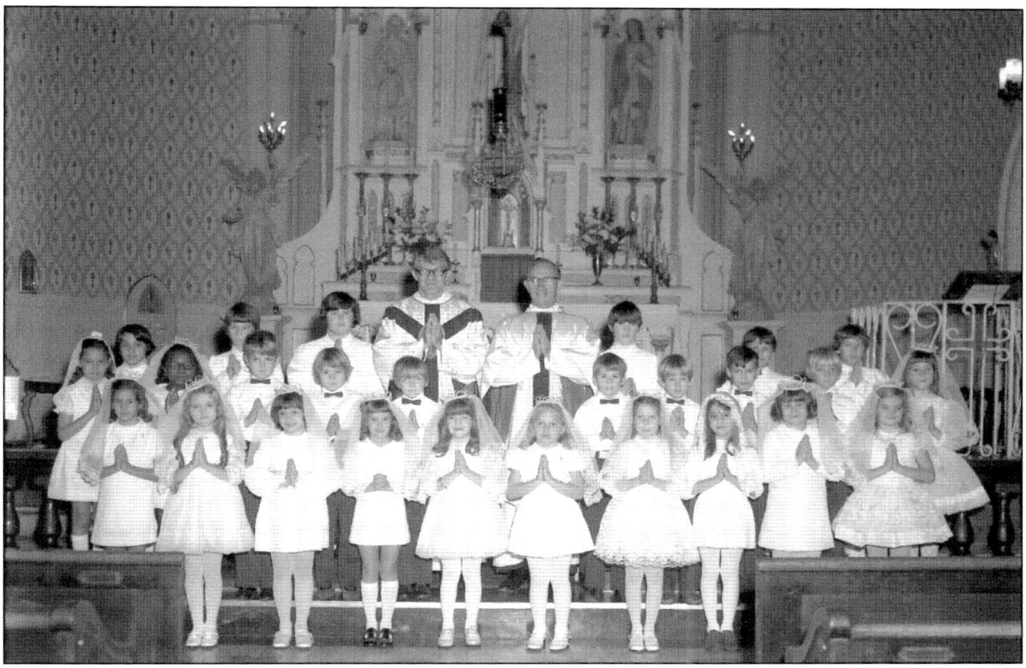

FIRST COMMUNION. A milestone of spiritual life, these young girls and boys celebrated their first communion at St. Joseph Catholic Church on December 10, 1979. Fr. Richard Powers (left) and Fr. Henry Willett officiated in the service as the lads and lasses took a first public step on their journey of faith.

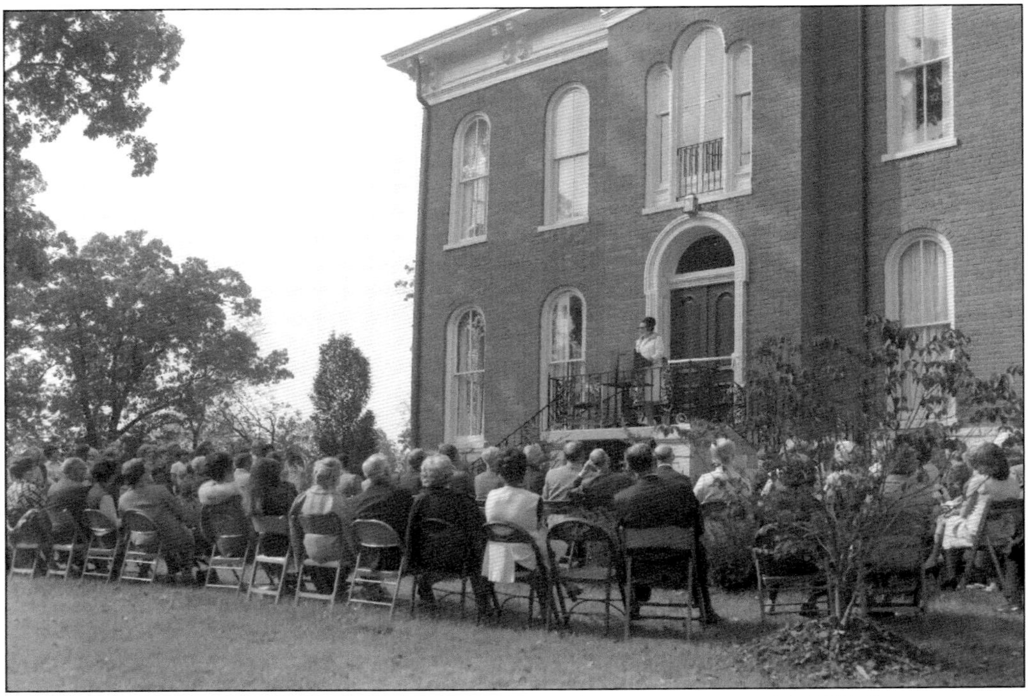

LOCAL LANDMARK. Members of the Hobson House Association met with U.S. Representative William Natcher, U.S. Senator John Sherman Cooper, Gov. Wendell Ford, and several hundred others at the October 16, 1972, dedication ceremonies held at Riverview. Henrietta Hines, president of the association, addressed the assembly, noting that seven years of dedicated work and contributions from local, state, and federal governments made the preservation of this historic landmark possible.

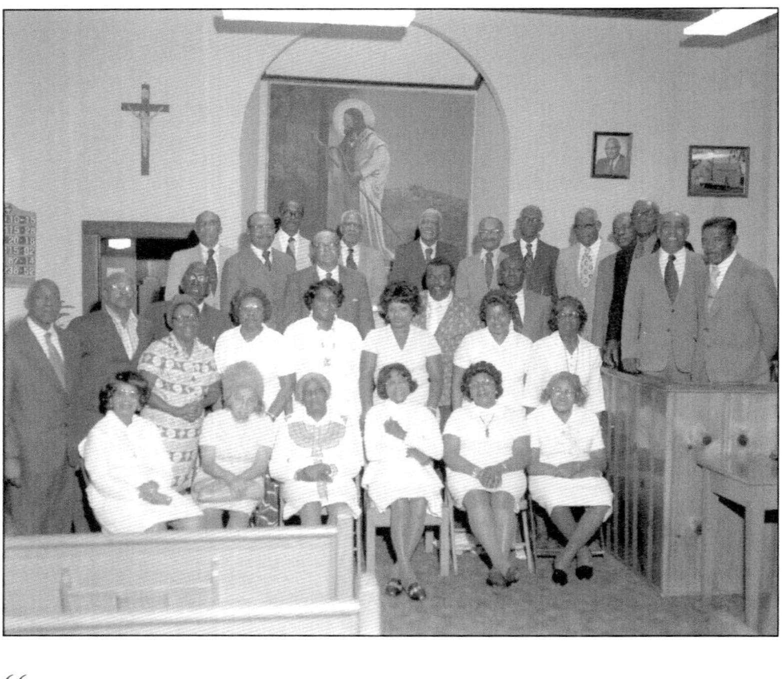

HEAVENLY HOME. Members of Eleventh Street Baptist Church and Pastor Herschel Halsell hosted the union district meeting on March 29, 1979. The church, then located at 874 East Eleventh Avenue, continues to be a vital part of the Bowling Green downtown church community, serving many generations of families.

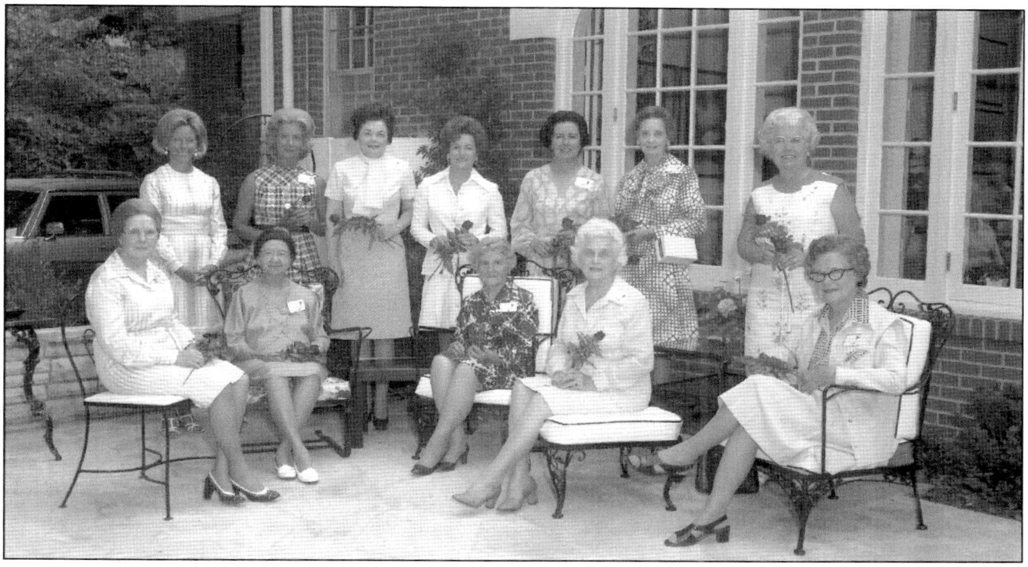

Grande Dames of the Garden. The Bowling Green Garden Club honored past presidents at a 40th-anniversary tea at the home of Carol McCormack in June 1974. These homegrown roses, dedicated to their mission of beautification of Bowling Green and of the state at large, include, from left to right, (first row) Ruby Berry, Mary O'Connor, Mabel Thomas, Ruth Rabold, and Kate Thompson; (second row) Judy Kirtley, Bette Barr, Nellie Brown, Carol Cooksey Malvey, Margaret Winkenhofer, Irene Sumpter, and Carol McCormack.

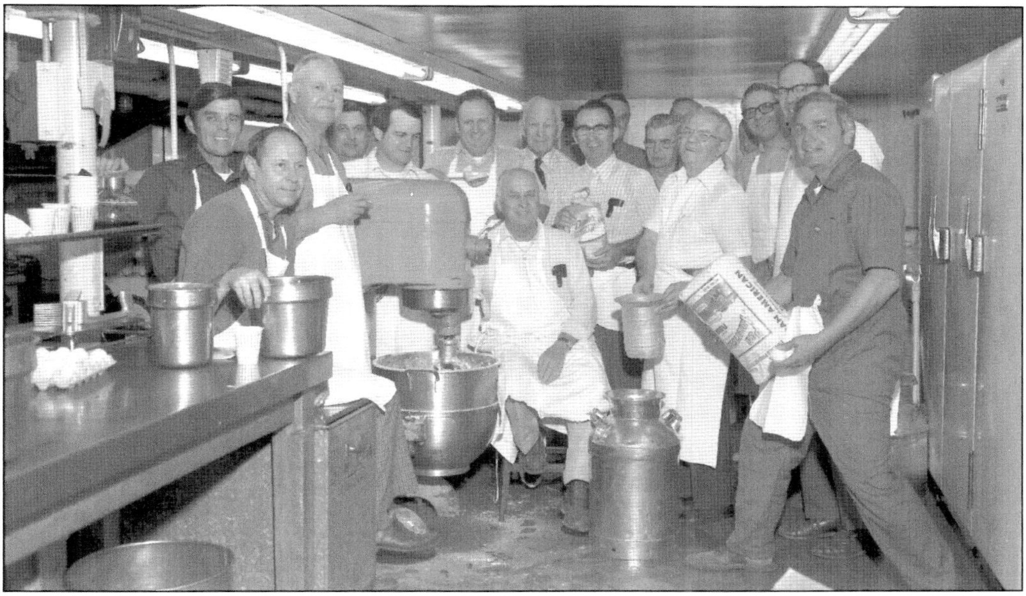

Lions Club Cuisine. Cooking it up for the Lions Club annual pancake fry, which has "been going on forever," members were ready to serve "all you can eat for $1.00" to hungry customers who gladly ate it up for a worthy cause. From left to right are Tom Webb (holding a bucket), Russell Goddard, John McGown, Warren Hines, Meredith Johnson, Cecil Watson, Charles Long (seated), unidentified, James Fisher, Furman Wallace, Bob Baldwin (holding a bowl), John Grider, John Jander, and John Moore.

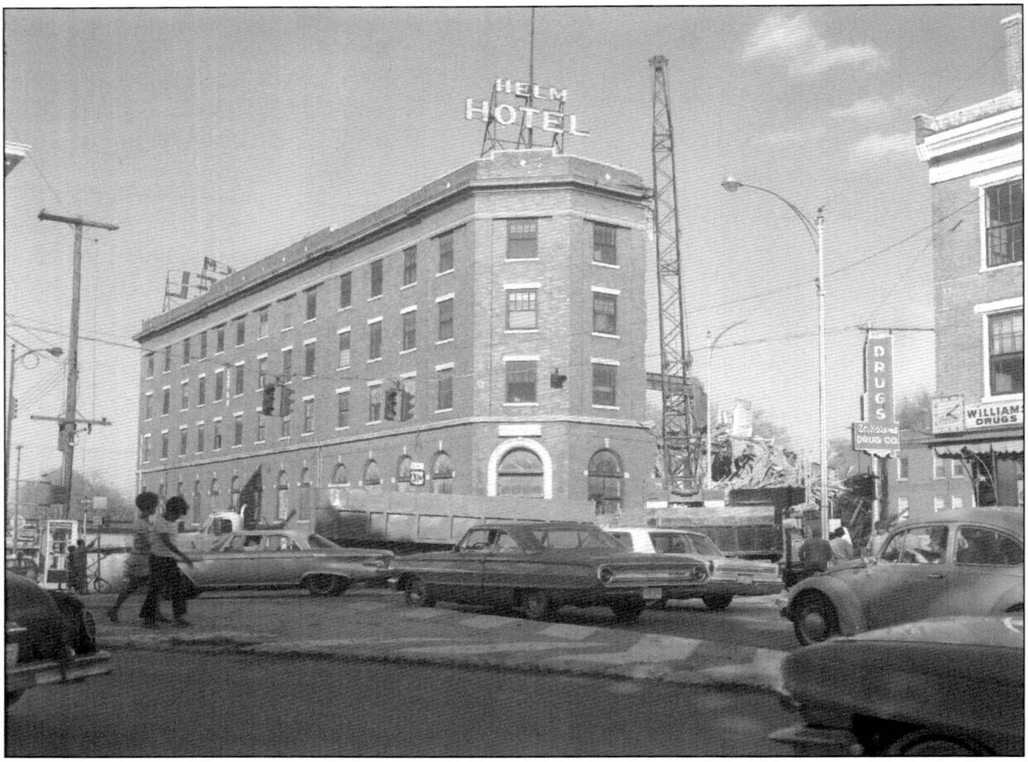

SOMEWHERE IN TIME. Hundreds if not thousands of weary travelers found rest at the Helm Hotel, originally built in 1923 at the hub of a bustling, thriving Bowling Green. Seen here on April 24, 1970, in the final stages of a 10-day demolition process, removal of the Helm to make way for a new Citizens National Bank building permanently changed the downtown Bowling Green landscape.

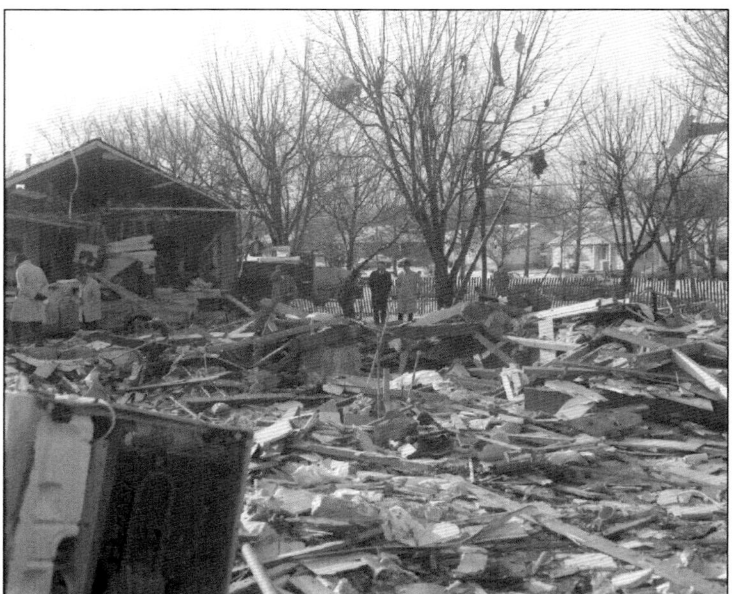

CATASTROPHE ON COVINGTON. A massive natural gas explosion at the home of Russell and Carole Miller at 604 Covington Avenue left death and destruction in its wake. A quiet Sunday afternoon, January 11, 1970, exploded in violence when a gas build-up at the Miller home erupted, causing damage to several homes and shattering windows in a block radius. A visitor to the Miller home did not survive, and five others were injured in the blast.

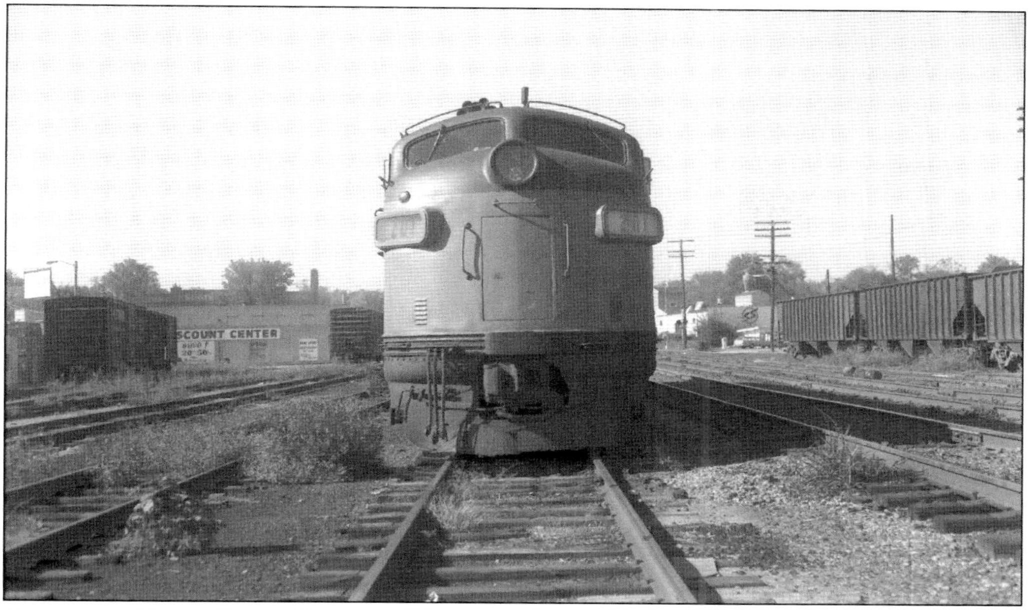

Riding the Rails. Pictured here in 1973, Louisville and Nashville Railroad engine No. 201 was ready with a valuable load of freight to depart from the train yard at the depot at 401 Kentucky Street. Opened in 1859, the depot helped to ensure Bowling Green's initial commercial success, serving as a hub of passenger and freight transportation for many years. The depot has been lovingly restored and remains a repository of the history of rail travel.

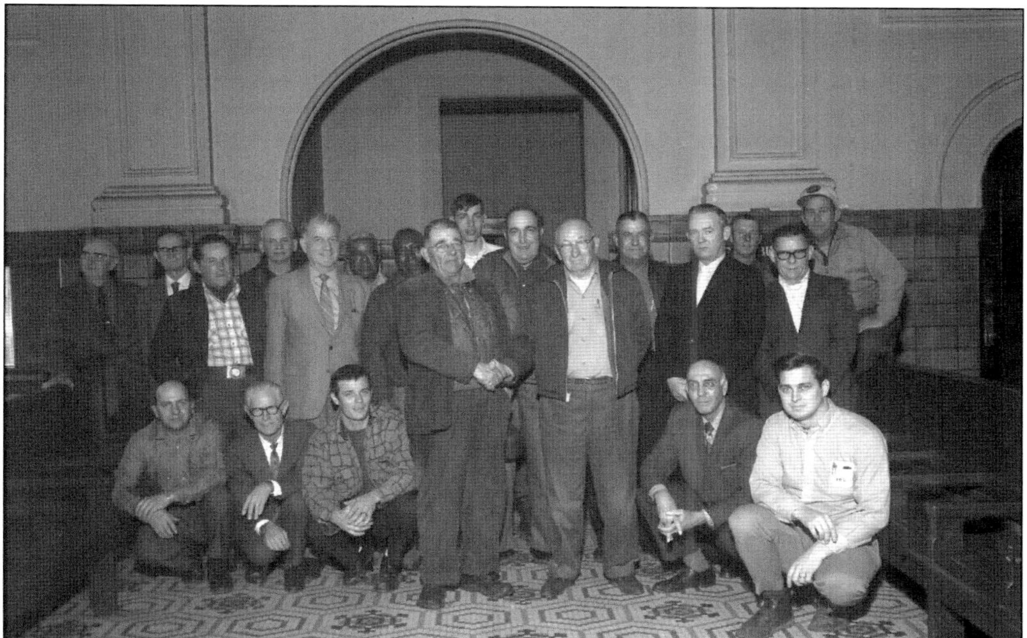

Rail Men. These men of the rails gathered inside the Louisville and Nashville Railroad depot at 401 Kentucky Street to bid an old year goodbye and to say farewell to familiar friends and faces during a retirement ceremony on December 31, 1970.

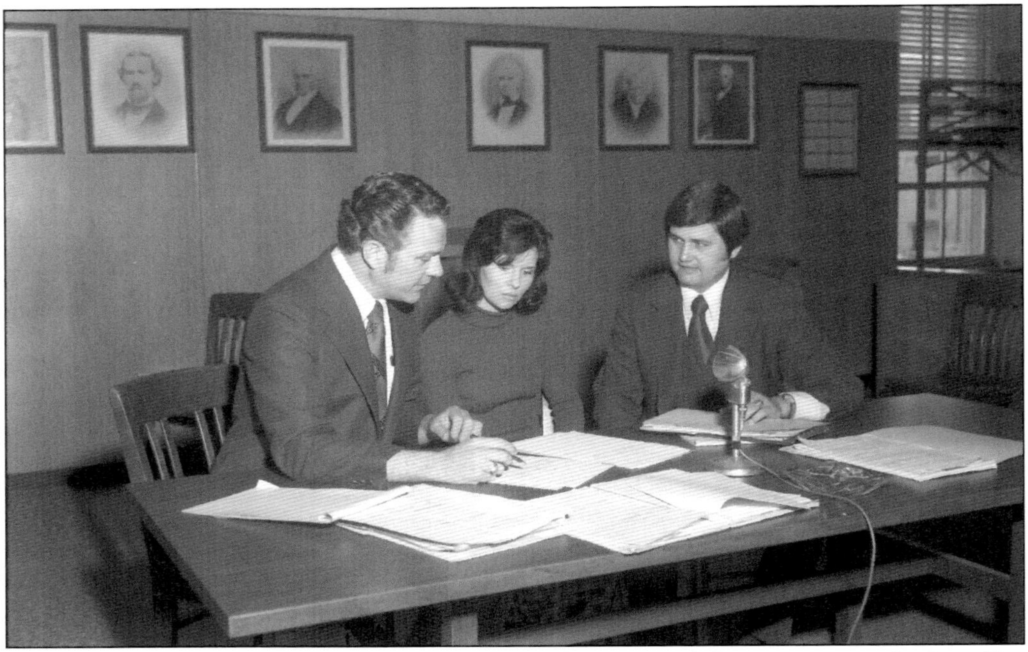

Legal Brief. Attorneys Gordon Johnson (left) and E. Kenneth Duncan met with client Eva Barnes on April 11, 1975, to discuss her ultimately successful legal case. Johnson served as the first public defender in Warren County.

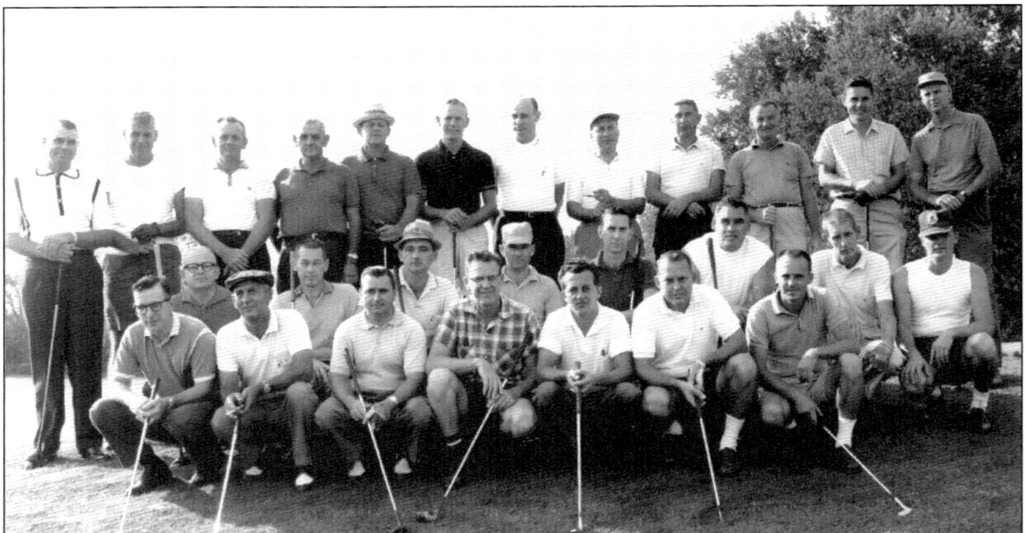

Power Built for Power Play. The Bowling Green Manufacturing Company Golf League met weekly for a day of camaraderie and competition on the links. Masters of the long drive and the short game in 1973 are, from left to right, (first row) Robert Kirby, Jim Jones, Jack Gillman, Neil Austin, Jerry Poston, Tom Montgomery, and Jerry Patton; (second row) Bill Snider, Charles Meeks, Rod Parrott, Jim Lowe, Jerry Manning, Tuffy Jeanette, Bob Tichenor, and Frank Moore; (third row) Jack Hawkins, Newt Robinson, Ed Hayden, Stanley Klabon, Watt Spencer, Johnny Upton, Ed Waggoner, George Bone, Don Peterson, R. L. Burnett, Bill Lindsey, and Paul Harrison.

FIREHOUSE HEROES. The brave men of the Bowling Green Fire Department gathered in front of the Central Fire Station in 1972. The department retired the brass fire pole from this location, where it had been in use since 1909, when the station was moved to its Fairview location in 1980. The pole will be installed in the new fire department administration headquarters for renewed use in a public education program.

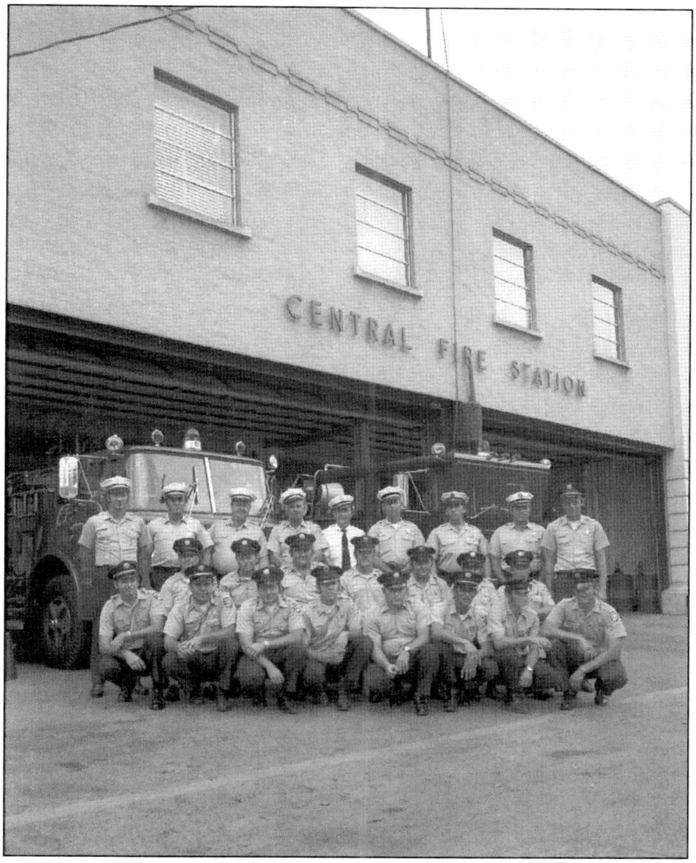

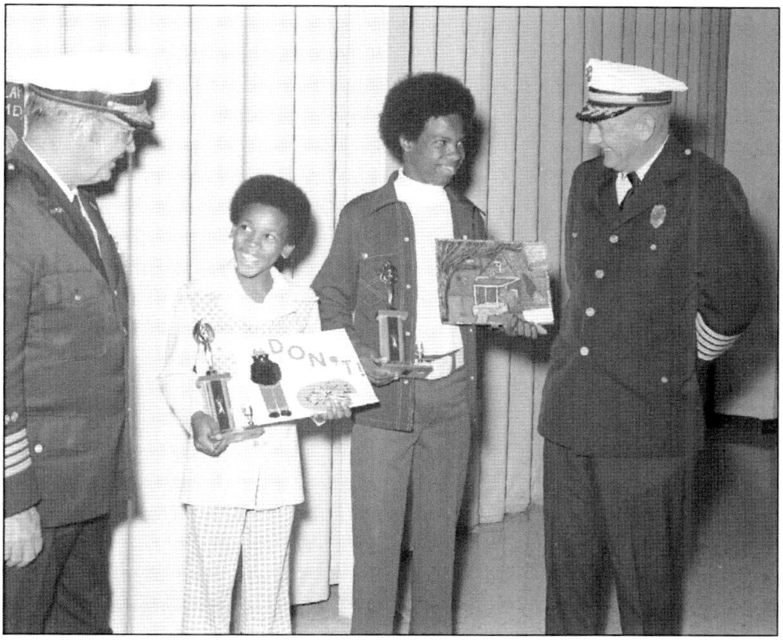

PRIZE ART. Bowling Green fire chief Lonnie Bellamy (right) congratulated two lucky artists on their winning entries in the December 1975 fire prevention poster contest. Smokey the Bear, originally created in 1944, would be proud to be a part of their artistically rendered campaign.

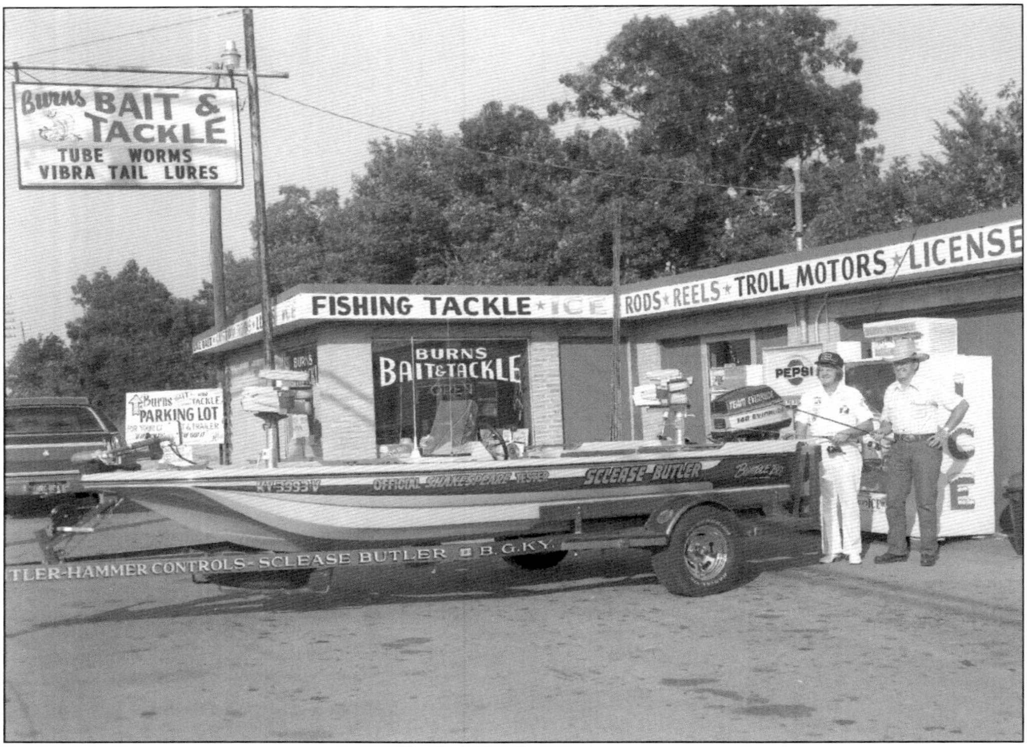

BASSMASTER. Professional angler Sclease Butler, with his prizewinning watercraft the *Bumble Bee*, posed with Harry Burns at Burns Bait and Tackle in 1975. Known for his expertise with rod and reel, Butler was an official Shakespeare tester and founder of the first bass club in the state of Kentucky in addition to being a prizewinning fisherman.

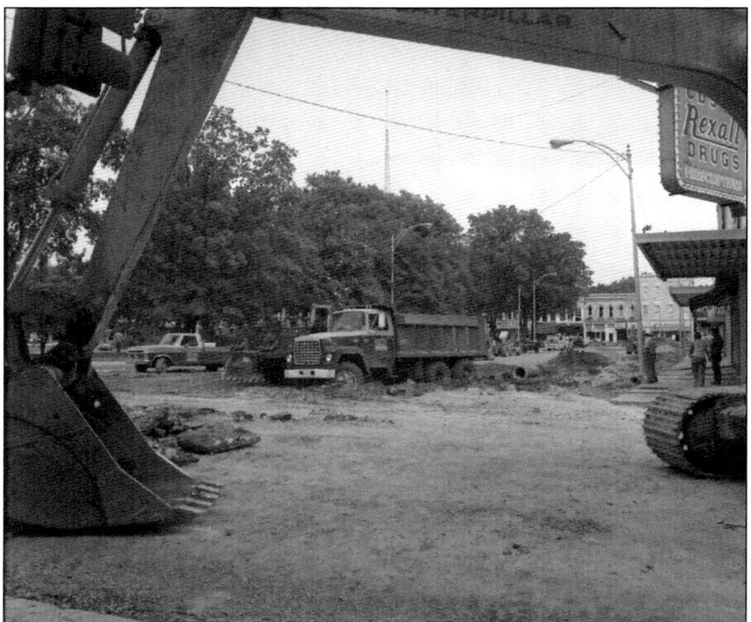

OPERATION TOWNLIFT. Just in time for the 1976 American bicentennial, the city of Bowling Green installed new sewer lines and sidewalks throughout the downtown area. Rough to live through but with lasting positive results, Operation Townlift was a major civic undertaking.

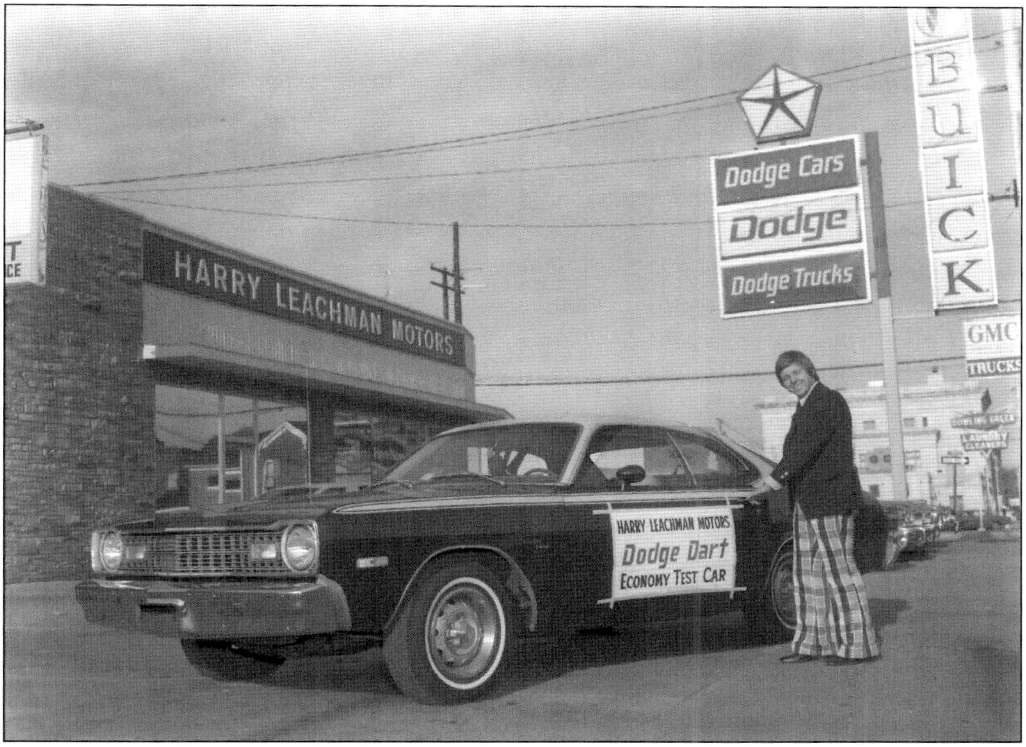

DECADE OF THE DODGE. Bill Leachman posed with this 1973 Dodge Dart economy test car at Harry Leachman Motors, then located at the corner of Tenth and Center Streets. Originally founded in 1946 by Harry Leachman, the family-owned company still provides Bowling Green citizens the latest in automotive transportation from its Scottsville Road location.

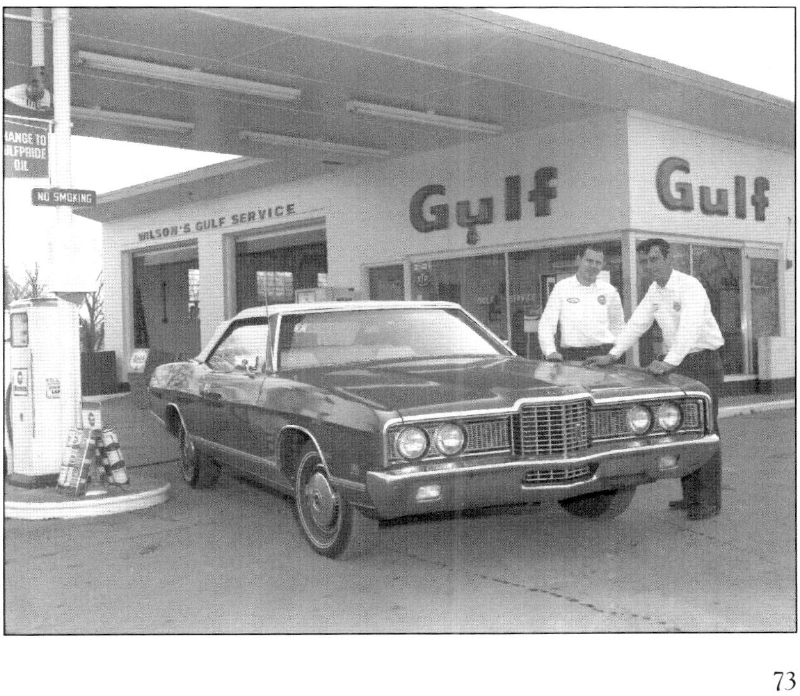

FILL IT UP. Melvin Wilson, owner of Wilson's Gulf Station at 730 Potter Street, offered a full array of service to busy travelers on December 29, 1971. From filling the tank and washing the windshield to airing up the tires and doing small repairs, motorists returned to the highway ready to travel.

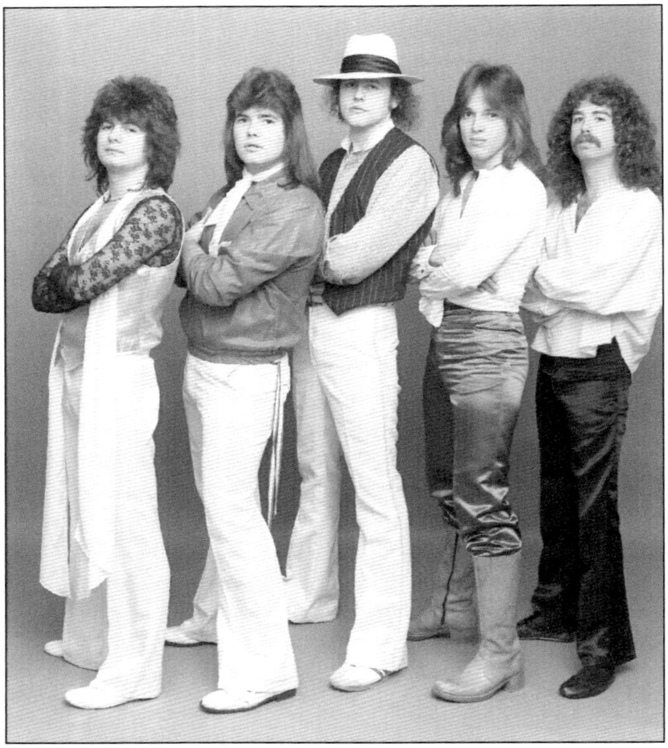

Rock On. Local band Ty Barc hit the charts in 1978 with *Whisper*, an original power ballad. Members, from left to right, are Tony Lindsey, Kyle Frederick, Jeff Brooks, Mitchell Plumlee, and David Dorris. Opening for Black Oak Arkansas, Brownsville Station, and Wet Willie, the band toured across the United States. Over 30 years later, Tony Lindsey, David Dorris, and Kyle Frederick, with drummer Fenner Castner, continue to write, record, and perform together as BoomTemple.

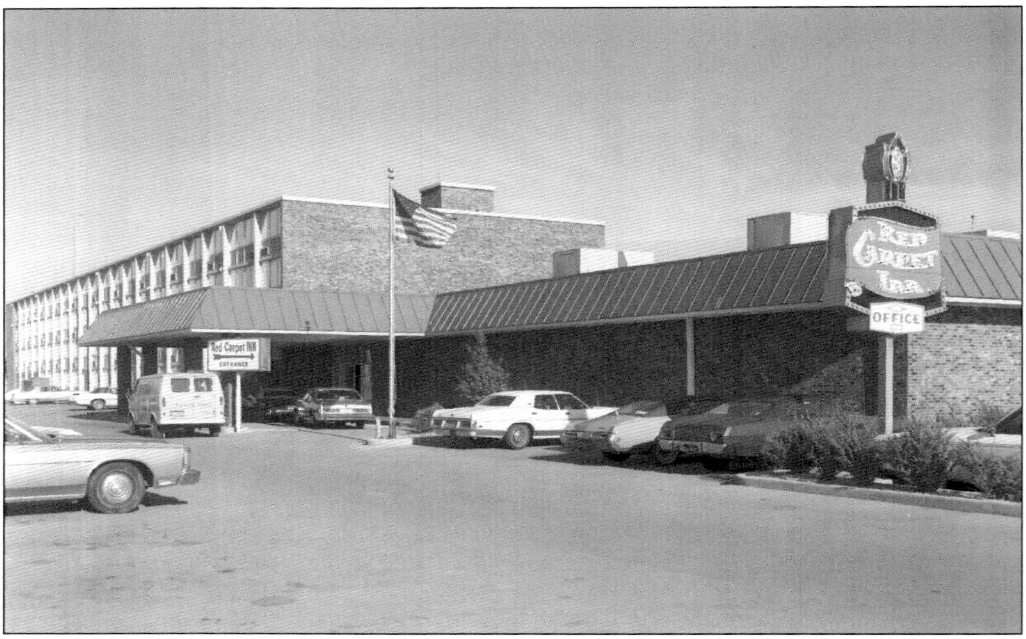

At the Red Carpet. A happening hot spot in 1974 Bowling Green, the Red Carpet Inn on Scottsville Road at Interstate 65 was the place to go for dances, graduation parties, banquets, or any other special occasion. Billed as "Bowling Green's major convention center," the Red Carpet offered live entertainment nightly and was the place for making memories.

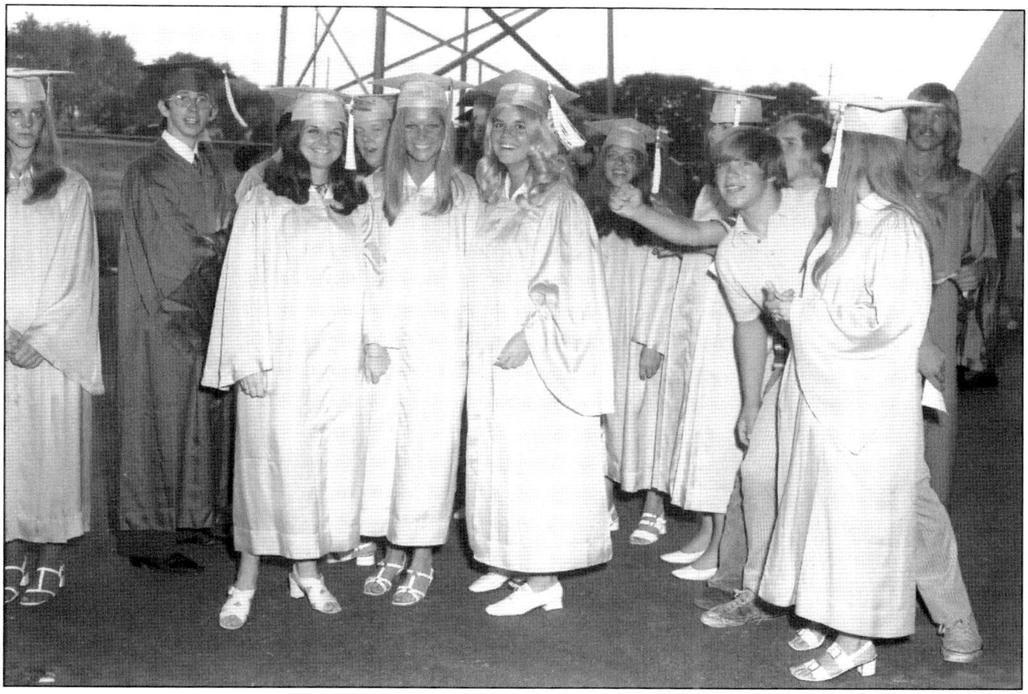

Pomp and Circumstance. On June 2, 1972, Bowling Green High School graduates celebrated their accomplishments with a little less pomp and a lot more circumstantial fun. The unquenchable smiles of new alums, from left to right, Beverly Davenport, Jane Manar, and Lisa Gary lit up this post-graduation gathering.

Disco Fever. Sizzling hot fashion and mesmerizing music made this 1972 dance a memorable night for Bowling Green High School students Marcia Harpool (seated, left) and (standing, from left to right) William White, Deborah Claypool and Stephanie Halsell.

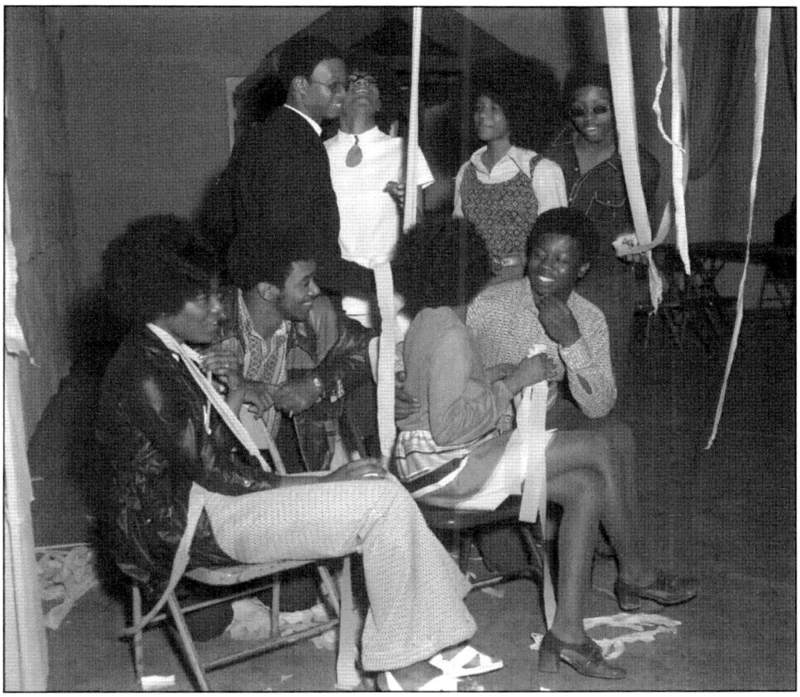

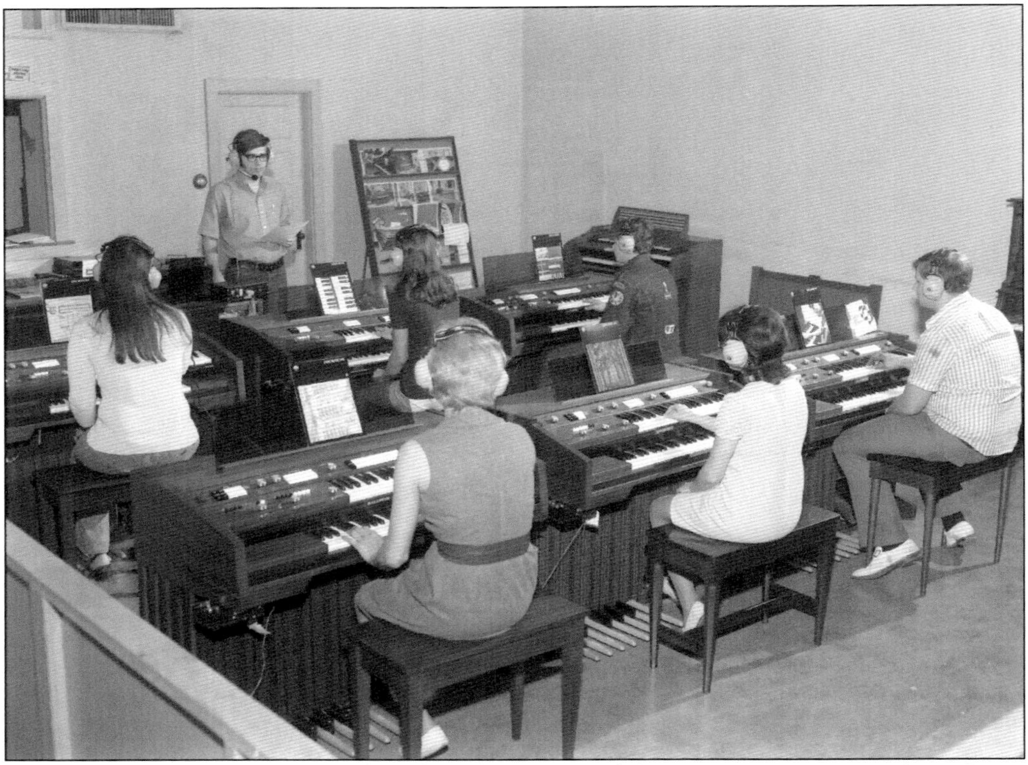

FINDING MIDDLE C. Students at the Etherridge Piano and Organ Company at 1029 State Street listened attentively to their instructor through state-of-the-art headphones on May 6, 1972. Group learning centers and laboratory instruction were popular music teaching methods of the time.

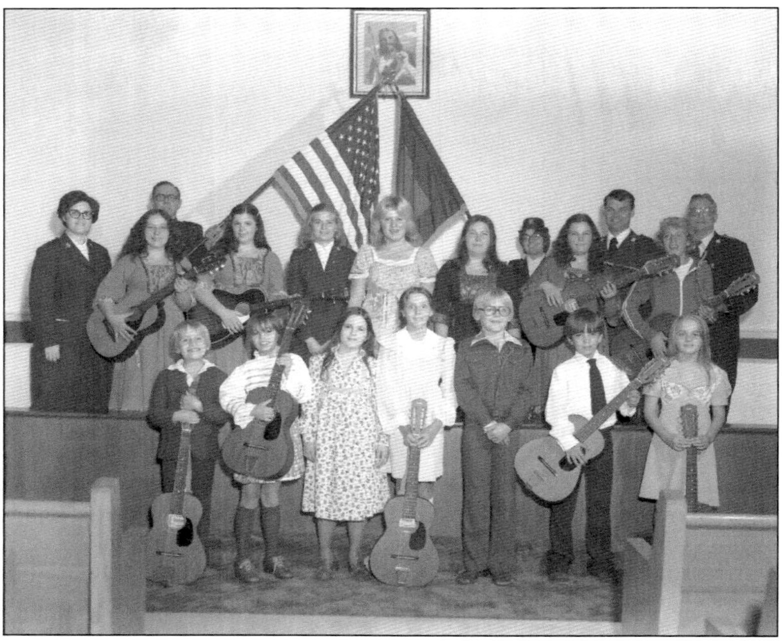

SALVATION SOUNDS. The Salvation Army Band met for rehearsal on October 8, 1978, at 401 West Main Street. Committed to serving those in need, the band provided a haven for musical creativity as well as an accompaniment for years of dedicated work and service to the community, which included almost 7,000 meals served.

Garish Ghouls. Jeff Feix (standing) and Peter Bryant were all set for Halloween haunting in 1972, when they sported fierce fangs, facial lacerations, and blank, zombie stares. Feix (son of Western Kentucky University football coach Jimmy Feix) went on to obtain a doctorate in forensic psychology, while a much less frightening Bryant became the silver-tongued station manager of WKYU-FM.

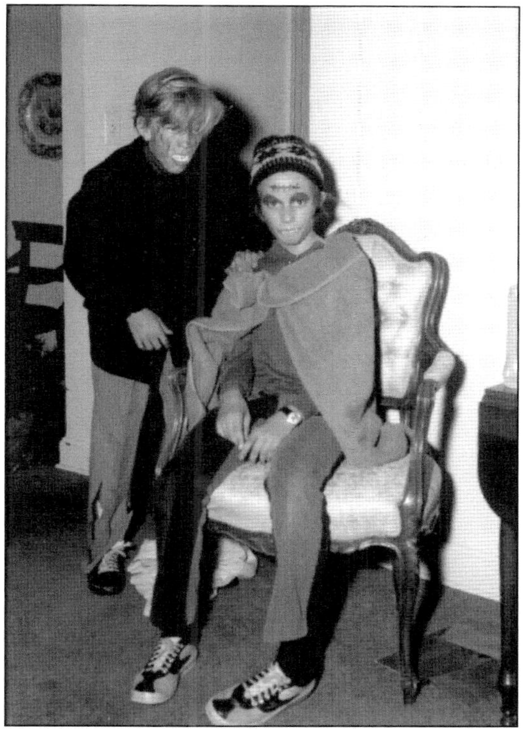

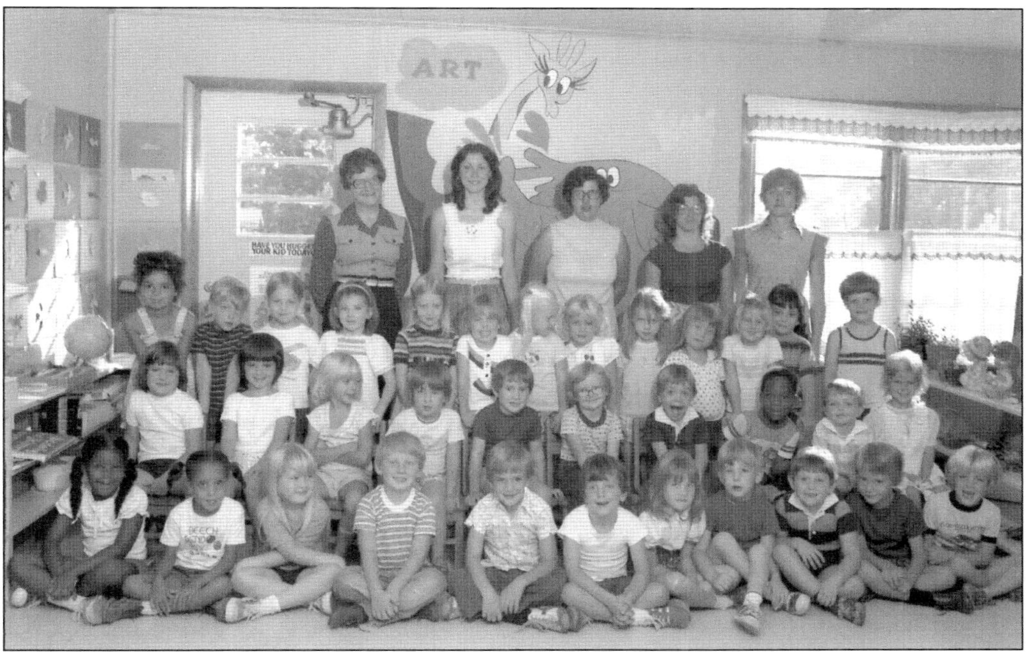

Sunny School Days. Jolly Time Pla Skool, owned by Rubye Dodd at 923 East Tenth Street, was ready for back-to-school time in September 1978. The preschool and day care provided generations of Bowling Green children a sunny, happy place for fun and games as well as lessons in the alphabet, art, and mathematics.

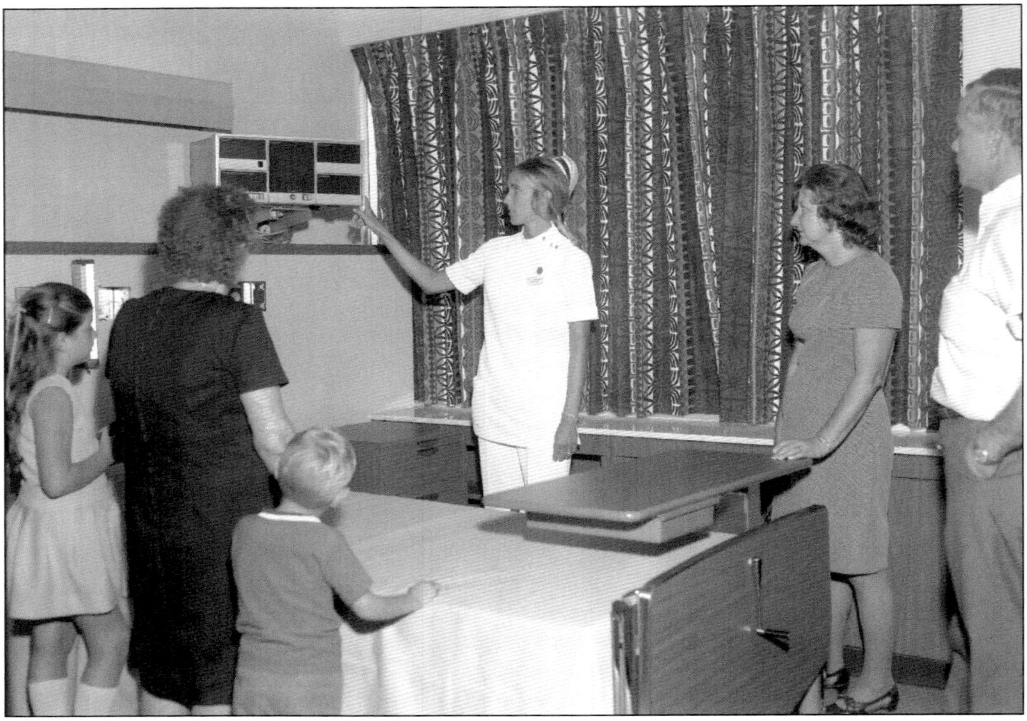

Greenview Gala. A Greenview Hospital nurse explained the latest in medical technology during an August 27, 1972, sneak-peak tour prior to the hospital's September 1972 opening. Over 3,000 attendees were on hand for tours of the new facility, while keynote speaker Dr. Dero Downing, then president of Western Kentucky University, cited the great regional economic impact to be provided by the facility. The day was made complete by the ceremonial cutting of a ribbon of medical gauze.

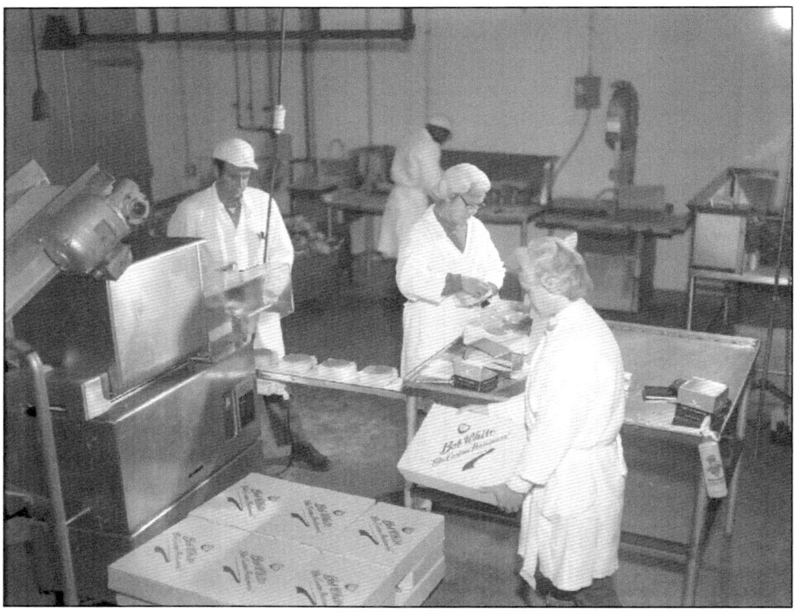

Meat Packing Mecca. The Bob White Packing Company, under the management of Robert A. Hardy at 1218 Boat Landing Road, was a hive of activity where "the custom portioners" went about the business of providing meats throughout the region in 1972.

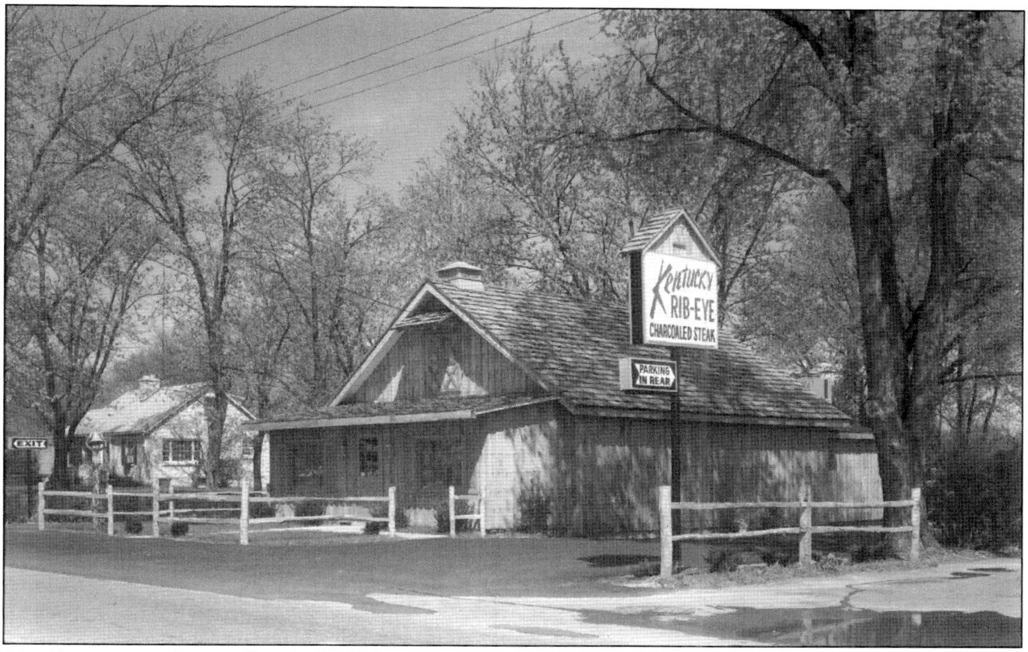

The Place for Steak. Kentucky Ribeye, at 956 Fairview Avenue, was the place to dine on April 19, 1970. Owned by Sonny Barr, John Logan, and Herb Smith, the restaurant was known for its succulent steak, cut to order at the patron's table, and delicious loaves of steaming hot, homemade bread.

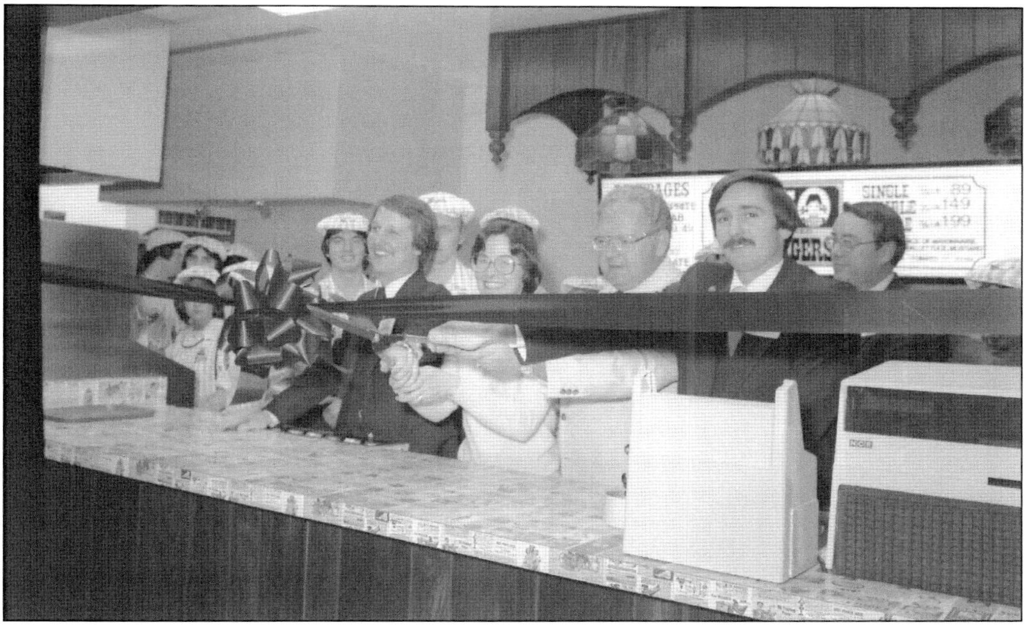

Fries and a Frosty, Please. Restaurateurs Dan Davis (front row, left) and David Mason (front row, right) cut the ribbon at the grand opening of their Wendy's franchise on Scottsville Road on January 22, 1979. Wendy's founder Dave Thomas and Mayor Pro Tem Patsy Sloan wielded the scissors at the event, when a single was only 89¢. Davis and Mason went on to establish the Rafferty's restaurant chain.

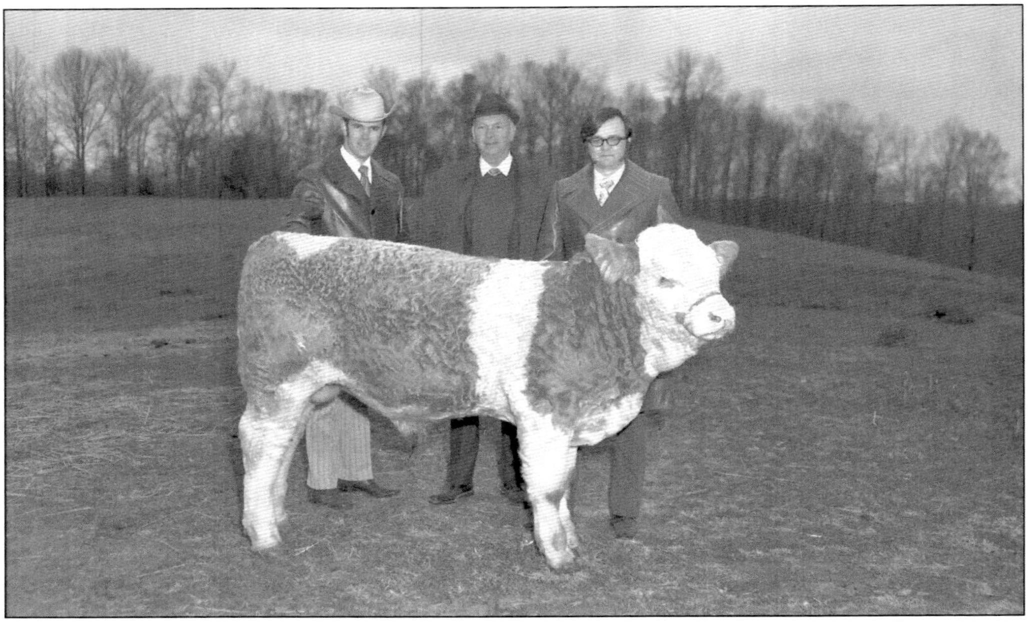

Blue Ribbon Bull. Warren County beef and dairy farming has long been an essential component of Bowling Green's agricultural economy. Dr. John Tapp (far right) successfully embarked in the development of breeding stock. He posed here in 1974 with, from left to right, Mack Jones, Ernest Tapp, and a prizewinning specimen.

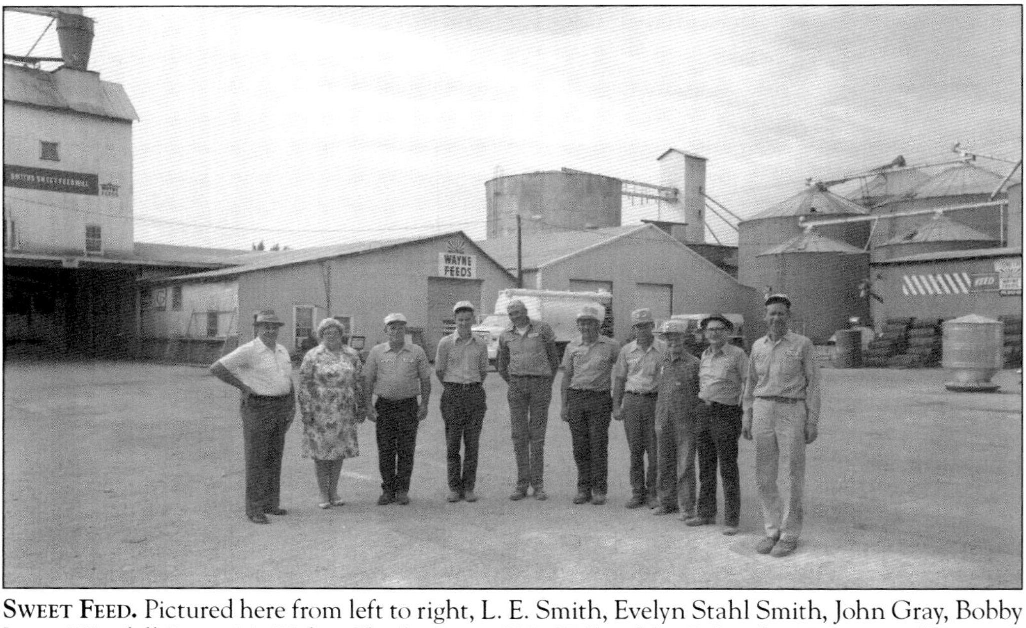

Sweet Feed. Pictured here from left to right, L. E. Smith, Evelyn Stahl Smith, John Gray, Bobby Jones, Wendell Scott, Mr. Haley, Charles Jones, Kyle Willoughby, Talmadge Hodges, and Kenneth Manley were active participants in the Bowling Green farming community. The Smiths were owners of Smith's Sweet Feed Mill at 1267 Adams Street. Their contribution to Kentucky farming extended all the way to Frankfort, when their son Billy Ray Smith became the commissioner of agriculture for the state of Kentucky.

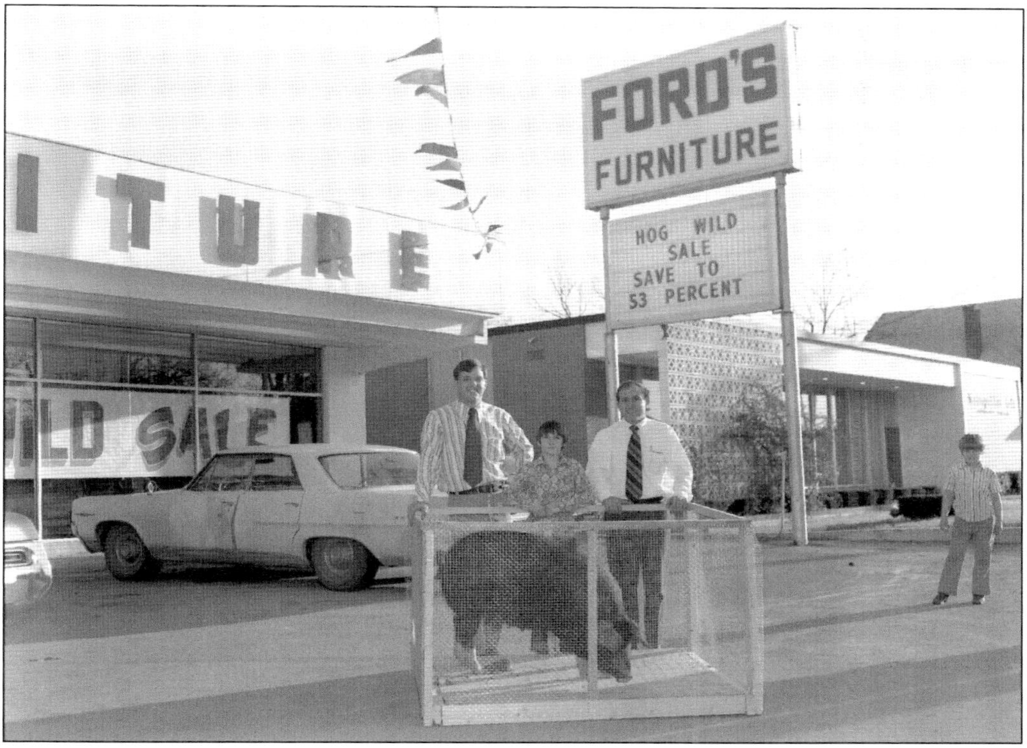

Hog Wild. Springtime in 1973 was when Harry (left) and Alvin Ford went hog wild at Ford's Furniture Store, then located on Laurel Avenue. Sixth-grader Jay Schaeufele, son of John and Martha Schaeufele of Alvaton, was the lucky winner of this 283-pound hog at the conclusion of the guess-the-weight contest on March 31, 1973. The Ford brothers continue to meet the furniture needs of Bowling Green and surrounding communities from their new location on Scottsville Road, with a little less pork.

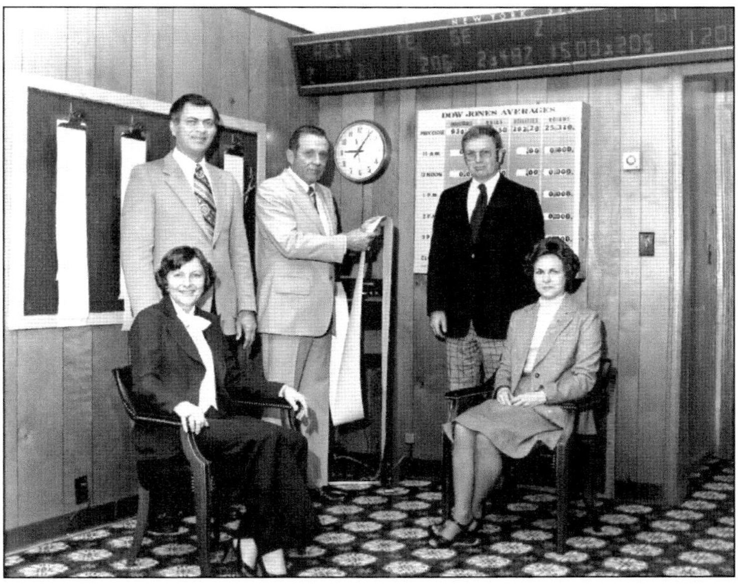

Market Report. Ticker tape and a hand-updated number board with 1978 Dow Jones averages were staples of the stock brokerage business when Hilliard Lyons professionals managed their clients' accounts. From left to right are (seated) Linda Denning and Carole Helton; (standing) Richard Jackel, Murray Hill, and Pete Mahurin.

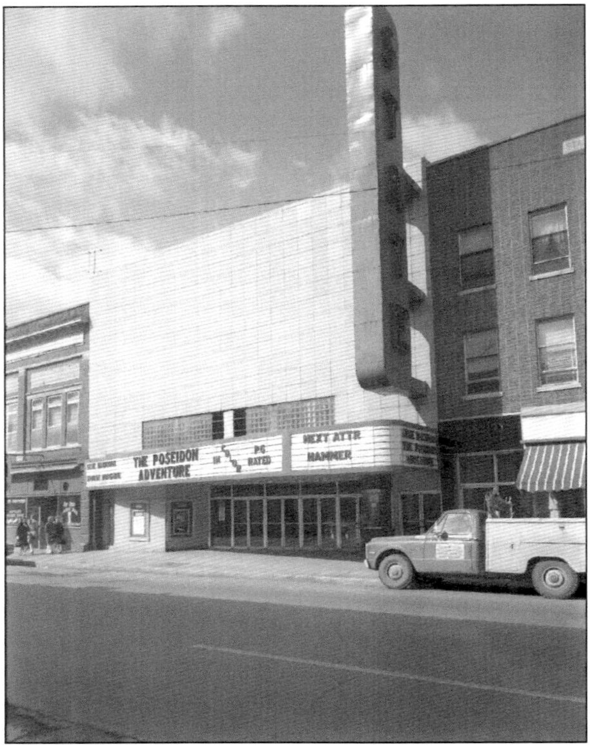

Modern Cinema. Showing on February 19, 1973, at the State Theatre at 929 College Street was *The Poseidon Adventure*, an early disaster movie that registered titanic success with its story of a doomed ship's watery demise. Not to be overlooked in its attention to modern technology, the marquee denotes that the *Poseidon*'s unlucky end could be viewed "in color"—still worth mention in 1973.

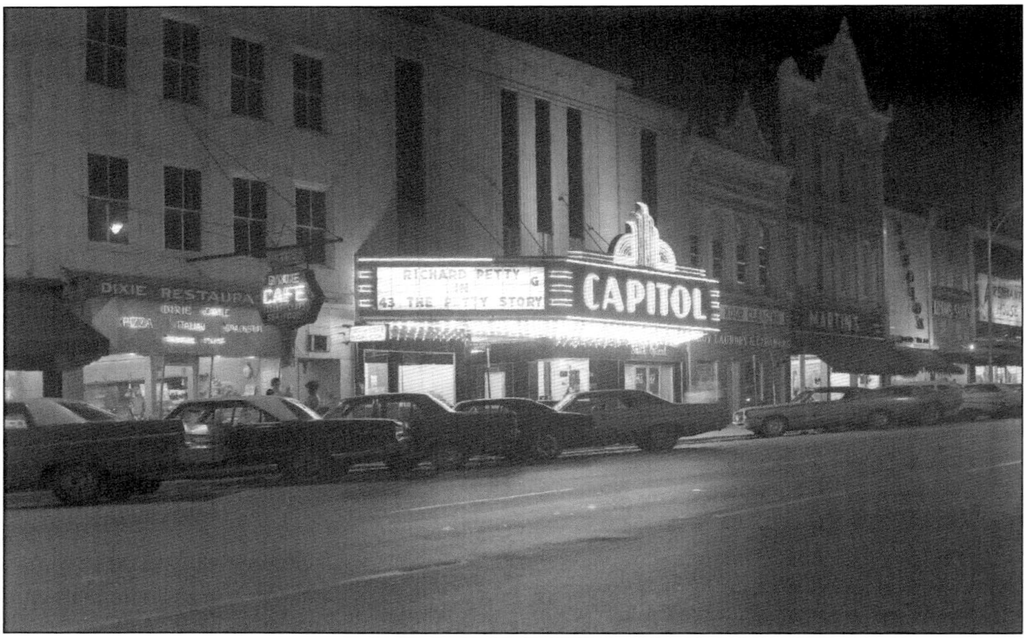

Bright Lights, Big City. The marquee at the Capitol Theatre at 416 East Main Street brightly burned, inviting all passersby to see Richard Petty in *43: The Petty Story* on October 13, 1972. The theater, originally called the Columbia, operated as a cinema for many years and remains open to the public today as a venue for the performing arts.

Abracadabra. Wandi the Magician (played by Jim Wilkins, left) wowed audiences throughout the Bowling Green region with his sleight of hand and original magic. Assisted by daughter Becky Wilkins Harrell and sons Nick and Andy, Wandi was an integral feature of south-central Kentucky entertainment. His legacy lives on in Broadway the Clown, originally created and still characteristically portrayed by Nick Wilkins in venues large and small.

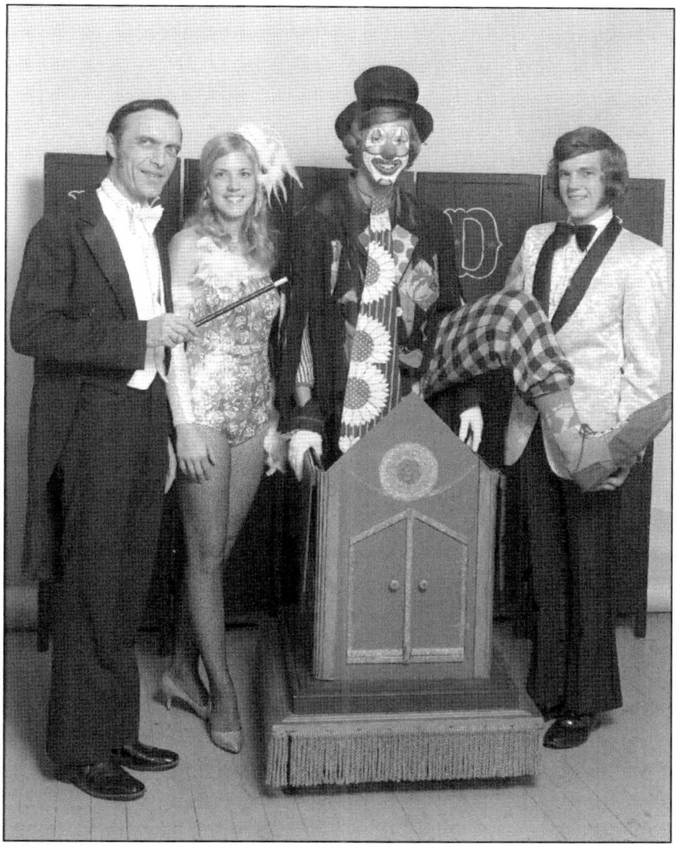

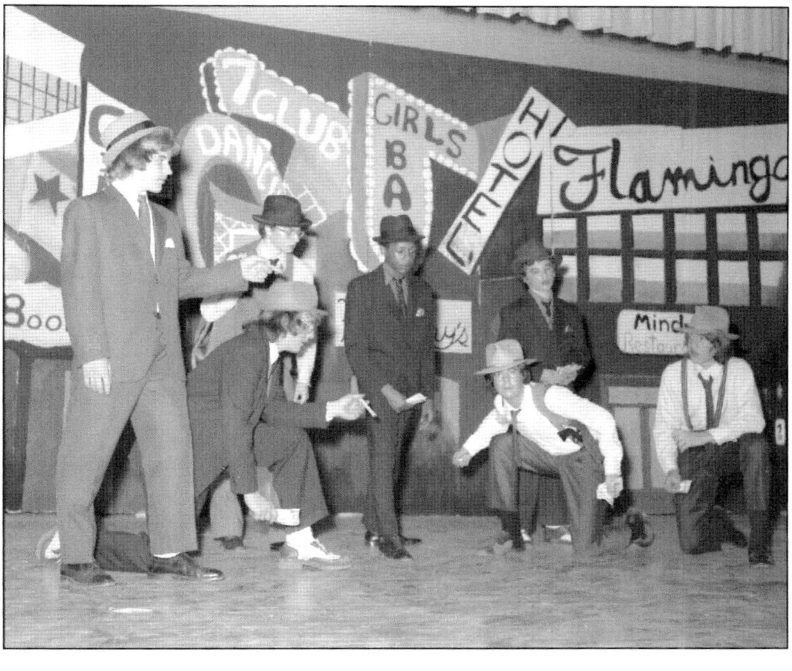

Stage Presence. These debonair young fellows were calling the odds and placing their bets in Bowling Green Junior High School's 1975 production of *Guys and Dolls*, directed by Jean Stark. Pictured from left to right are (first row) Fred Rich, David Holland, and Craig Martin; (second row) Tony Henon, Jeff Nash, Odell Wilson, and John Caudill.

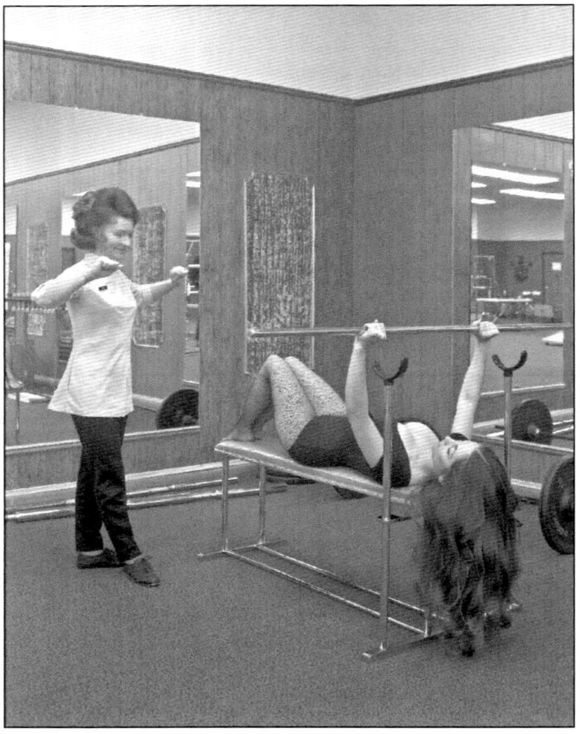

Pumping Iron. In 1971, getting in shape at the Imperial Health Spa at 1901 Russellville Road was sure to make fitness enthusiasts "look better and feel better" at "Bowling Green's only private health club for men and women."

Lois-Glyn Ladies. A weekly visit to the Lois-Glyn Beauty and Tot Shop at 912 State Street was a must in many a Bowling Green lady's personal calendar. Founded in 1932, the shop was an entrepreneurial innovation, incorporating a children's clothing store and beauty salon in one location. Pictured from left to right, owner Rebecca Williams, Janet Carver, Linda Harrod, Ruth McBride, and Lena Milam stayed current on the latest 1972 styles and techniques.

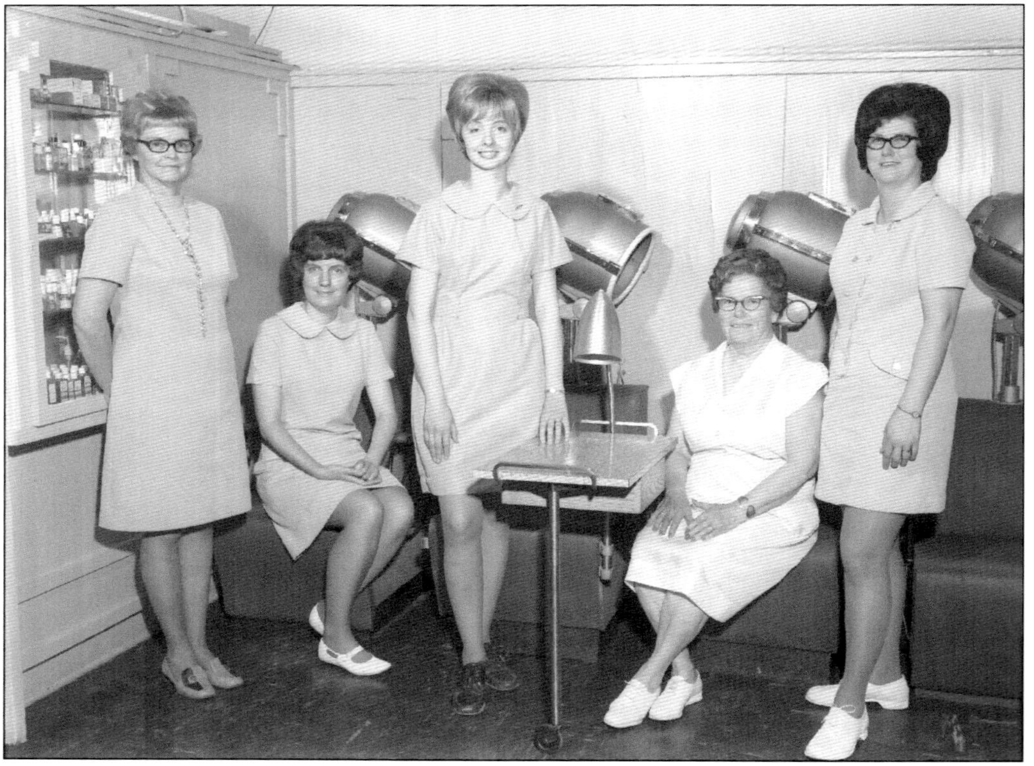

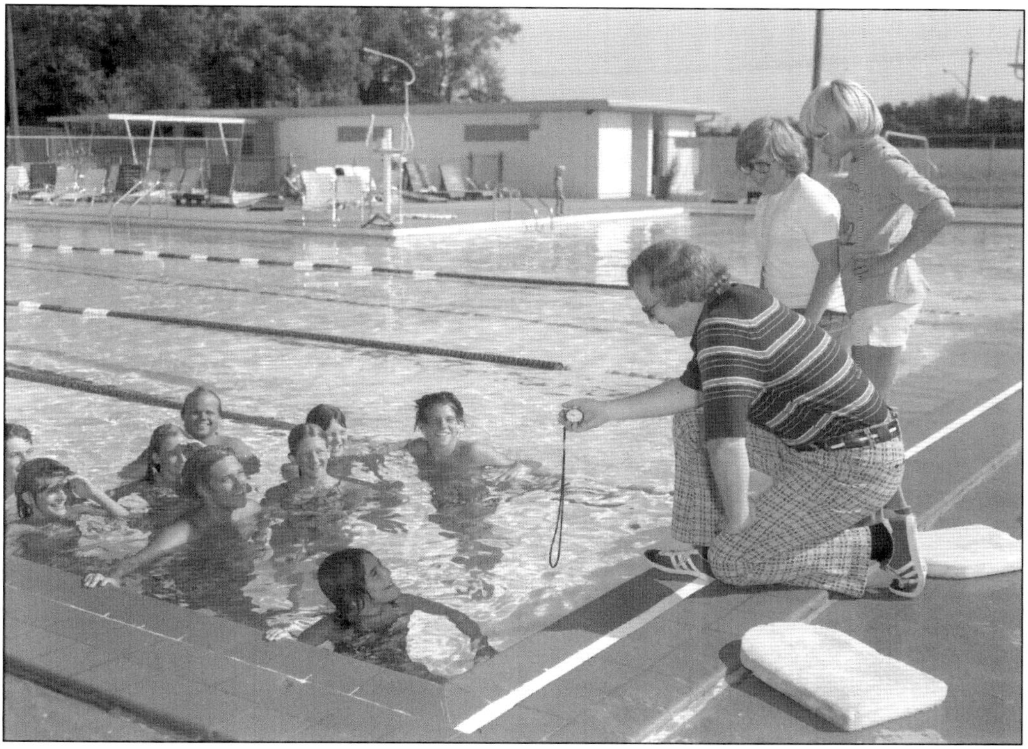

Free Style. Coach Craig Dodson kept the clock as members of the Southland swim team perfected their times at a June 4, 1974, practice. The private swimming club is still in operation, and the Southland Sharks continue to compete in regional swim events throughout the area.

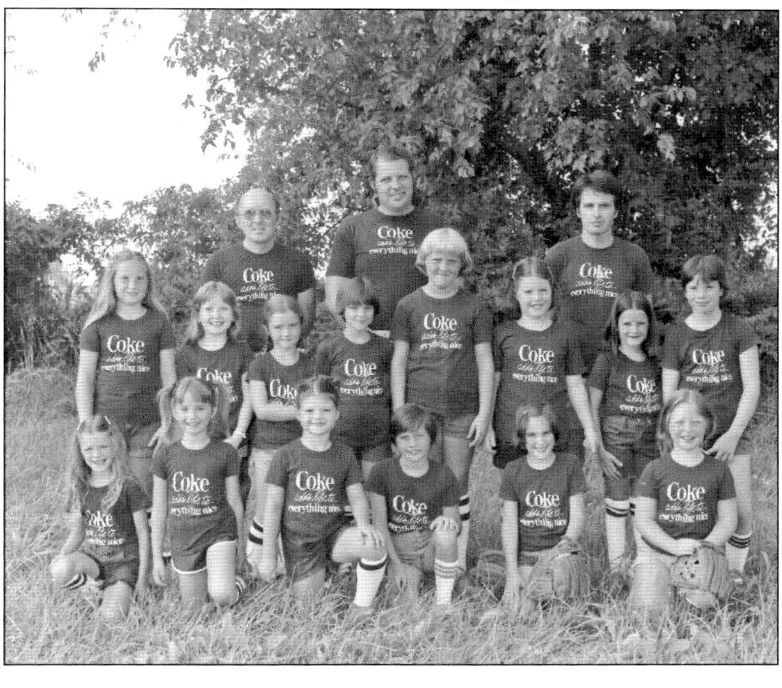

Saints of Softball. Enjoying a summer of softball fun, with the generous sponsorship of Coca-Cola, were the tube sock–sporting Saints, a Bowling Green team under the coaching leadership of Bob White (left), Larry Elmore (center), and Larry Smith.

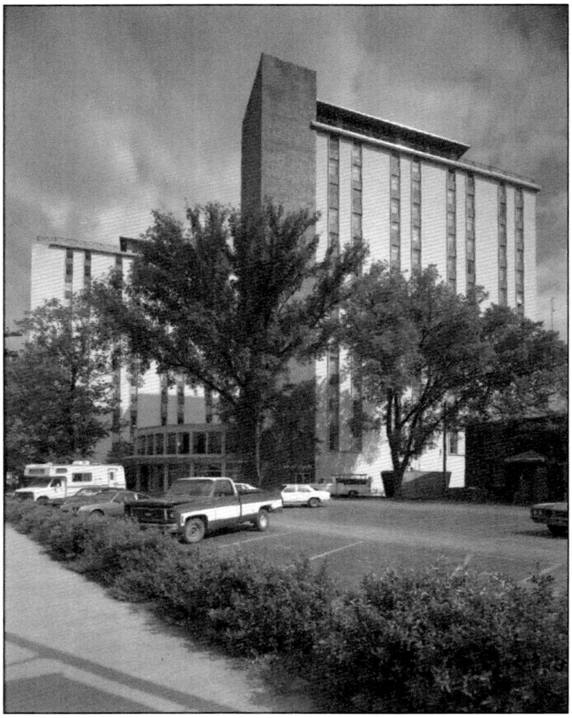

High-Rise Living. The College Inn at 1149 College Street was originally designed as state-of-the-art college housing, with a pool and many other amenities for the modern college student. The facility is still a hub of life, providing housing for an older generation as Bowling Green Towers.

Hearth to Home. Warren County Realty Company urged potential home buyers to go "hearth" shopping in December 1977. Pictured some 30 years after its 1947 establishment, members of the firm from left to right are (first row) D. C. Riley, Howard Poindexter, George Justice, and David Williams; (second row) Willard Thomas, Marion Thomas, Frances Graham, Judy McCoy, Gilbert Biggers, Beverly Crow, Joan Miller, Sammye Riley, Dot Brown, Violet Perkins, and Tom Runner.

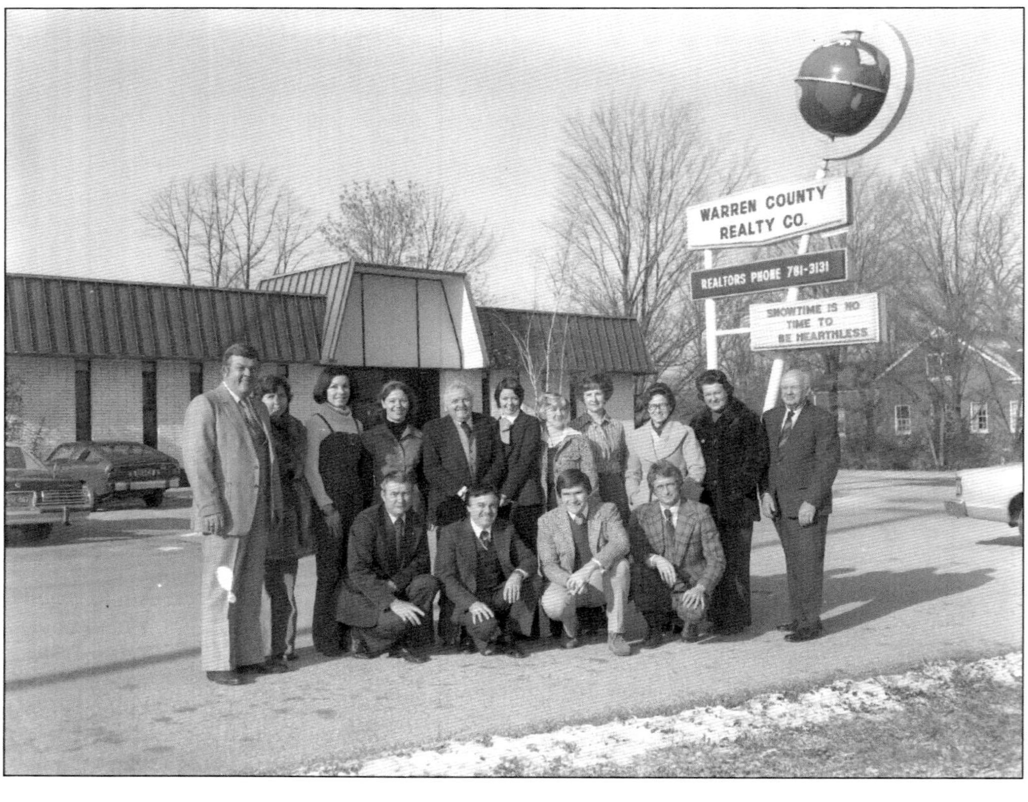

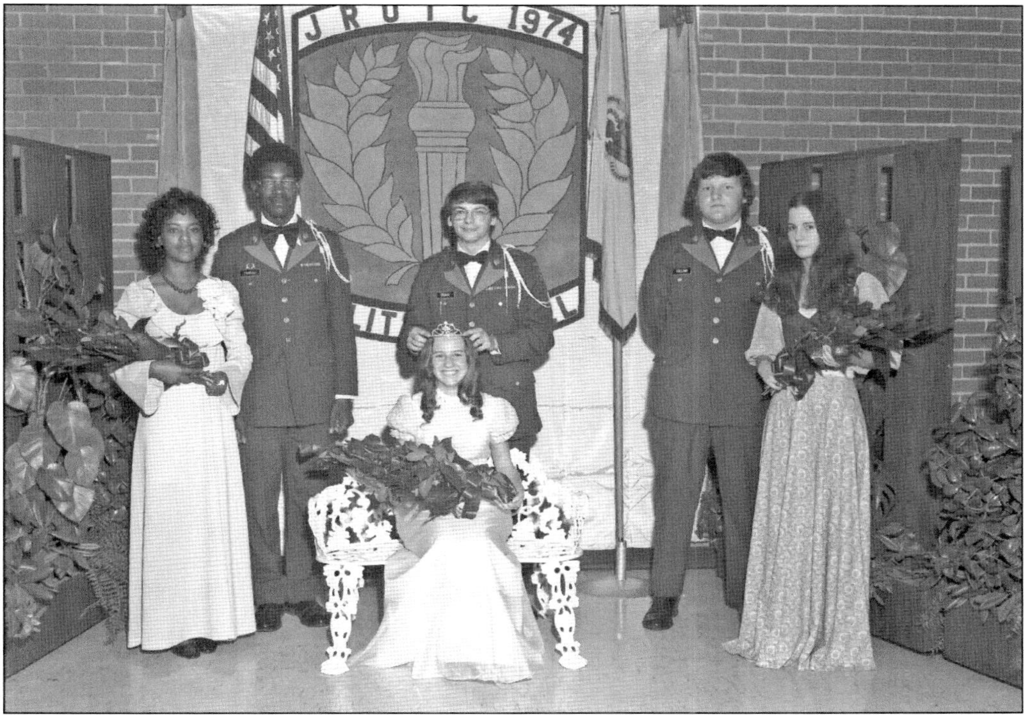

Royal Roses. Patricia Talley, the smiling queen of the Bowling Green High School ROTC dance, was crowned on March 30, 1974. She was attended by members of her royal court; from left to right are Penny Patterson, William Parrish, battalion commander David Roach, Phillip Holland, and unidentified.

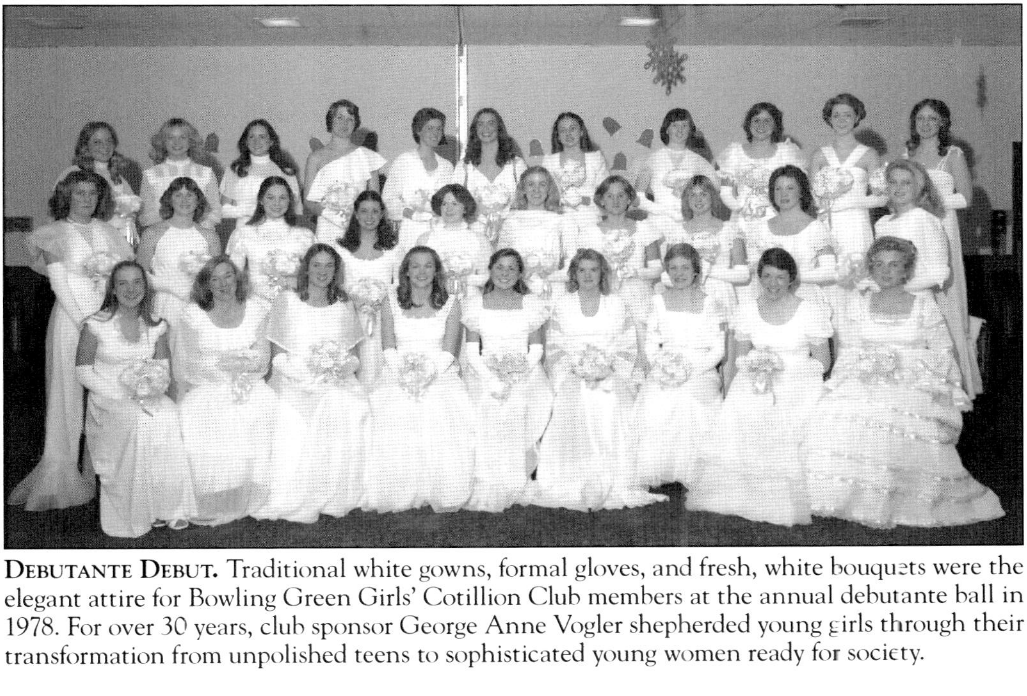

Debutante Debut. Traditional white gowns, formal gloves, and fresh, white bouquets were the elegant attire for Bowling Green Girls' Cotillion Club members at the annual debutante ball in 1978. For over 30 years, club sponsor George Anne Vogler shepherded young girls through their transformation from unpolished teens to sophisticated young women ready for society.

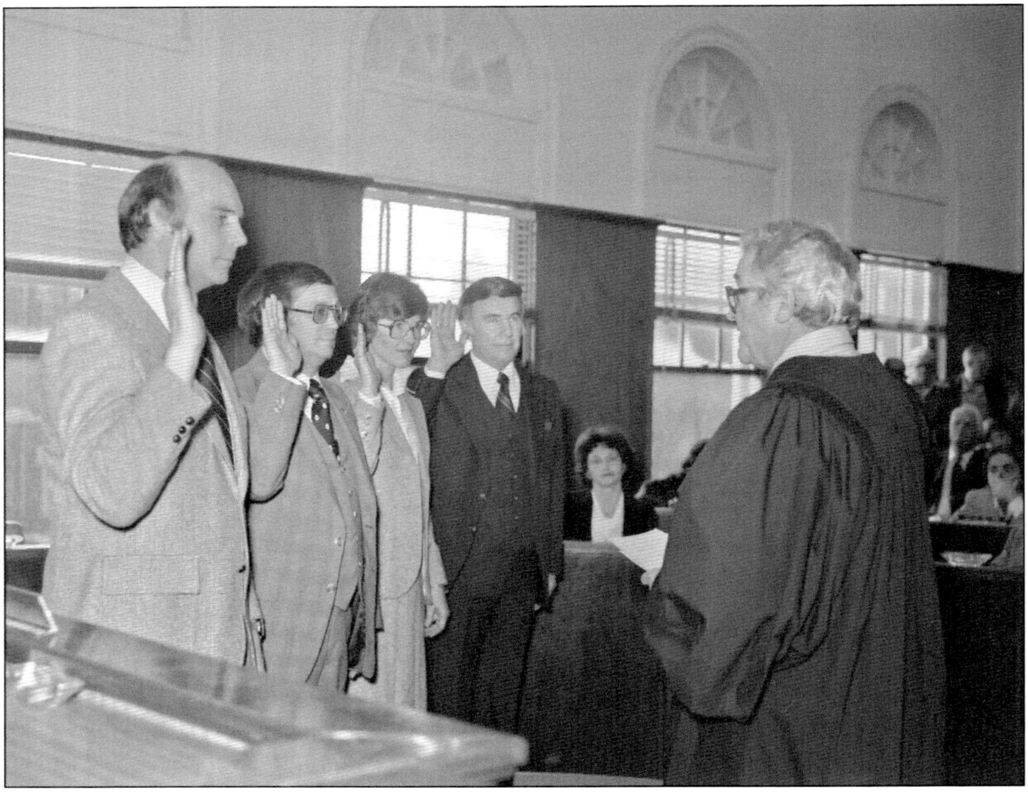

Oath of Office. Judge J. David Francis administers the oath of office to Bowling Green city commissioners in 1978. From left to right are Harold Miller, Charles Ray Woosley, Patsy Sloan, and Charles Wilson. The first woman elected to a seat on the commission, Sloan went on to win the 1987 election to mayor of the city.

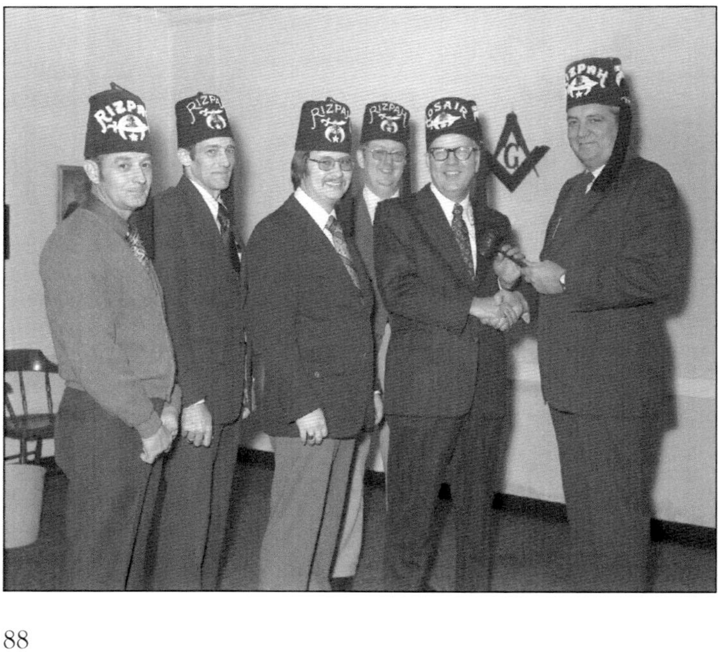

Regal Rizpah. Shriners of the Rizpah Temple, an organization dedicated to providing charitable health care for children, met in December 1974 for the official installation of new officers. Pictured from left to right are David Miller, secretary; Ralph White, treasurer; William D. Stevens, second vice president; Donald G. Meredith, first vice president; Jack D. Sublett, president; and James E. (Jim) Boucher, past president and installing officer.

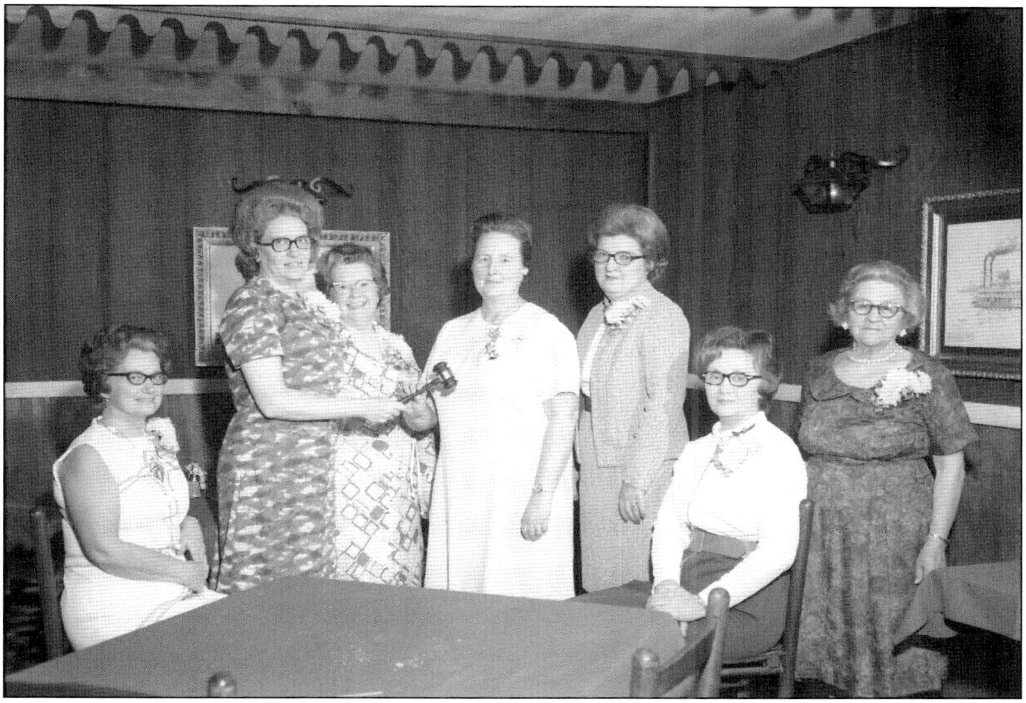

PASSING OF THE GAVEL. Members of the Bowling Green Business and Professional Women's Association met in 1972 for the installation of new officers. From left to right, new leaders are Mrs. Tackett, unidentified, Elizabeth Sharer, Erma Stargel, Marie Martin, Sandy Bailey, and Rachel Dozier. Originally formed in 1924, the association is the largest group in the world devoted to the affairs of businesswomen.

REACHING NEW HEIGHTS. The board of regents of Western Kentucky University was charged with oversight of the university and with ensuring that the future of education on the hill would be one of growth and excellence. From left to right, board members in 1978 were (first row) J. David Cole, Dr. Dero Downing, and Hugh Poland; (second row) unidentified, Bill Buckman, John Ramsey, Tom Emberton, Ron Sheffer, Bill Kuegel, Ronnie Clark, Carroll Knicely, and Georgia Bates.

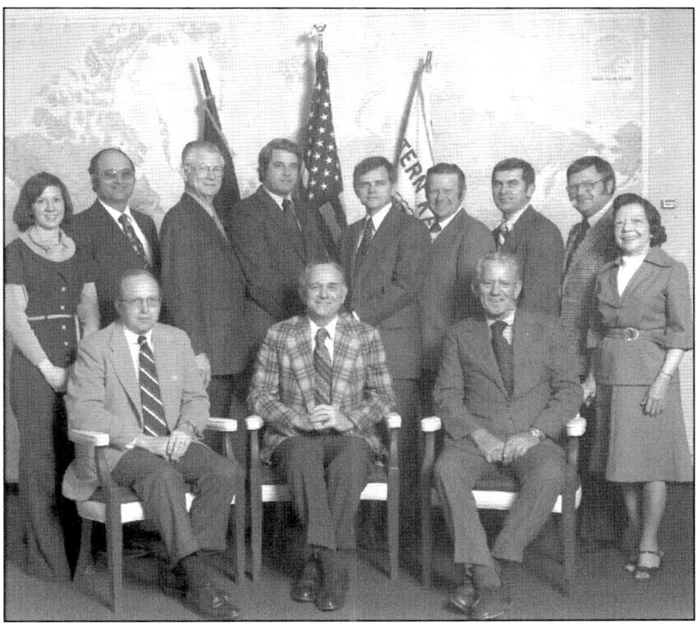

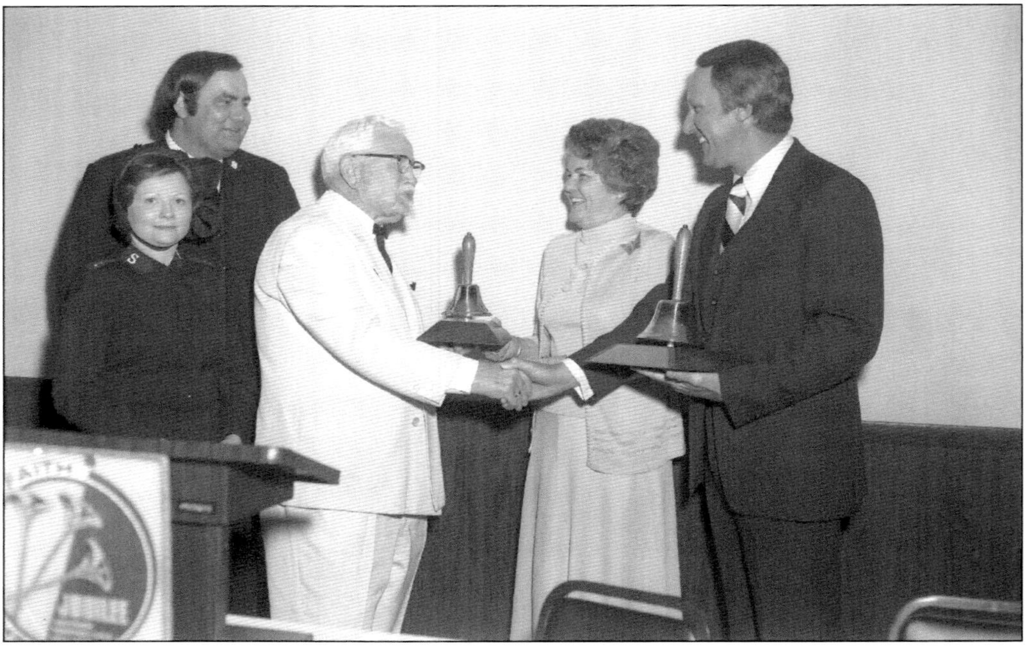

Kentucky Fried Award Winners. Salvation Army Bell Ringer award recipients Juanita Milton of the Altrusa Club and Clyde Payne of the Kiwanis Club were pleased to receive their bells of recognition from Col. Harlan Sanders in 1977 while Salvation Army captain David Birmingham and his wife looked on.

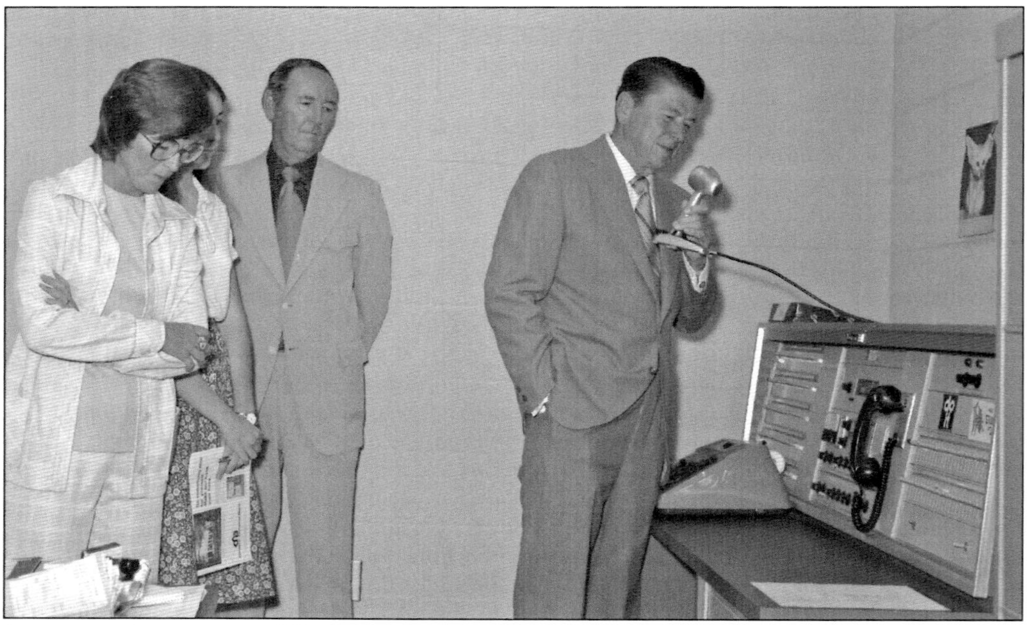

Pledging Allegiance. While on a 1978 pre–presidential campaign national tour, Ronald Reagan made an unscheduled stop at Bowling Green High School to lead the student body in the Pledge of Allegiance. Standing by were Social Studies Department head Patsy Sloan and principal Denval Barriger.

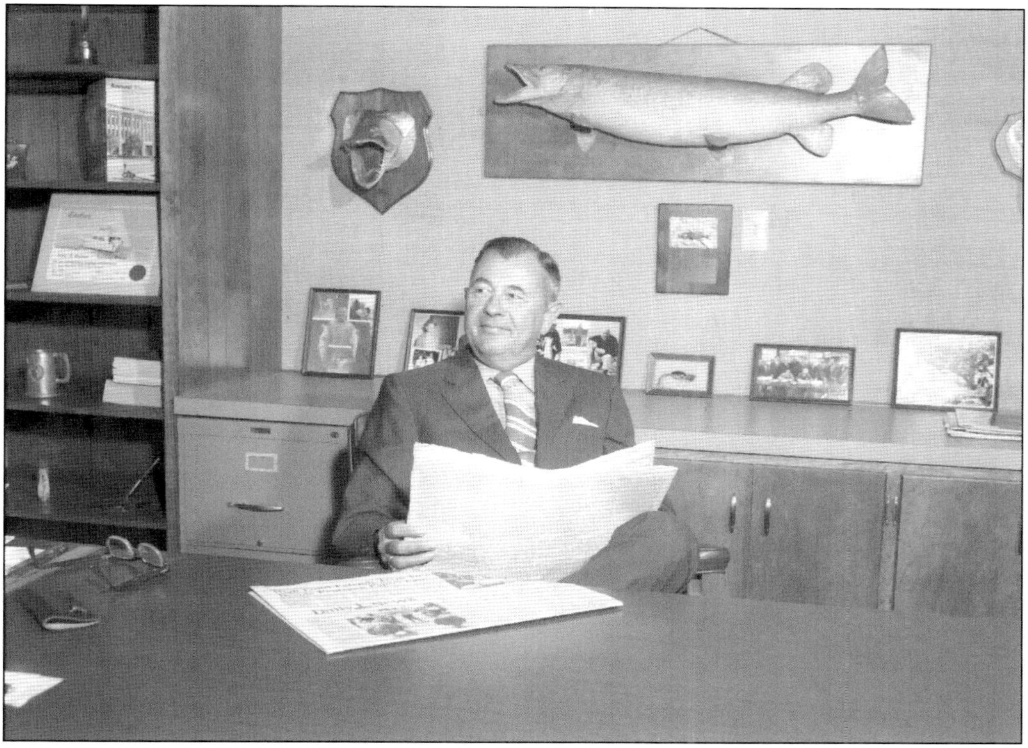

Park City Publisher. John Gaines, publisher of the *Park City Daily News*, paused on June 29, 1971, in his office at the newspaper's newly enlarged publishing facilities at 813 College Street. With a paid circulation in 1971 of 15,000, the *Park City Daily News* has been published by members of the Gaines family since it was first established in 1882 under the name *Daily Times* and remains a regional source of print news today.

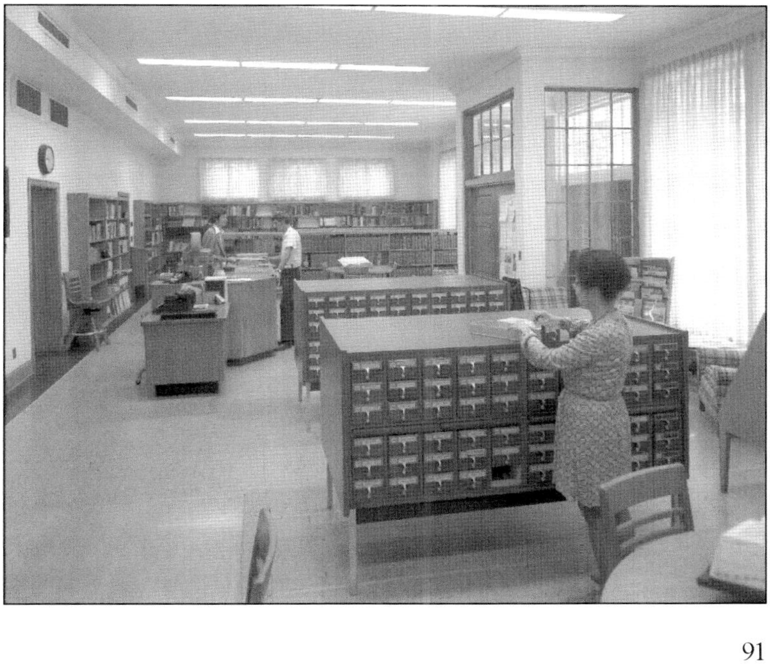

Lending Library. Director William Bolte and the staff of the Bowling Green Public Library at 1225 State Street were ready to assist patrons with all of their reference and library needs in September 1973. A prominent feature in all libraries of the day, the card catalog was a necessity for finding one's way through the literary treasures in the stacks.

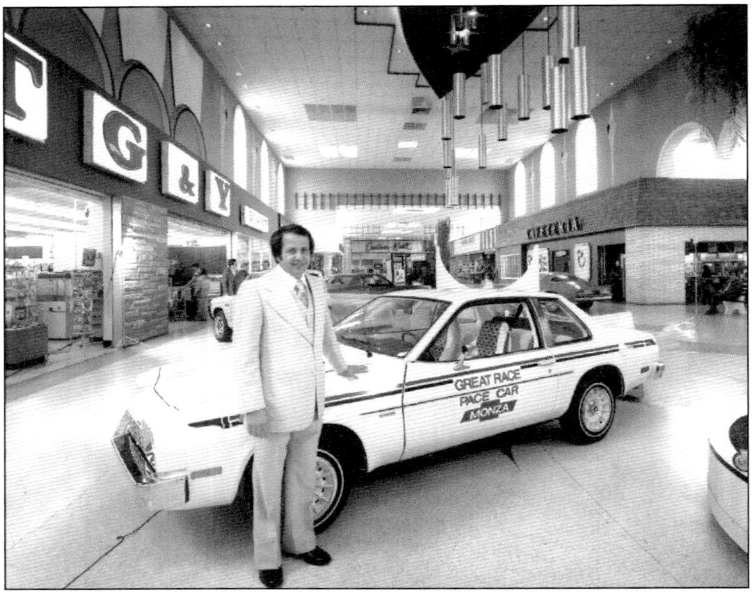

MOTORING AT THE MALL. Jimmie Greenway, president of Greenway Chevrolet, posed with a Great Race Pace Car at Bowling Green Mall on Nashville Road. With parking for over 2,000 vehicles, the mall was an omen of the vast changes in store for Bowling Green. Now owned by Western Kentucky University, the mall has become a storehouse of educational pursuits.

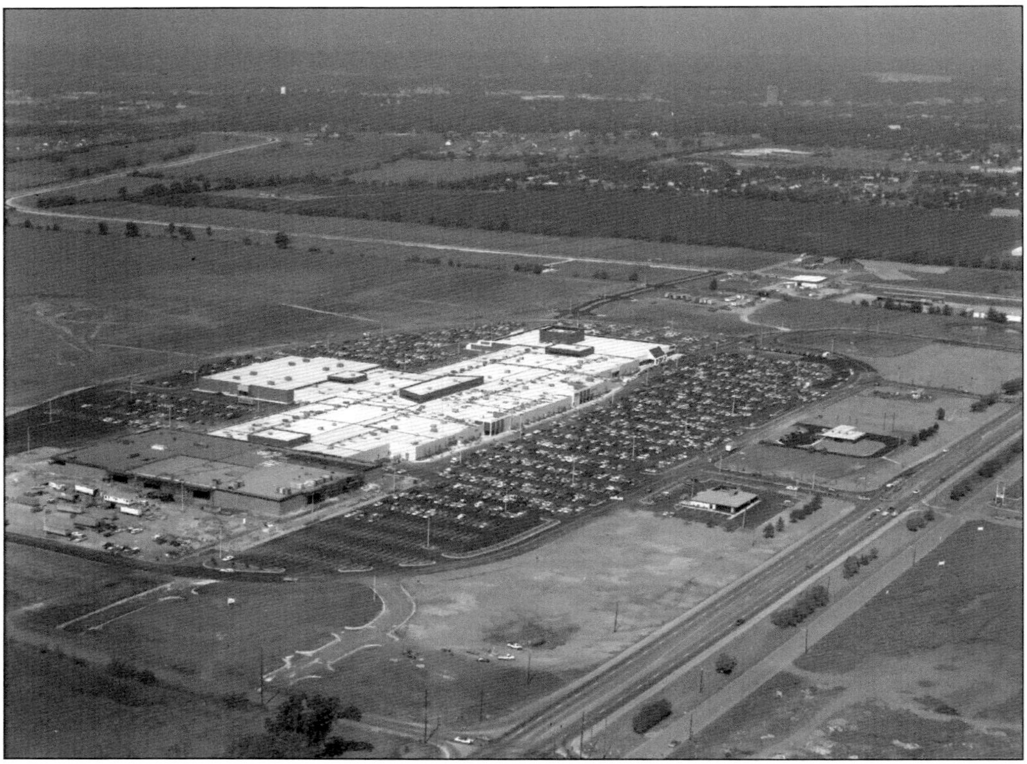

GREENWOOD GROWTH. Opening day at Greenwood Mall, September 12, 1979, was a major event, as Bowling Green mayor B. G. Steen and other officials gathered at the 575,000-square-foot facility to cut a bright green ribbon festooning the mall's central court. In this aerial view, it is evident the mall literally broke new ground in what had been the Warren County countryside, as a then-quiet Scottsville Road and undeveloped Campbell Lane cut through the rural landscape.

Four

The 1980s
The Wonder Years

A study in contrasts, the 1980s was a time of trivial pursuits and Tiananmen Square. It was the end of the cold war and the destruction of the Berlin Wall, symbolizing to the world the death of communism. It was the beginning of a kid-centered economy, symbolized by the addition of Toys-R-Us on the Bowling Green retail scene. The world was getting smaller, and Bowling Green was getting bigger.

Perhaps no single development changed the economic and social face of Bowling Green like the 1981 opening of the General Motors plant. The only plant in the world to produce the Corvette, deemed by many to be the classic American sports car, General Motors brought new tastes and new ideas to the area, which culminated in the late-1980s planning and development of the National Corvette Museum.

Kentucky lawmakers wrestled and fought the Kentucky Education Reform Act onto the law books, changing the way schools were structured and the way Kentucky children were educated. A new public golf course, centrally located at the former farm fields of Hartland, was completed, and work was begun on a controversial convention center. Bowling Green was fast becoming a small city—no longer a small Kentucky town with small Kentucky ways, the city had big-town assets and big-town problems.

With big hair and big plans for economic prosperity, the people of the 1980s rode the wave of Ronald Reagan–era success until it bottomed out on October 19, 1987, Black Monday, when the stock market experienced a precipitous fall. They grieved when the space shuttle exploded, a bloom of frothy white against a brilliant blue sky. They made Eddie Murphy a household name and sang along with a red-haired mermaid who yearned to be part of another world.

The vicissitudes of an ever-changing world made themselves known, even in Bowling Green. An active, bustling part of what was rapidly becoming a global, CNN-reported economy, Bowling Green went about its business of growth and change, and when Halley's Comet streaked across an inky black 1986 sky, Tommy Hughes was hard at work, busily chronicling this once-small town's development into a 20th-century city with big ideas for the future.

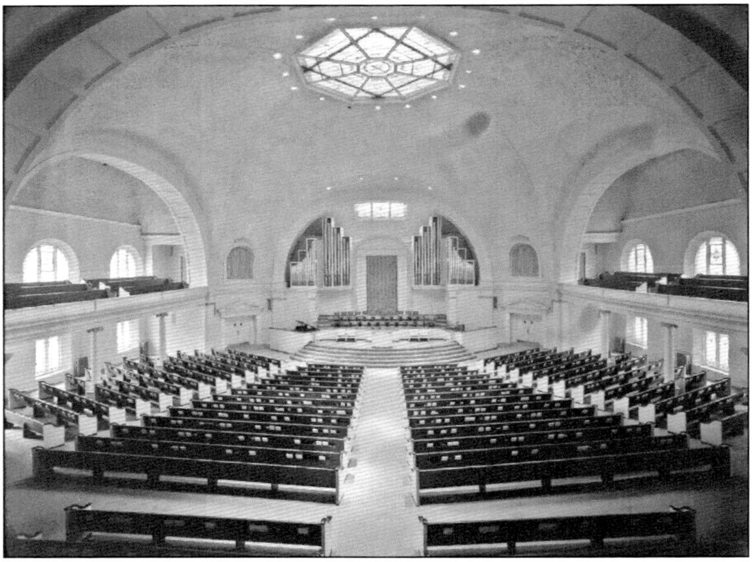

White Temple. Congregants of First Baptist Church, originally established by a group of dedicated members from Providence Knob Baptist Church, built a new spiritual home at 621 East Twelfth Avenue in June 1915. Stunningly simple architectural details made this serenely beautiful auditorium a focal point of landmarks in 1980 Bowling Green.

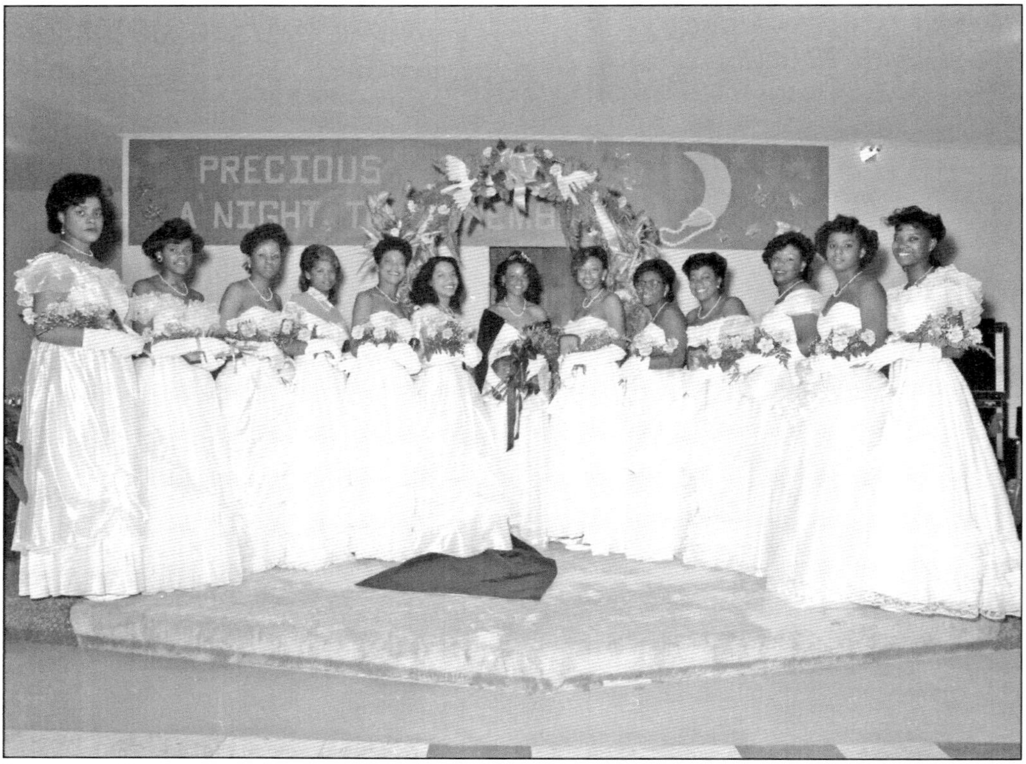

Precious Night, Precious Debutantes. Lovely young Alpha Kappa Alpha debutantes shone brighter than any heavenly stars at the 1988 debutante ball sponsored by the members of Omicron Sigma Omega chapter of Alpha Kappa Alpha sorority. Elegant in satin and pearls, from left to right are Cheryl McKinney, Sherry Smith, Tyra Coleman, Delphia Satterfield, Tonya Carr, Kathryn Lewis, Terra Burnam, Minyarn Pratt, Antonio Ray, Candice McLean, Larecia Denning, Carla Bradley, and Nicole Carver.

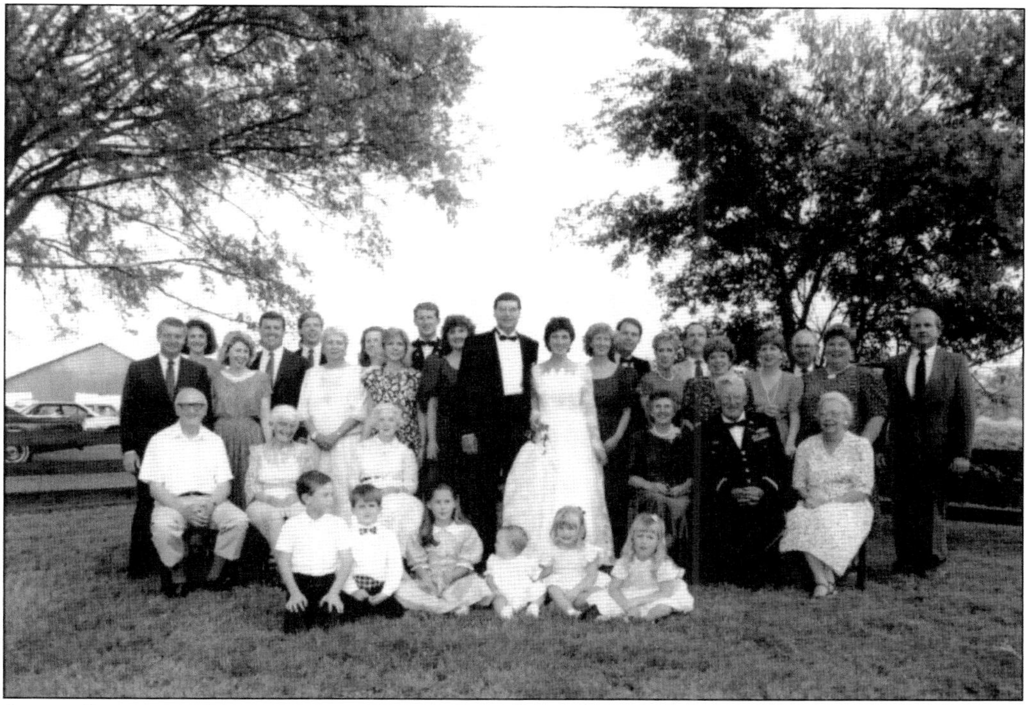

Sweet September Memories. Nancy Gates Spiller and Gerald Joseph Lozinsky celebrated their September 9, 1989, wedding surrounded by the dearest of family and friends. After a ceremony performed by Rev. Howard Surface and Rev. Anne Louise Reed at 3:30 p.m. at Christ Episcopal Church, the wedding party gathered in Oakland at the home of Col. Robert and Cora Jane Spiller, parents of the bride, for an old-fashioned outdoor reception under the oaks.

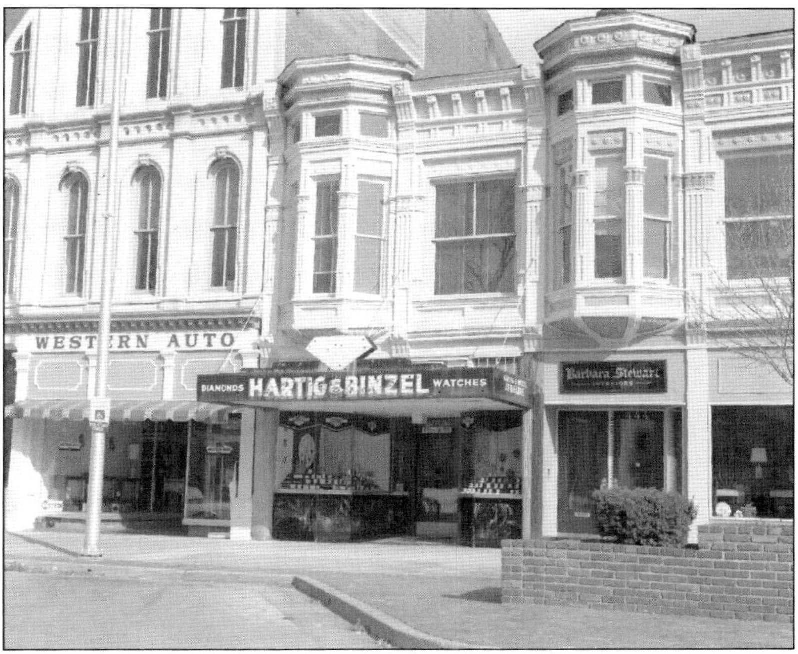

Jewel of the City. Hartig and Binzel at 442 Main Street was the place to shop for fine diamonds and classic watches. Master jewelers serving Bowling Green since 1919, the store remained a staple of city society in 1983.

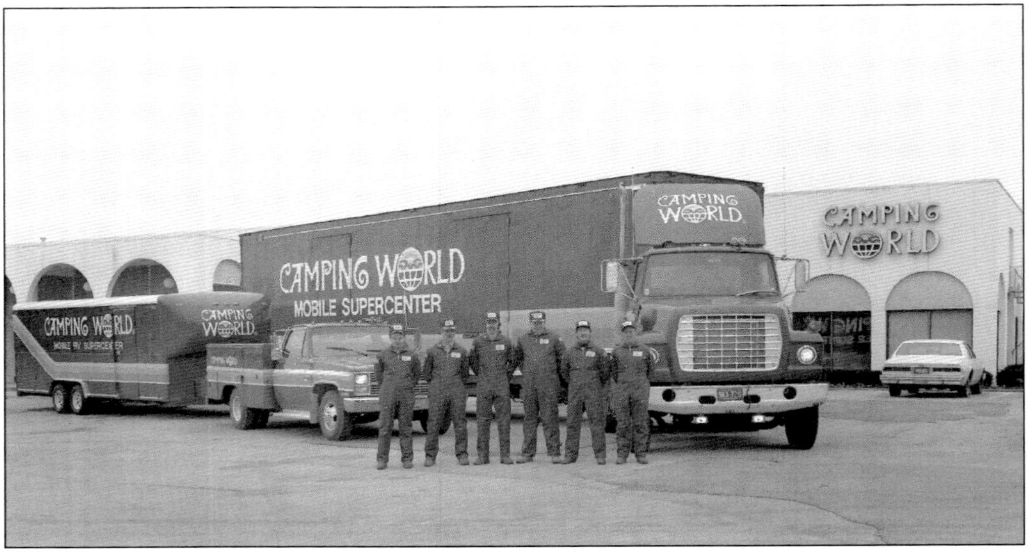

Camping World Crew. Members of the 1983 Mobile RV Supercenter Crew, from left to right, Bobby Reynolds, Kenny Shoemake, Buddy Steele, Jerry "Peanuts" Gaines, Jeff Morris, and Ray Sylvia, posed in front of their big rig at the 134 Beech Bend Road location. The crew traveled throughout the country, serving as a mobile Camping World store at recreational vehicle rallies and at grand opening festivities of new Camping World retail locations.

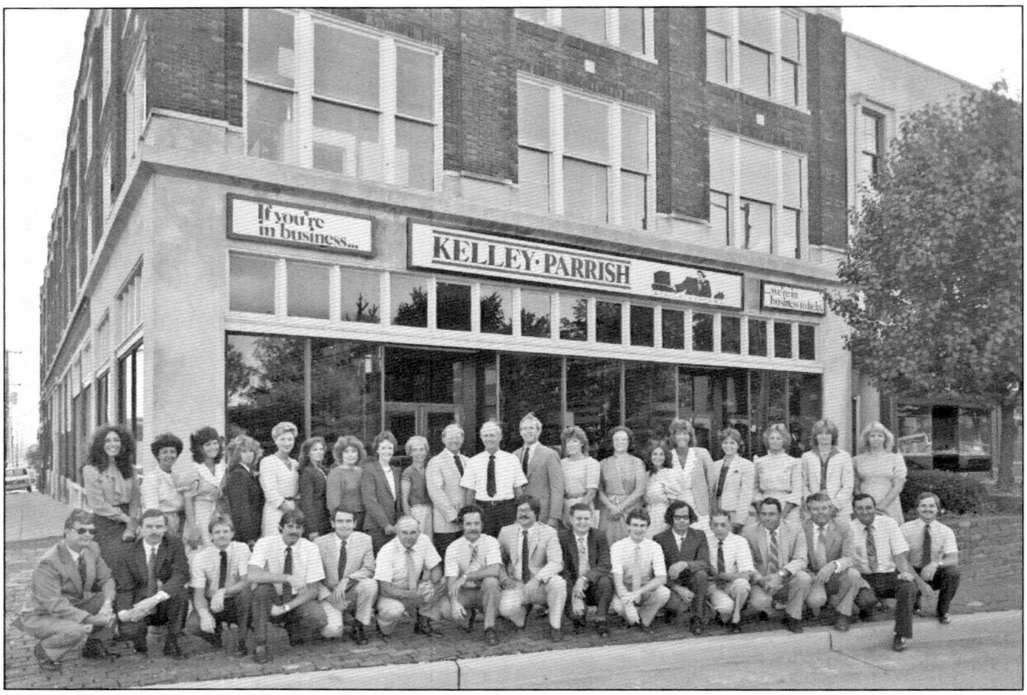

One-Stop Office Shop. Team members of Kelley-Parrish Office Systems at 400 Main Street gathered in front of the company's downtown location on September 4, 1984. An essential part of business life in Bowling Green, Kelley-Parrish provided office furniture and supplies throughout the area with the philosophy, "If you're in business, we're in business to help."

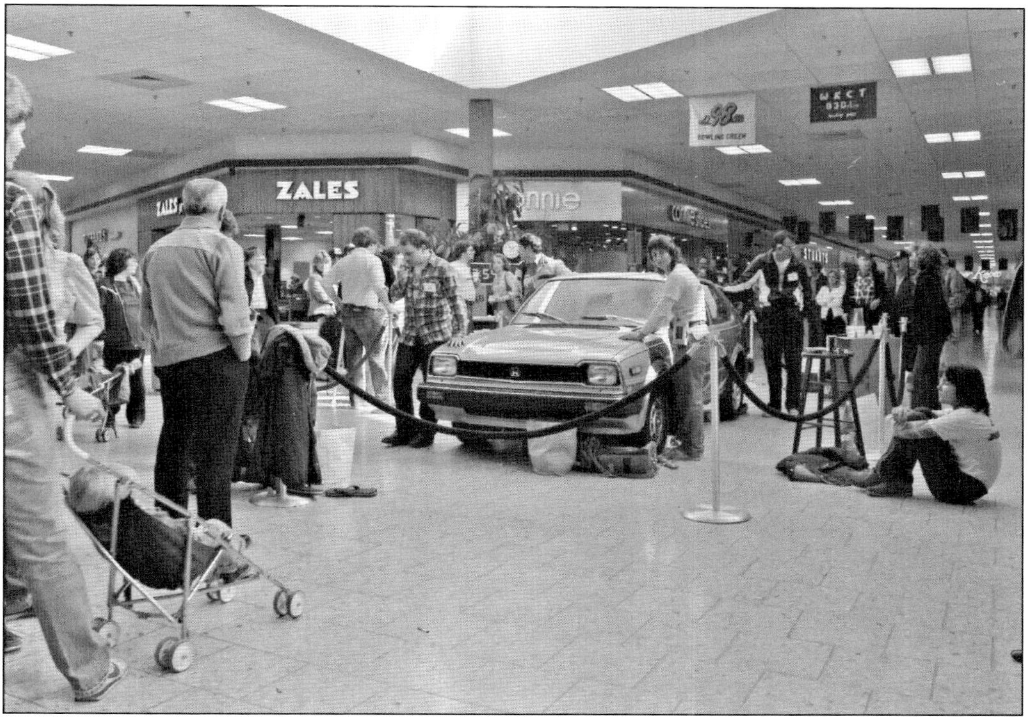

Hands-Down Winner. Sleepy contestants competed to win a 1983 Honda Civic hatchback from WKCT and D-98 radio stations at Greenwood Mall. Winning contestant Louis Naas, a Western Kentucky University student, outlasted 28 contestants by keeping his hands firmly planted on the Honda for a record 84 hours and 12 minutes.

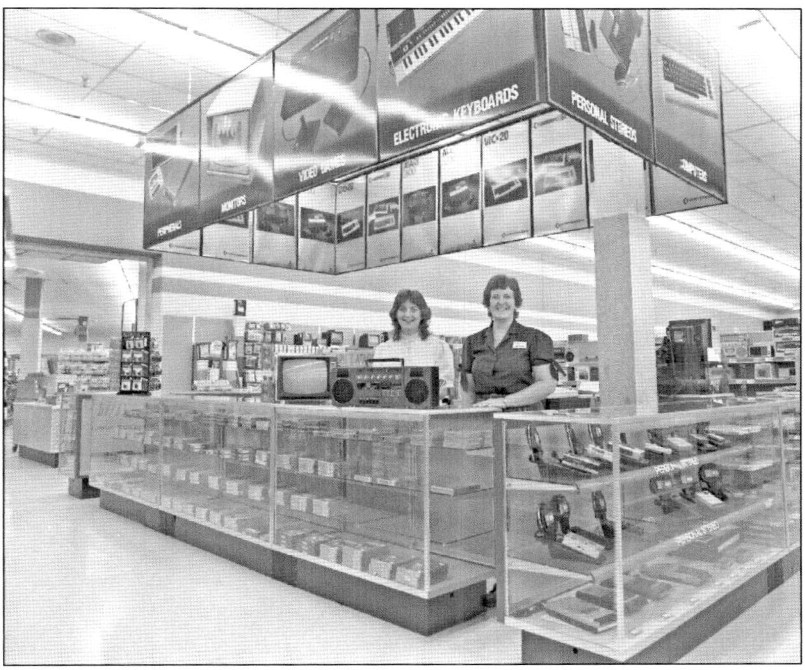

Blue Light Special. K-Mart celebrated its 1984 grand opening at 480 Fairview Plaza. Hot items of the day were boom boxes and portable television sets, many still equipped with rabbit ears.

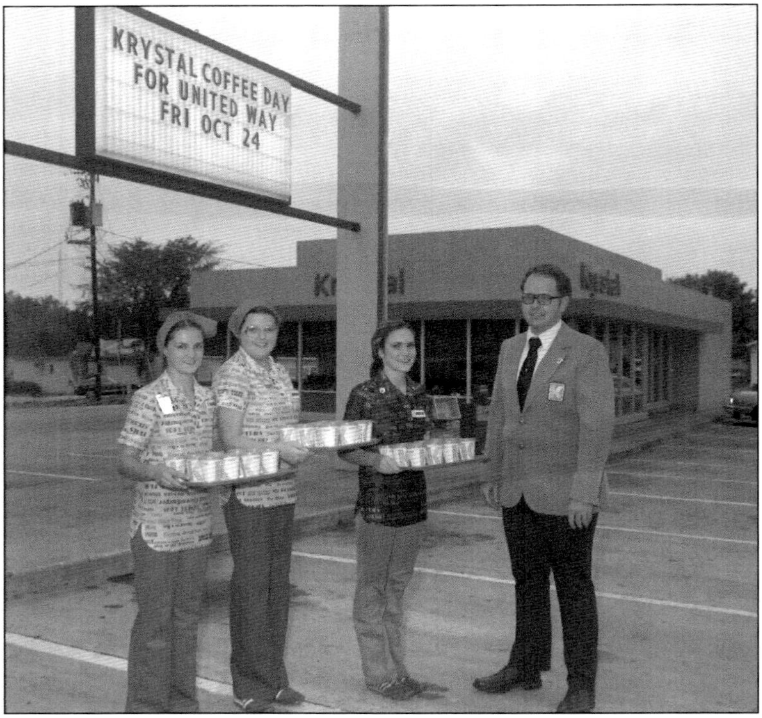

Coffee at Krystal's. Patrons of Krystal's enjoyed hot coffee for a good cause during the United Way fund drive on October 24, 1980. Located at 1511 U.S. 31-W Bypass, Krystal's was a proud supporter of the United Way and its many projects.

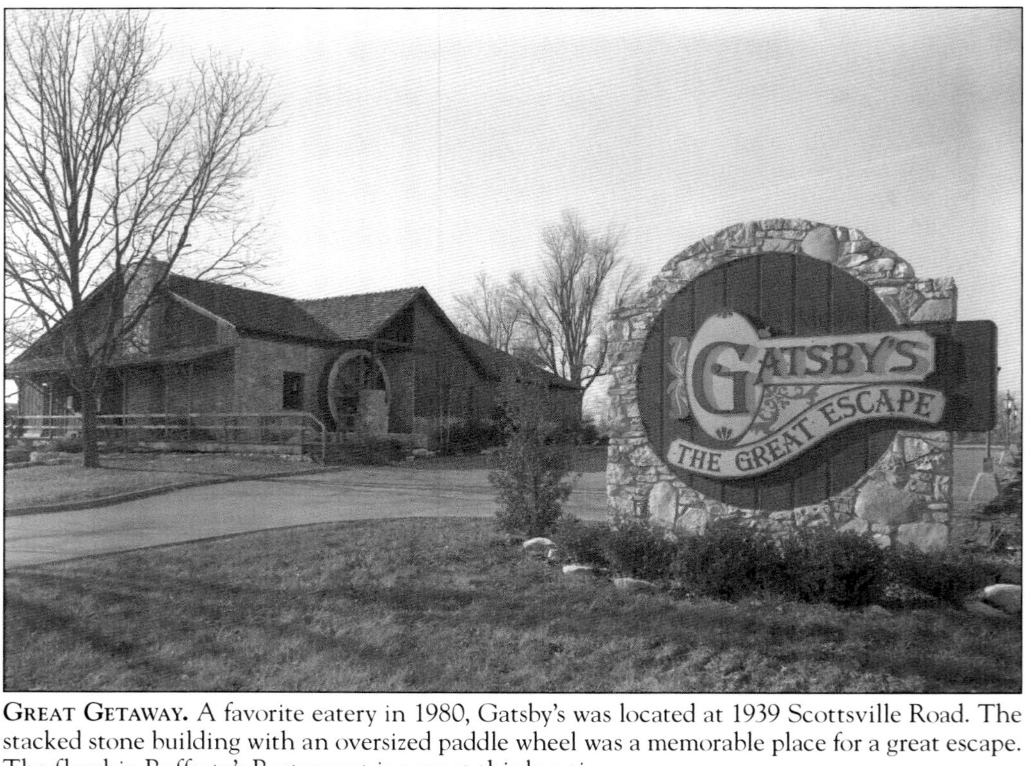

Great Getaway. A favorite eatery in 1980, Gatsby's was located at 1939 Scottsville Road. The stacked stone building with an oversized paddle wheel was a memorable place for a great escape. The flagship Rafferty's Restaurant is now at this location.

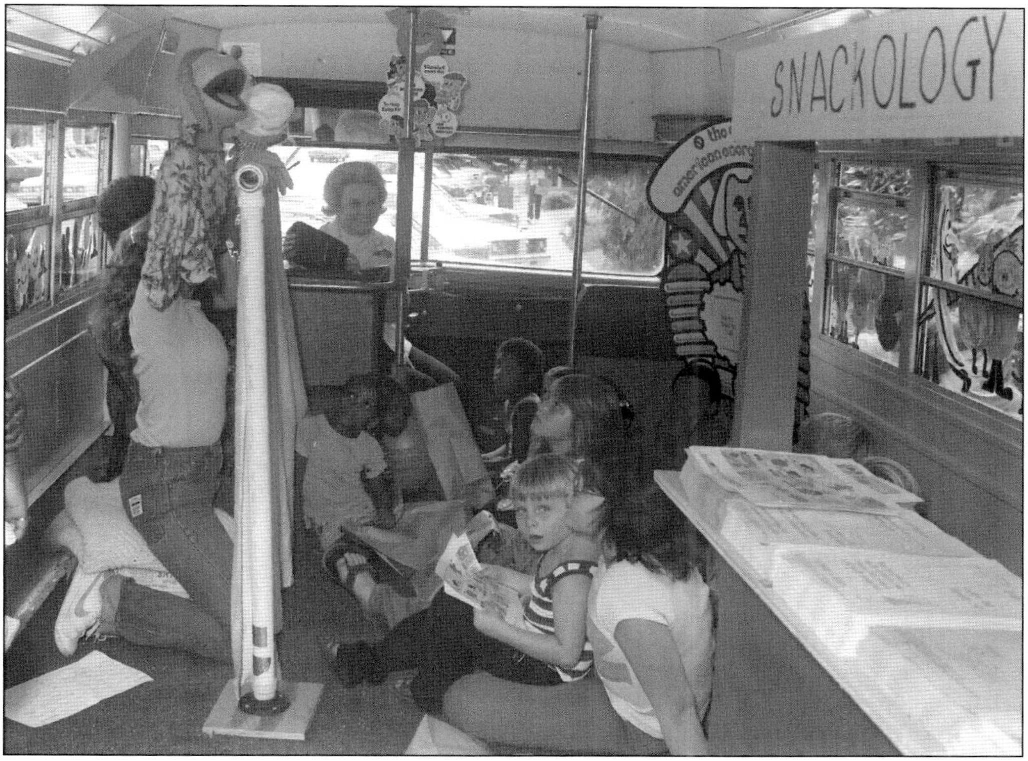

Brain Food. Doris Pruitt, director of food service for Warren County Schools in 198C, cheerfully gestured with a prop as children enjoyed a puppet show aboard the Nutrition Bus, where students could pursue their studies in "snackology."

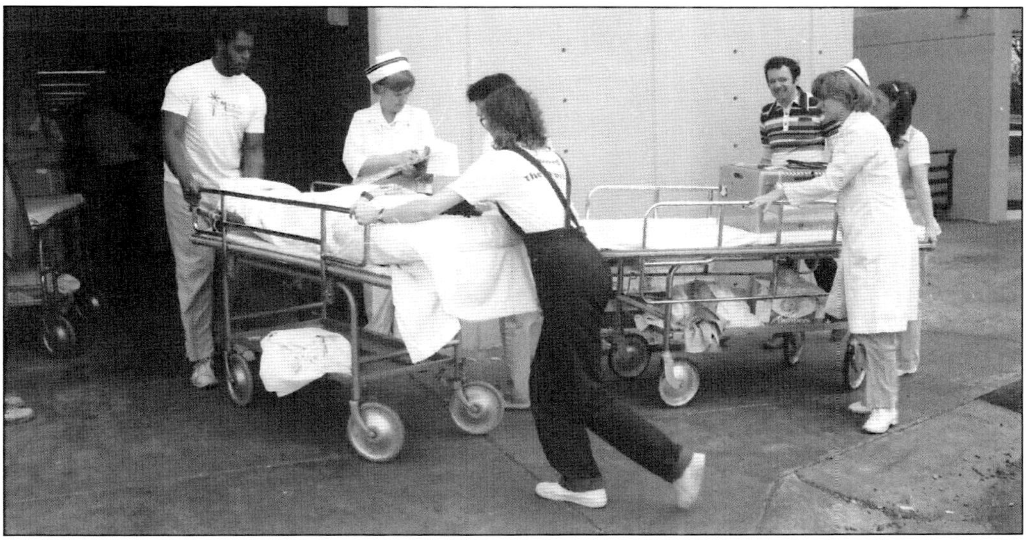

Medics on the Move. On the morning of March 8, 1980, staff of the Medical Center made the move from the former City-County Hospital on Reservoir Hill to shining new facilities located on Park Street. All hands were needed to accomplish this logistical feat, and staffers wore shirts proclaiming "I moved the hospital."

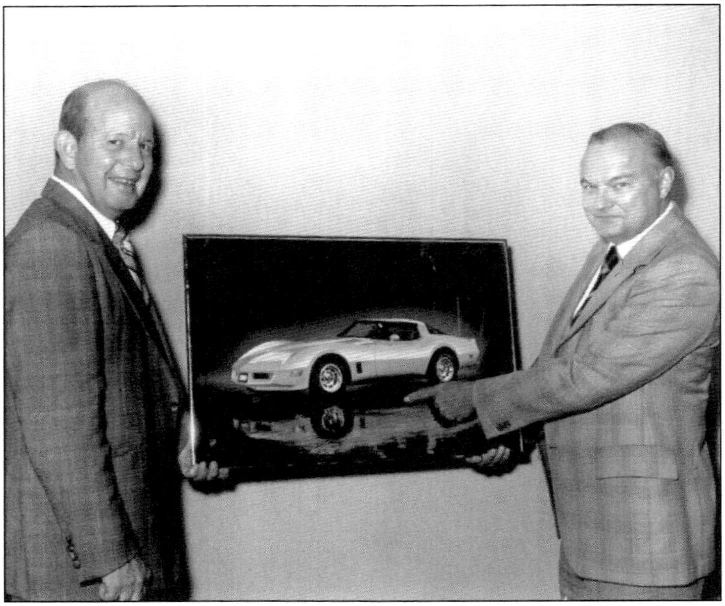

LITTLE RED CORVETTE. David Chestnut (left), executive vice president of American National Bank, and Earl Harper, first manager of Bowling Green's General Motors plant, posed with a picture of a symbol of America's love of automobiles: the Corvette. The car has been manufactured exclusively in Bowling Green since 1981, and the annual national Corvette homecoming fills Bowling Green streets with beautiful, high-powered collectibles.

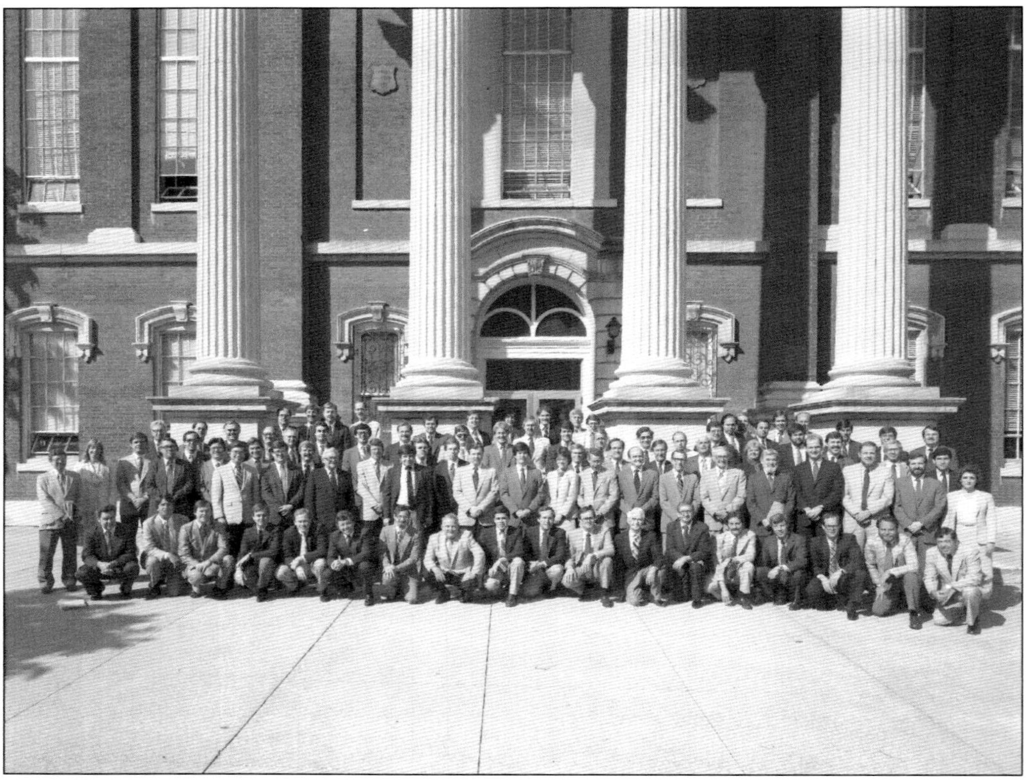

MEMBERS OF THE BAR. Members of the Bowling Green/Warren County Bar Association put aside their briefs to assemble together at the courthouse on a sunny May 15, 1984.

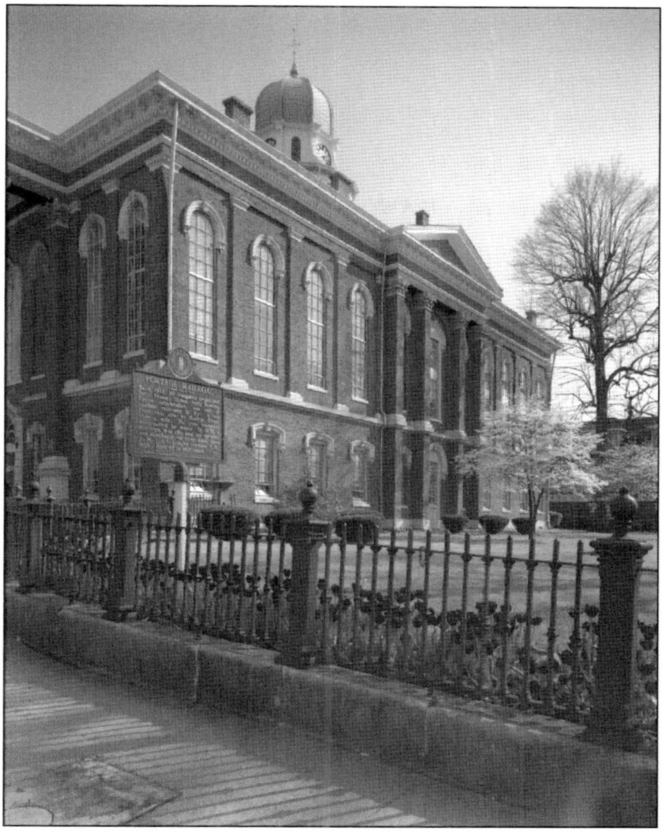

HALLS OF JUSTICE. The Warren County Courthouse at 429 East Tenth Street was completed in 1868 and still sparkled in the 1983 springtime sun. Designed by D. J. Williams in classic Italianate style, the courthouse was officially certified in the National Register of Historic Places in 1977 and remains in public use today, as thousands of Warren County feet continue to leave their mark on the steps entering this historic building.

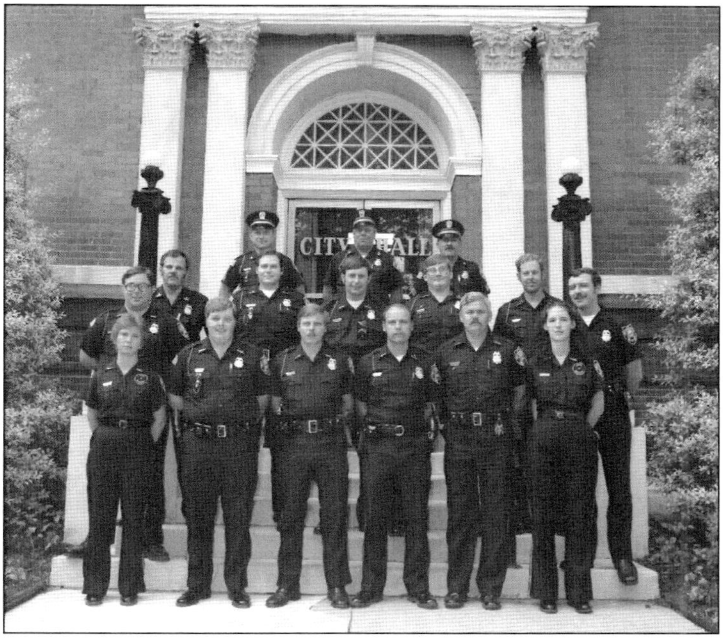

OFFICERS OF THE LAW. Men and women in blue, committed to the dual tasks of protecting and policing, gathered at Bowling Green City Hall on June 6, 1980. Pictured from left to right are (first row) Margaret Johnson, David Herrman, Danny McGown, Phil Crick, Cecil Beach, and Mary Peel; (second row) Pat Johnson, Danny Jenkins, Mark Johnson, Grover Hubbard, John Patterson, Bobby Oldham, and Mark Williamson; (third row) George Scott, Doc Hightower, and Carlos Lobb.

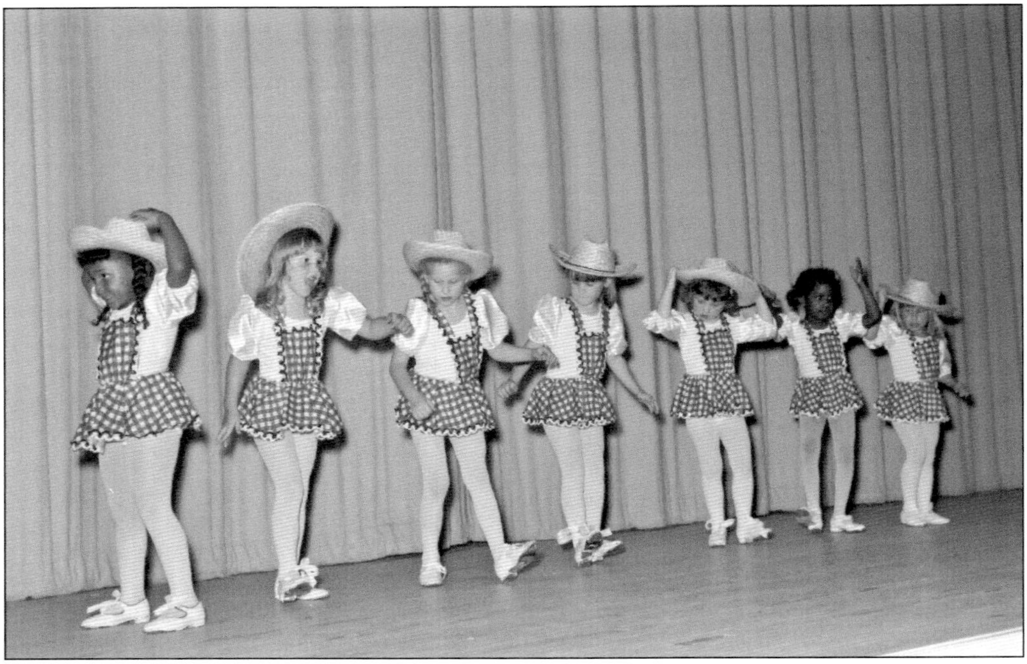

Toe Tapping. Students of Ms. Paula's Dance Studio strutted their stuff during a May 27, 1988, recital, except for one distracted little diva who could not tear her eyes away from the off-stage mirror.

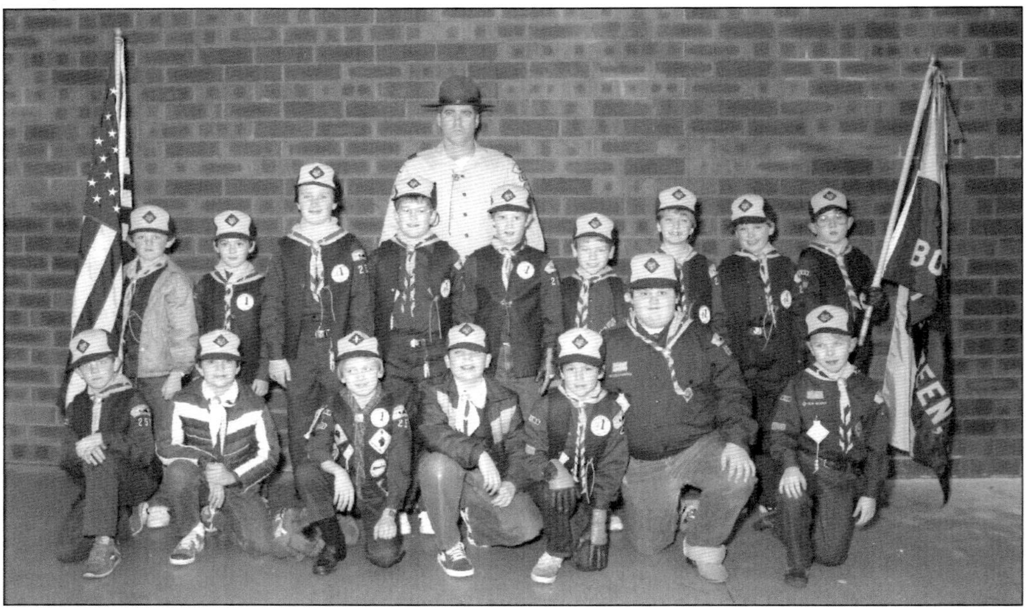

Pack Pride. The young men of Cub Scout Pack 259 posed with cubmaster John Jamison at Potter Gray Elementary School in 1983. Pictured from left to right are (first row) Robbie Schulten, unidentified, Jason Smith, unidentified, Clay Rudolph, Donnie Robinson, and Donnie Violett, (second row) Jason Belek, Nick Fisher, Brock Denton, Josh Wells, Bill Price, Hunter Stewart, R. D. Lightfoot Jr., Craig Calkins, and Shea Sparks. Having sworn the Scout's oath of honor, they were dedicated to fulfilling the creed.

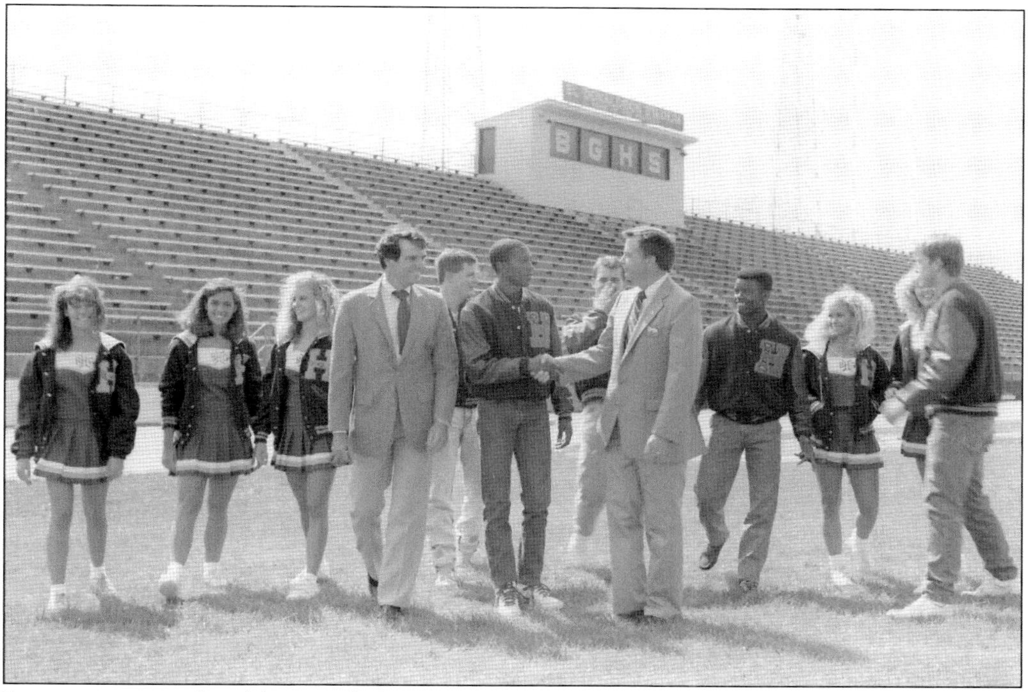

LETTERMEN. Purple athletes and cheerleaders celebrated the 1987 football season with Buddy Adams (right), of Century 21 Real Estate, and Ray Cobb.

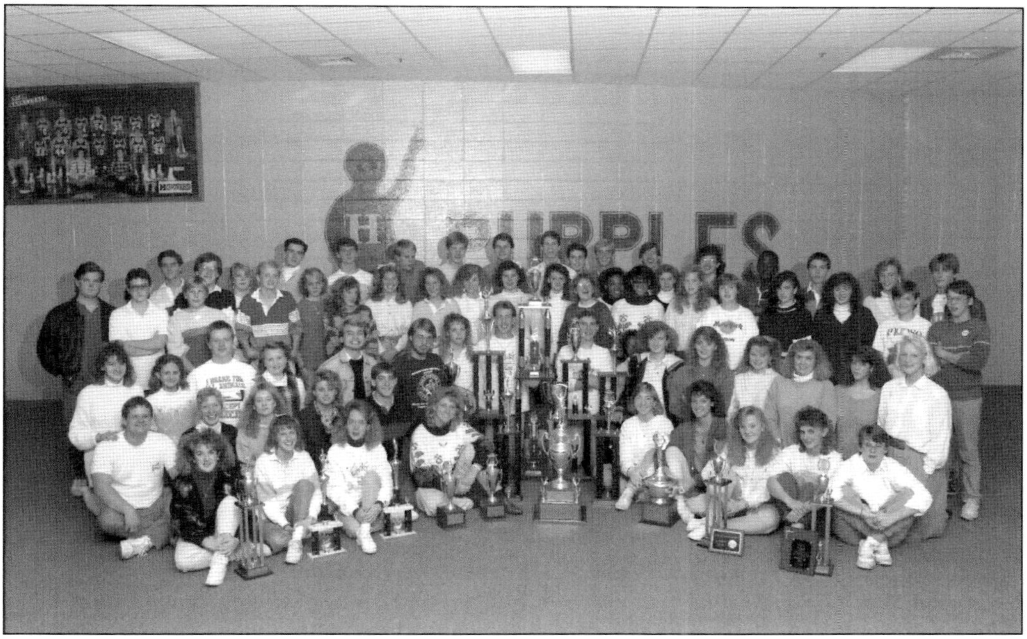

BIG BAND. Bowling Green High School marching band members gathered to recognize the many awards they earned on November 7, 1988. Under the direction of Brant Karrick (son of longtime director and composer Cecil Karrick), the marching Purples gave musical heart to the familiar strains of "All Hail to Dear Old Bowling Green High."

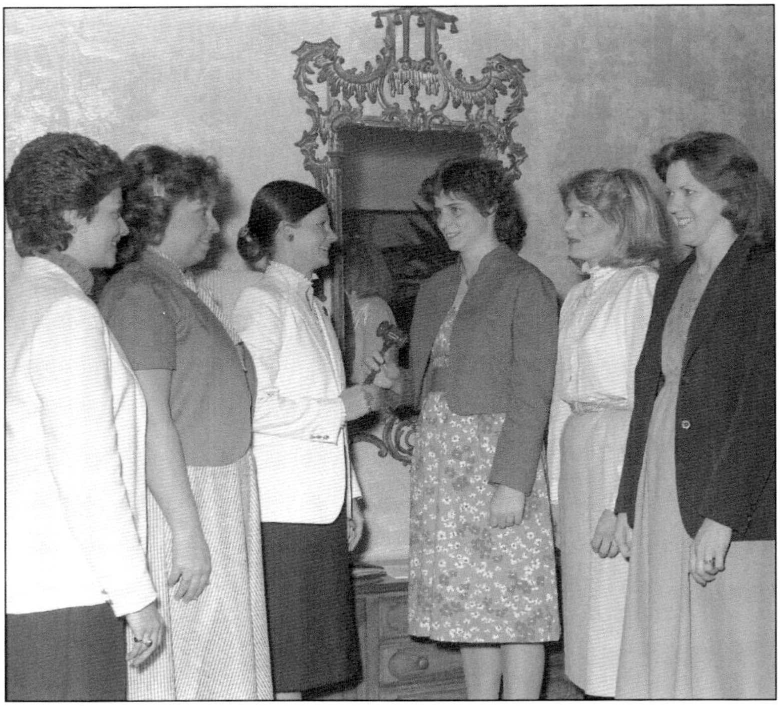

Oath of Office. Bowling Green Junior Women's Club officers were inducted into the service organization in 1983. Dedicated to civic projects for the betterment of the community, new officers include, from left to right, Lou Graham, Jo Goff, Alice Ford, Colleen Hathaway, Libby Milliken, and unidentified.

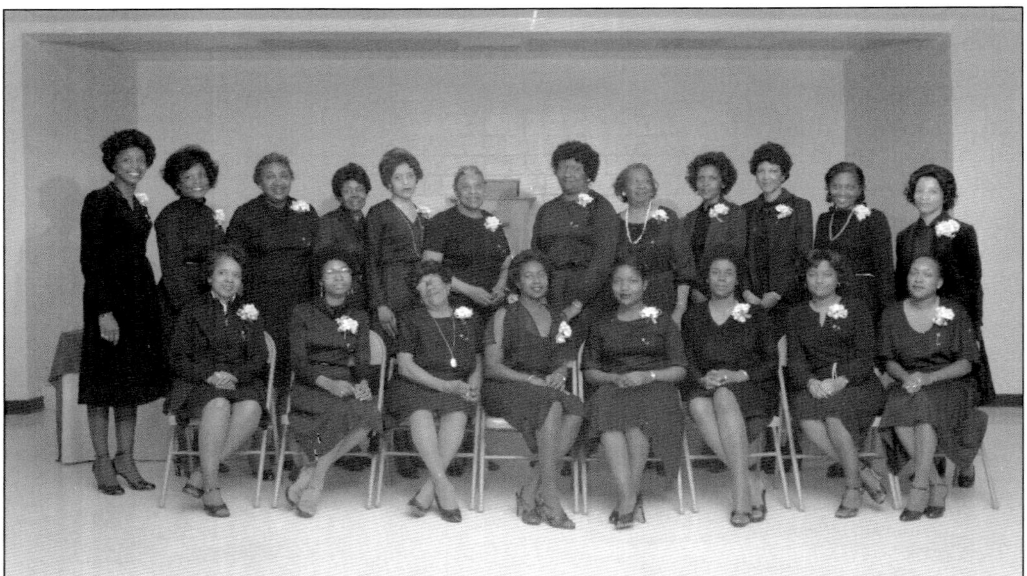

Sisterhood. Members of the Beta Rho Omega chapter of Alpha Kappa Alpha sorority met in 1980. They were the image of refined elegance, with dedication to the cultivation of the highest scholastic and ethical standards for young girls and fellow women. Pictured from left to right are (first row) Gladys Sivels, Marilyn Mitchell, Elizabeth Dorsey, Emma Forte Kendrick, Shirley Malone, unidentified, Brenda Bell, and Lavinia Peavey; (second row) Betty Esters, Shirley Sisney, Irene Barlow, Mary Thompson, Sylvia Payne-Goodner, Amanda Barlow, Sarah Sweatt, four unidentified, and Ersa Austin.

History in the Making. The Eloise B. Houchens Center, at 1115 Adams Street, was officially placed on the National Register of Historic Places in June 1980. From left to right, Representative Jody Richards, Secretary of State Frances Jones Mills, Romanza Johnson, Ervin Houchens, Kathryn Garrison, unidentified, Clyde Payne, and Riley Handy gathered at the center to mark the event. The historic structure was built in 1904 by Francis L. Kister, cobuilder of St. Joseph's Catholic Church, and was preserved in perpetuity by Ervin Houchens in 1976.

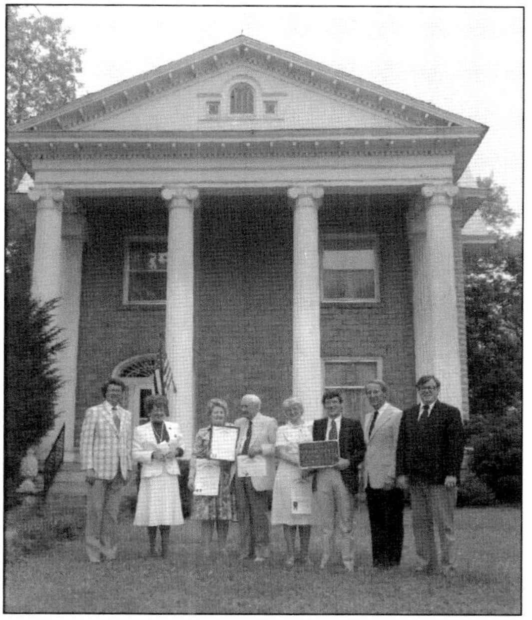

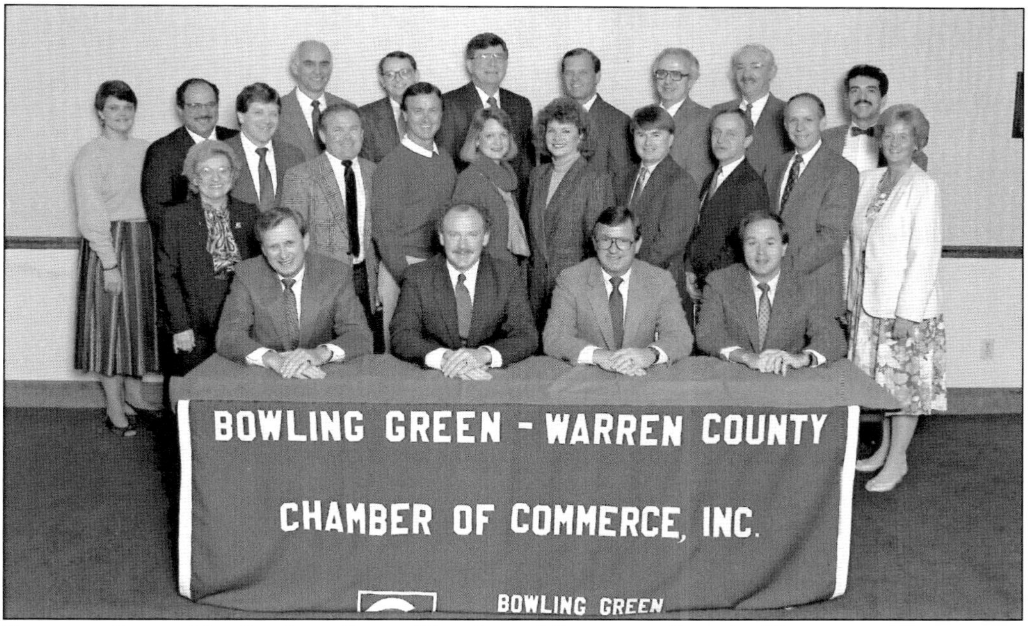

Business Sense. The Bowling Green Chamber of Commerce Board of Directors were pictured on December 9, 1988, in the chamber offices at 438 East Tenth Street. From left to right are (first row) Eddie Beck, Gary Dillard, Harold Brantley, and Dennis Griffin; (second row) Margaret Garris, Doug Nelson, Buster Stewart, David Garvin, Sarah Glenn Grise, Peggy Loafman, Scott Blann, Rick DuBose, Dr. Paul Cook, and Flo Sullivan; (third row) Ann Burke, Cornelius Martin, Bill Jackson, Fred Hensley, Joseph Huddleston, David Wiseman, Joe Hunt, B. J. Booth, and Jim Holton. Long recognized throughout Kentucky as an outstanding example of business development, the Bowling Green Chamber of Commerce has provided leadership and vision to the continued progress of business and industry throughout Warren County.

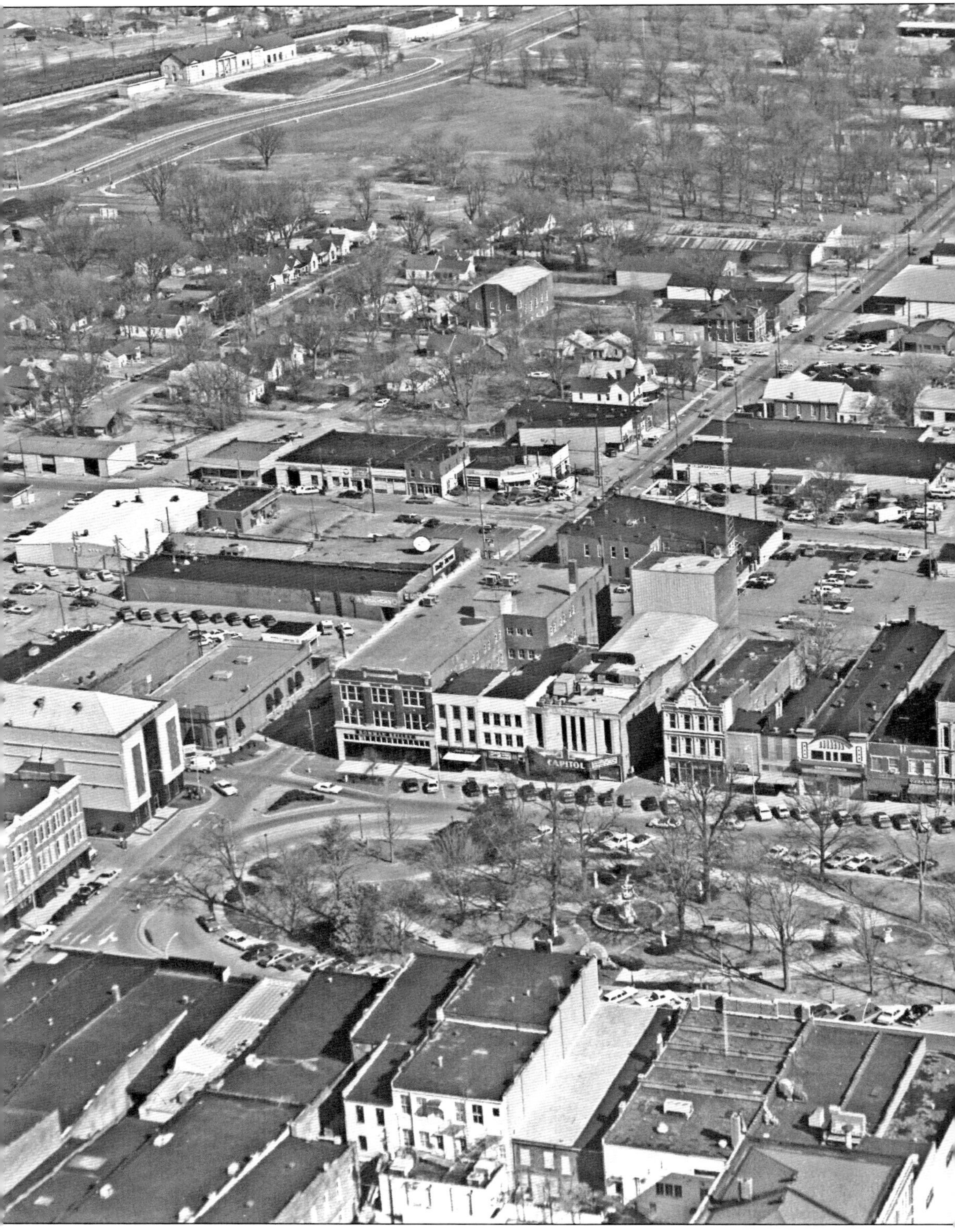
CAPITOL

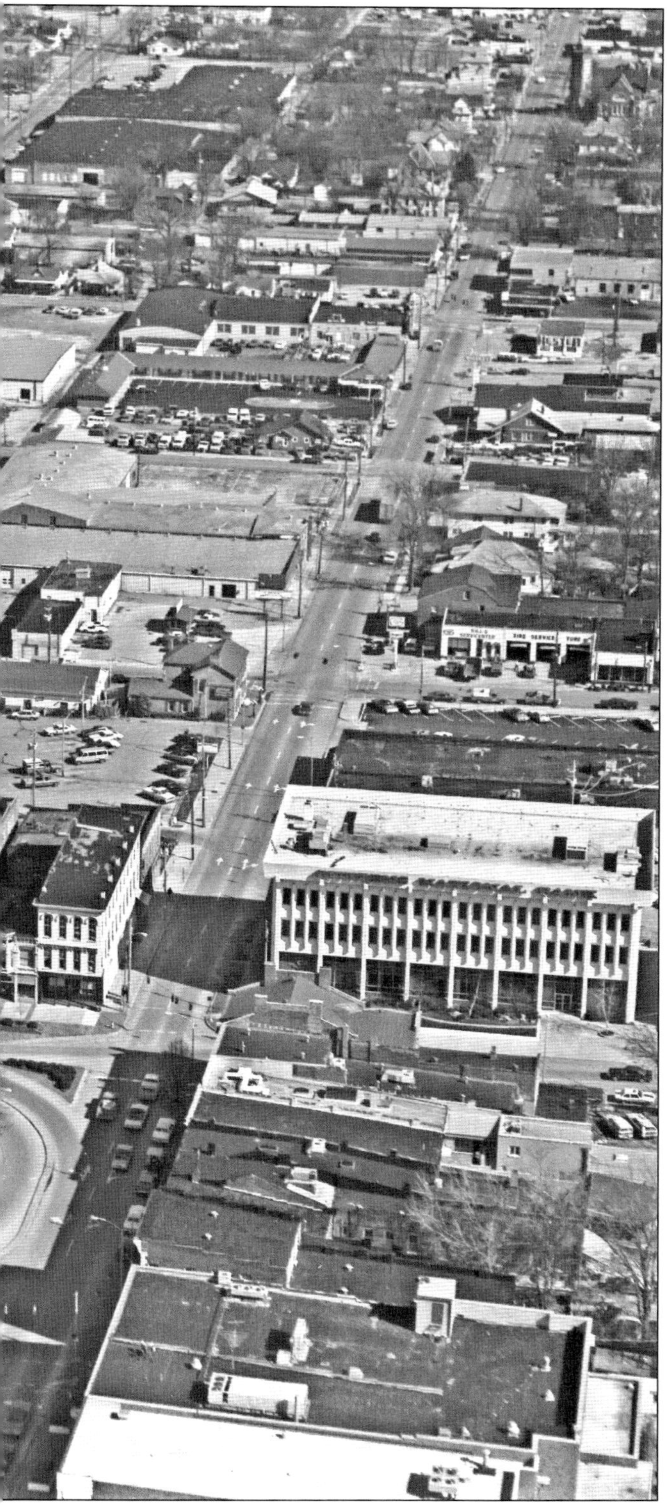

URBAN GROWTH. A February 14, 1984, aerial view of downtown Bowling Green highlighted the centerpiece of the city: Fountain Square Park. A perfect oval in design, perfectly envisioned by Warren County ancestors, it remains in use today as a cool, shaded gathering space It earned Bowling Green the moniker of "park city" by Louisville editor Henry Watterson in 1882. Encroachment of parking throughout the downtown area was readily apparent from the air, as historic structures had been razed to make way for vehicles. The Louisville and Nashville Railroad line visible in the upper left is evidence of the early importance of rail travel to the development of the city. Even in mid-winter, the leafless trees of Bowling Green provided a natural relief from the busy streetscapes, while a view from above today would include the newly formed Circus Square Park and the Hot Rods baseball stadium.

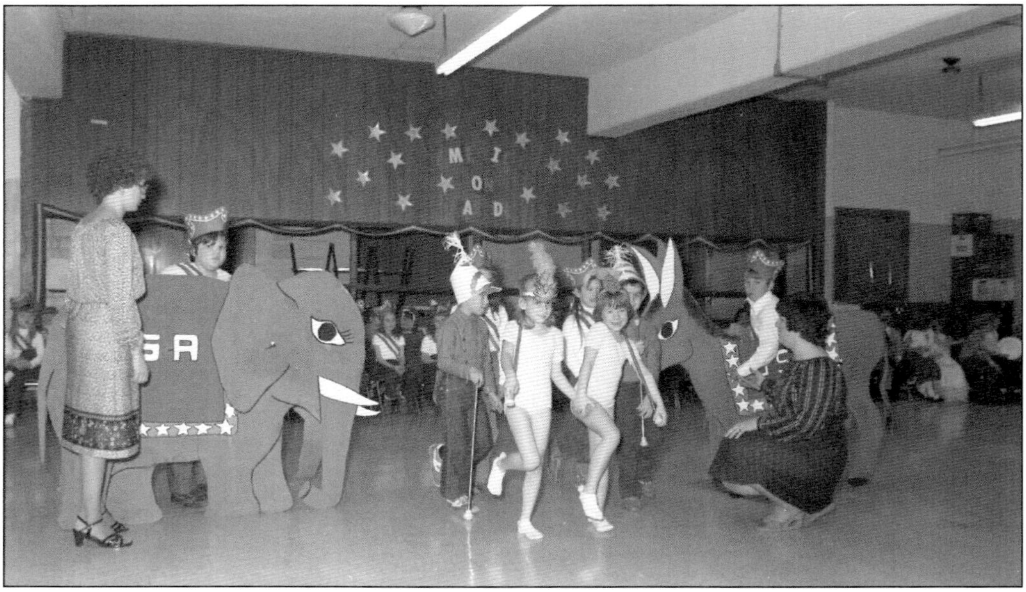

Political Conventions. Warren County elementary students celebrated "America on Parade" in 1980, with equal time and equal talent given to both major political parties.

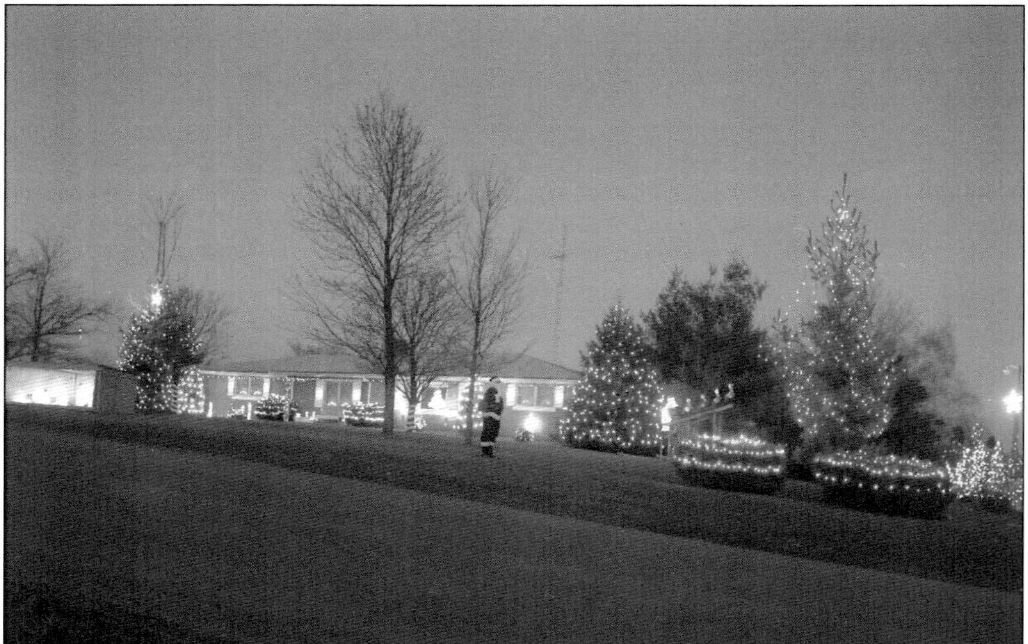

Holiday Lights. Jolly old St. Nick (also known as Richard Cassady) and Mrs. Claus (his wife, Geneva) made a lifetime of Christmas memories for others at their 1166 Blue Level Road home. Begun in 1946 with simple candles in the windows, the Cassady family tradition grew throughout the years to require a second fuse box, parking assistance from high school students, and the gift of as many as 300 candy bars each night that were hand-delivered to carloads of starry-eyed Bowling Green children.

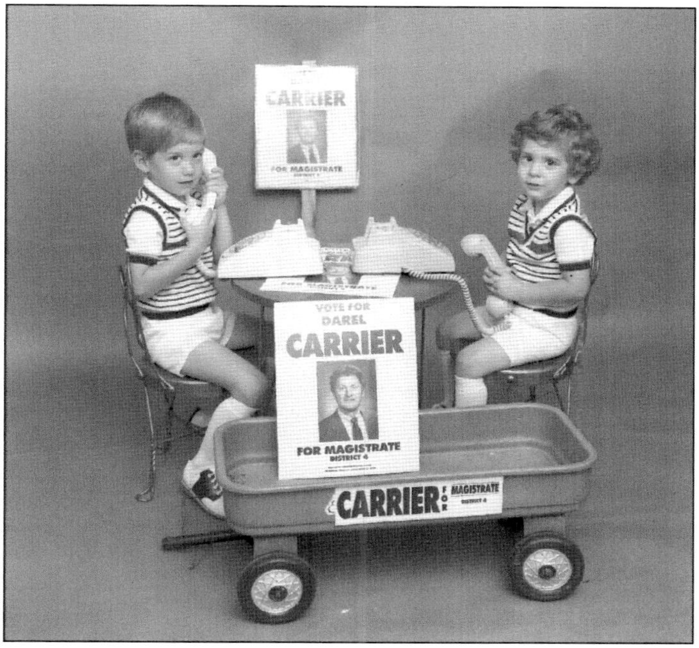

Phone Bank. These young lads were ready to work the phones for their dad's campaign. Jonathan Carrier (left, age four) and Joshua Carrier (age two), were "calling to remind [voters] to vote for [their] dad" in Daryl Carrier's successful 1985 bid for Warren County magistrate. A former Hilltopper all-American basketball star under coach E. A. Diddle, Daryl enjoyed a successful professional basketball career before his tenure in local leadership.

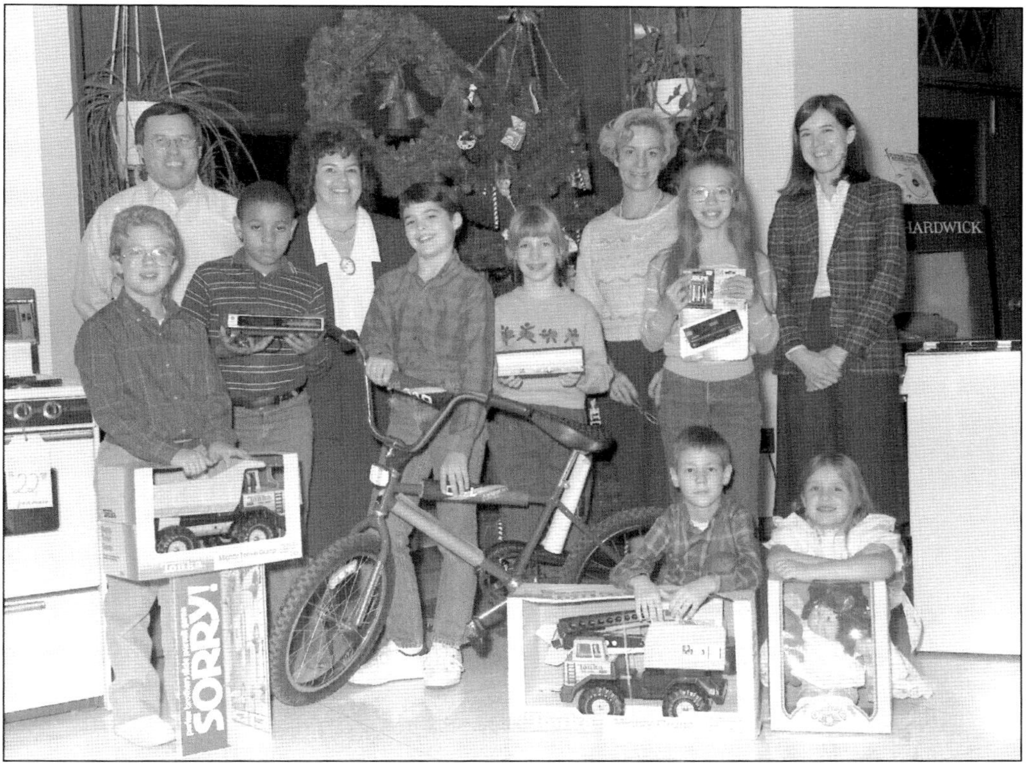

Dear Santa. In true holiday spirit, Western Kentucky Gas sponsored a letters to Santa contest, and lucky correspondents were the recipients of gifts and prizes on December 18, 1986. Volunteer holiday elves from left to right are Larry Brown, Judy Haynes, Tina Coates, and Pam Kielty.

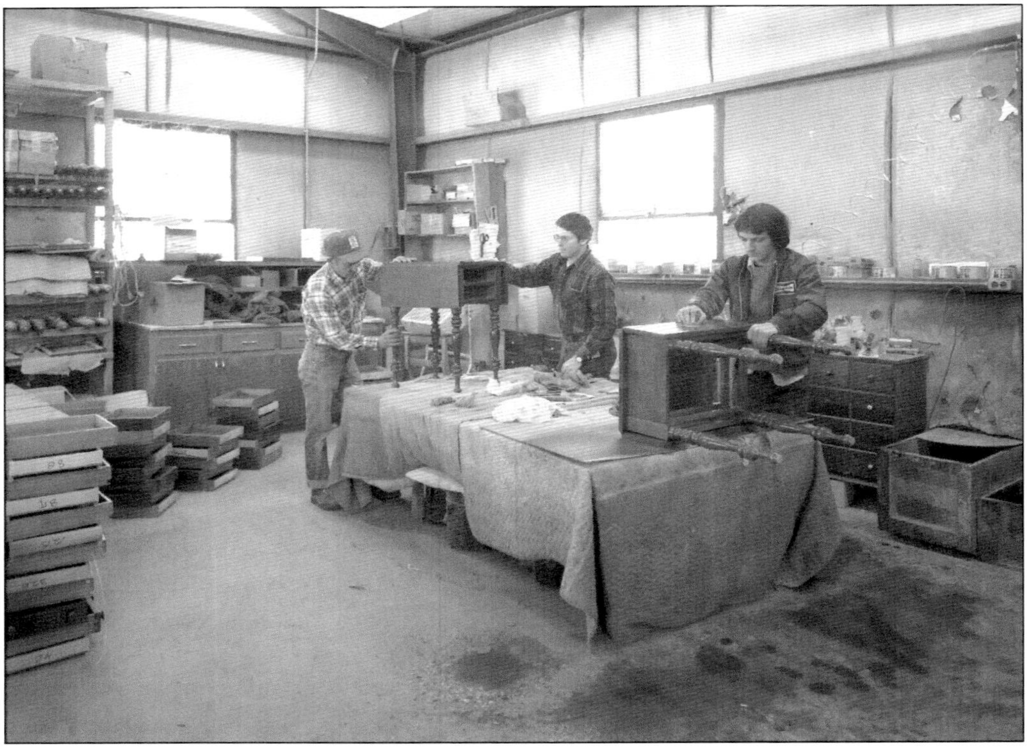

Family Heirloom. Handmade cherry reproductions from Cassady Furniture, founded in 1949 by Lloyd Cassady Sr. at 318 Louisville Road, were destined to become cherished family heirlooms. From left to right, dedicated craftsmen William Webb, Lloyd Cassady Jr., and Logan Estes put the finishing touches on solid cherry pieces built to last. Some 50 years after the first heirloom found a home, Cassady's continues to grace families throughout Kentucky with its craftsmanship.

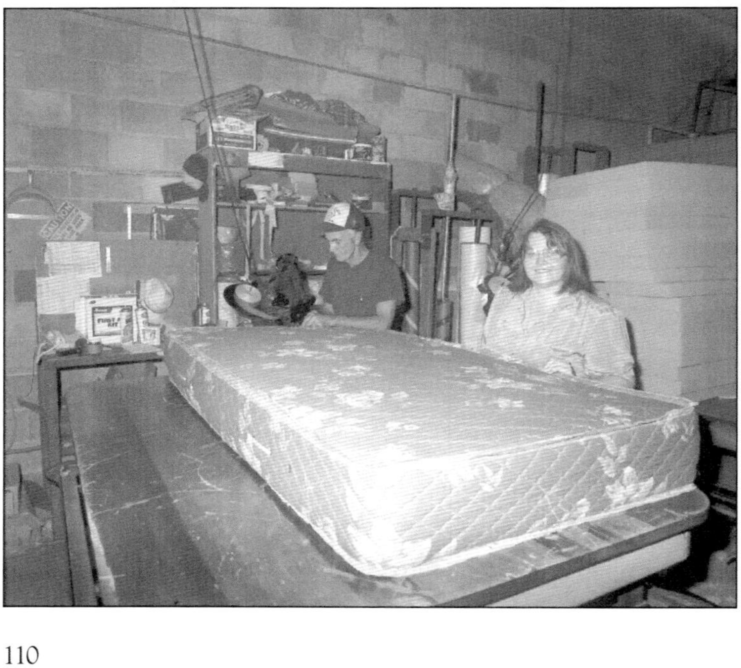

Mattress Makers. Mary Bandy (right), owner, and Kenneth Cowles put the finishing touches on a locally made mattress at Bandy Bedding. One of the only factories in Bowling Green founded and led by a woman, Bandy Bedding now includes three retail stores and continues to thrive under family ownership.

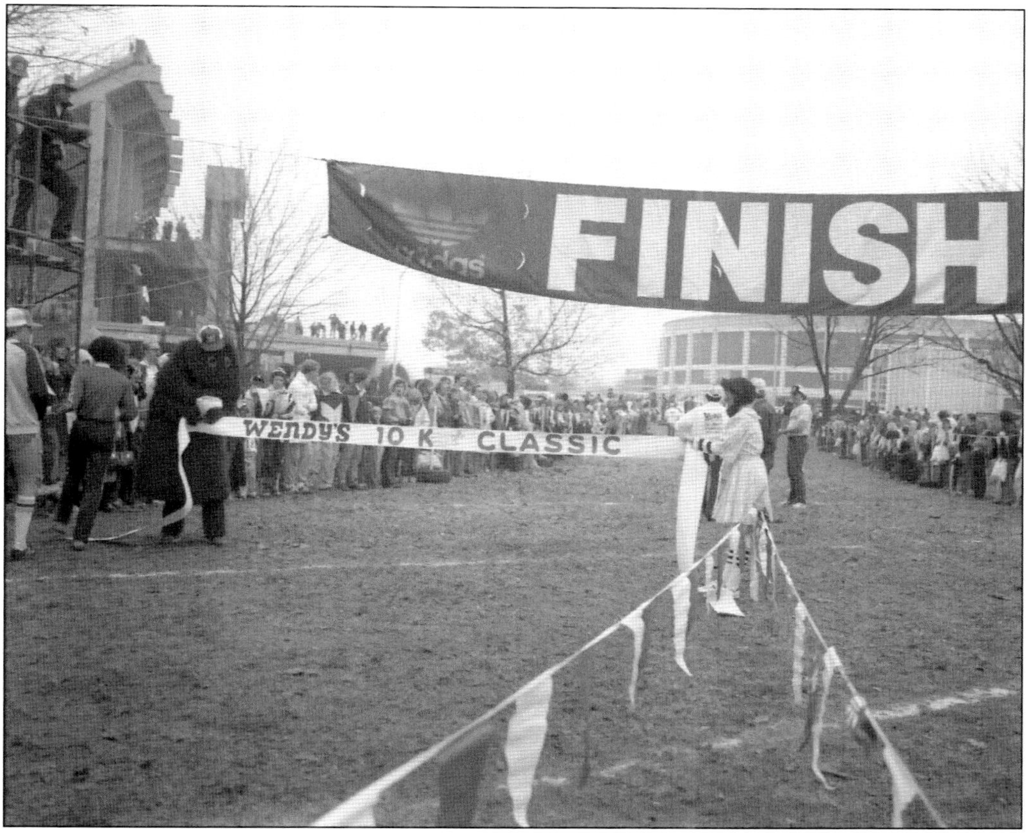

HOME STRETCH. Western Kentucky University mascot Big Red lent a hand at the finish line of the Wendy's 10-K Classic in 1980. A staple of Bowling Green athletic competition for 30 years, the classic annually attracts competitive racers from around the world.

ROCK ON. Pictured from left to right, Dixie Line Band members Tom "Bones" Kaelin, Tommy Johnson, Danny Dodson, Tommy Hendricks, and Chris Carmichael were ready to rock out in 1980. The group toured throughout the United States and recorded an original country rock album.

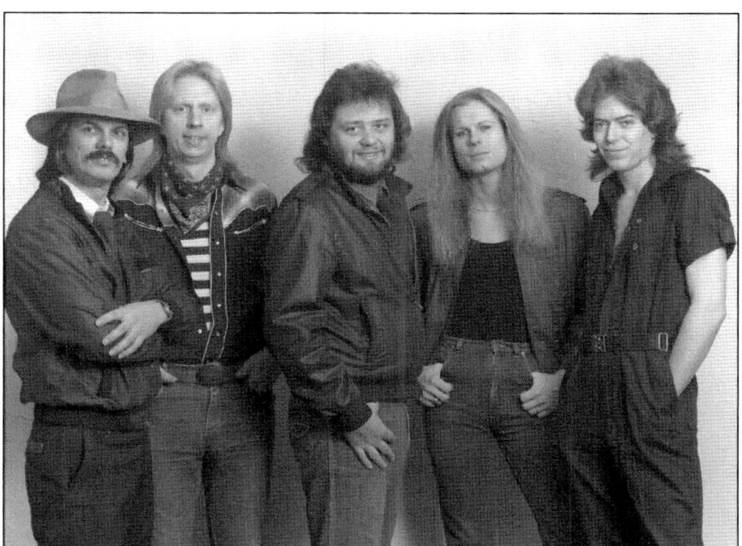

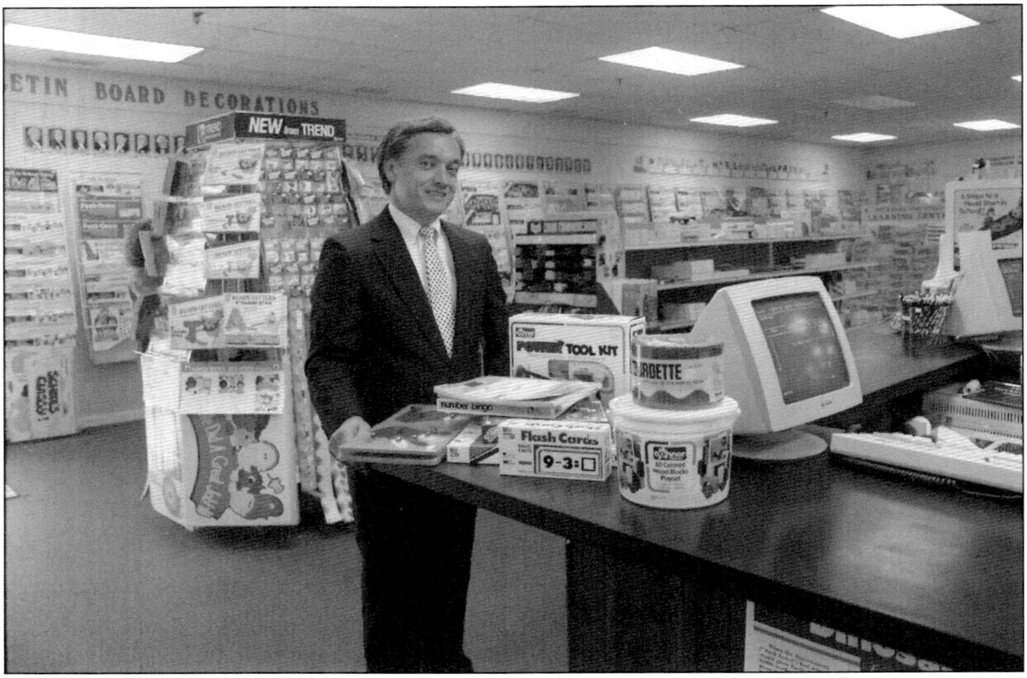

RESOURCE ROOM. Johnny Webb began Southern School Supply in his garage and personally delivered supplies from the trunk of his car. In 1987, the venture had grown to numerous retail outlets in several locations, and Webb mounted a successful bid to the office of mayor of Bowling Green.

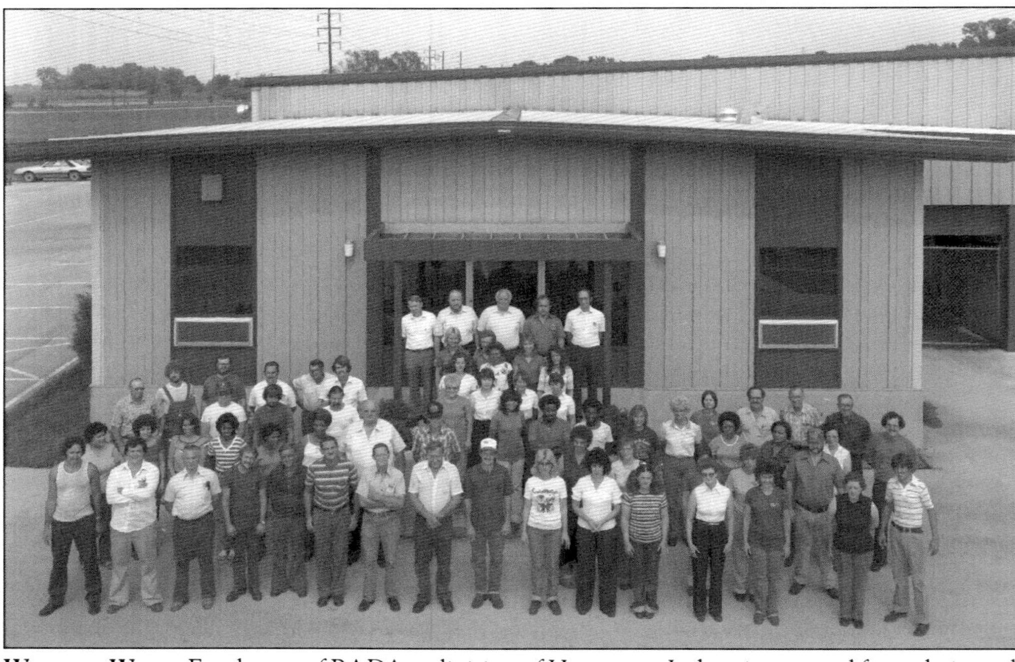

WEIGHTY WORK. Employees of BADA, a division of Hennessey Industries, paused from their work on July 14, 1982, at the company's location on U.S. 31-W North. Manufacturer of wheel-balancing weights, BADA was an essential part of the automotive industry.

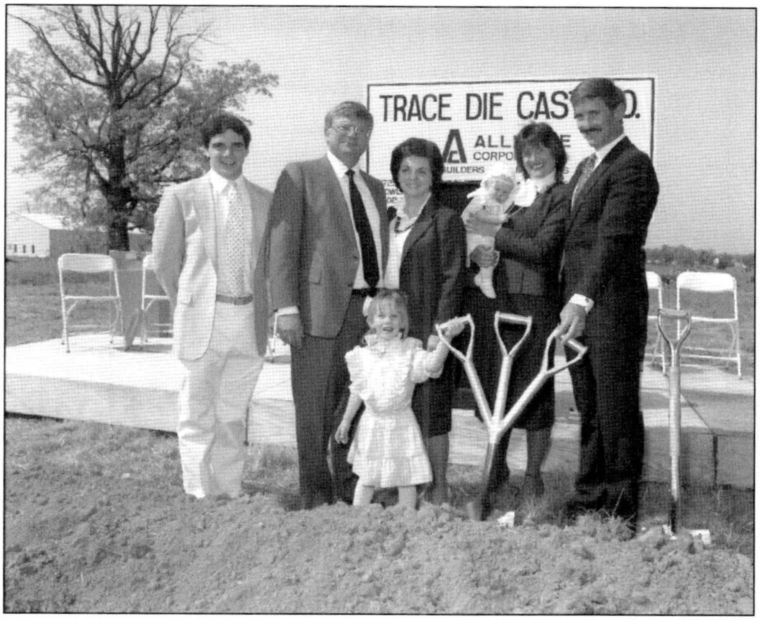

PUTTING DOWN ROOTS. Lowell Guthrie and his family members dug into life in Warren County when they founded Trace Die Cast in 1988. The supplier of high-quality aluminum die castings remains an integral component of the Bowling Green business community, and son Brett Guthrie now serves Bowling Green citizens as a U.S. representative.

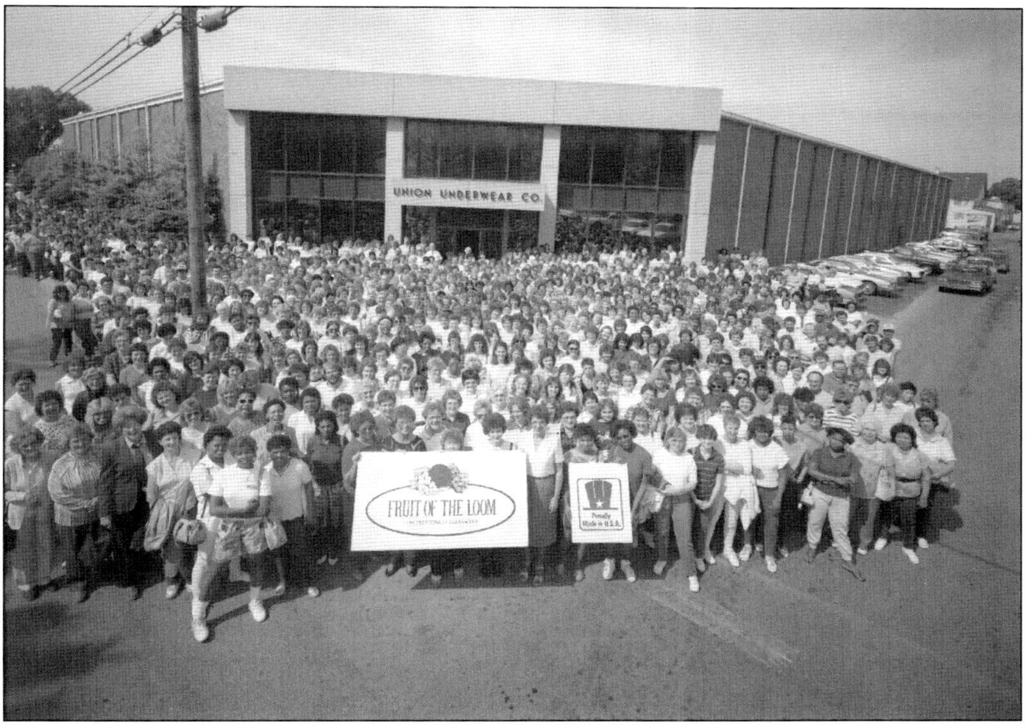

BUILDING SEAT COVERS. Union Underwear Company employees displayed the Fruit of the Loom moniker and "Proudly Made in the U.S.A." at the Church Street manufacturing facility on April 29, 1987.

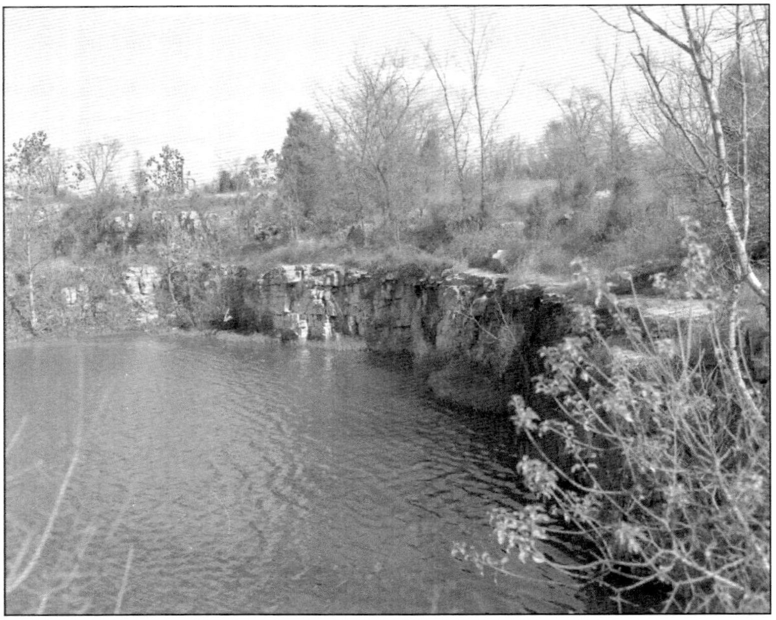

LIMESTONE LAKE. The serene, unruffled waters of Limestone Lake at 831 Woodford Avenue obscured what was once a bustling quarry where strong men carved out of the earth the white stone for which Bowling Green became famous.

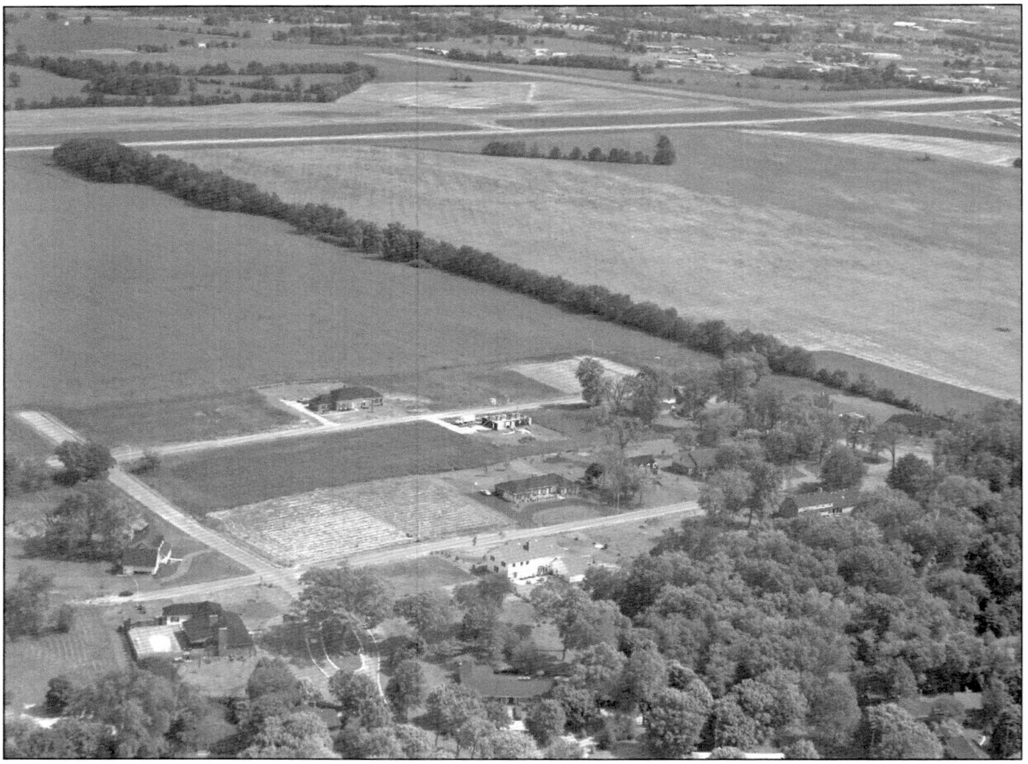

ROAD TO THE FUTURE. This May 2, 1983, aerial photograph highlighted the birth of Bent Tree, one of Bowling Green's most successful residential developments, and the undeveloped land that later became Hartland and Crosswinds Golf Course. Stub roads and a smattering of houses were quiet omens of the hustling, bustling life to come.

Five

The 1990s
Back to the Future

The last decade of the 20th century was one of ever more rapid change for Bowling Green and the world. Punctuated by violence and crime and accompanied by a proliferation of advertisements for anxiety medication, the world was moving fast, and Bowling Green was doing its best to keep in step.

A kid-centered economy continued to swell, with television networks exclusively devoted to juvenile programming and massive corporate marketing budgets geared to capturing juvenile dollars. At the same time, the disenfranchisement of the young became ever more apparent in the Columbine and Heath High School shootings, even while Harry Potter books turned the publishing world upside down and Disney became a global phenomenon, launching careers and setting fashion trends.

Desert Storm battles were fought in grainy night vision and seen on CNN with 24-hour access, and a burgeoning cyber world came home to Kentucky on the Internet, while cell phone towers dotted the rolling landscape. Bowling Green's connection to the world was permanent, vast, and far-reaching.

Downtown explosions and fires reminded citizens of their own town's vulnerability, while a violent hail storm damaged properties but thankfully took no lives. Local government wrestled with plans for a Tri-Modal Transpark, and citizens battled the American Civil Liberties Union for the right to display a Nativity scene in Bowling Green's historic centerpiece, Fountain Square Park.

As the decade neared its close, concern about a year 2000 cyber meltdown grew, businesses prepared for disastrous computer problems, the government planned for terrorist acts, and Bowling Green citizens stocked up on basic supplies, planning for the worst. The coming of the millennium passed peacefully enough, and after 50 years of lasting work, photographer Tommy Hughes was still on the streets of Bowling Green, camera in hand, while his astute eye remained on the lookout for the perfect shot.

A new generation of photography was born in the digital age, and an award-winning photojournalism school at Western Kentucky University ensures that Hughes's legacy of documenting life with humor and insight will live on in photographs of a town that has grown through the many decades and will continue to grow for many more.

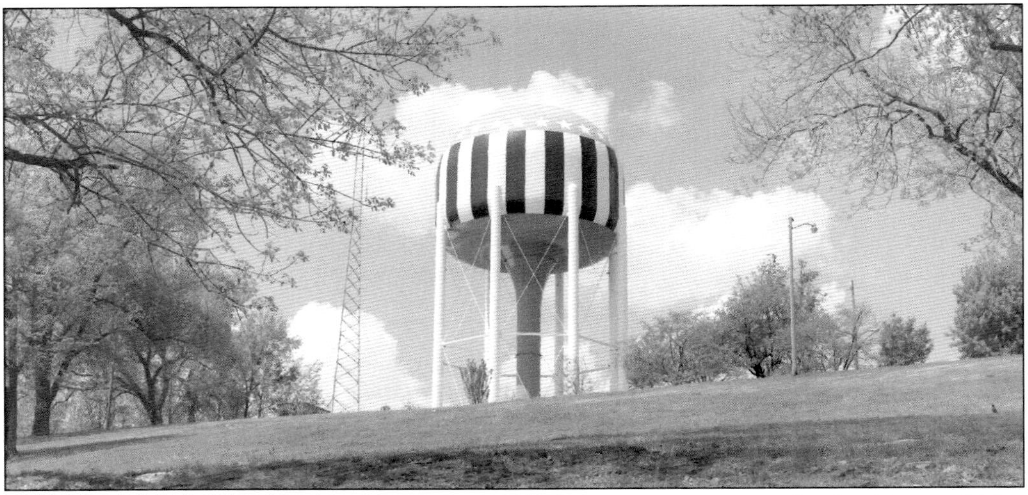

The Pride of Bowling Green. The Reservoir Hill water tower, painted red, white, and blue at the suggestion of a U.S. Marine Corps recruiter for the country's 1976 bicentennial, was first constructed in 1957. This well-known landmark was the inspiration for a song written by Ted Allen and recorded by the Hi Lites, and it remains a symbol of Bowling Green patriotism.

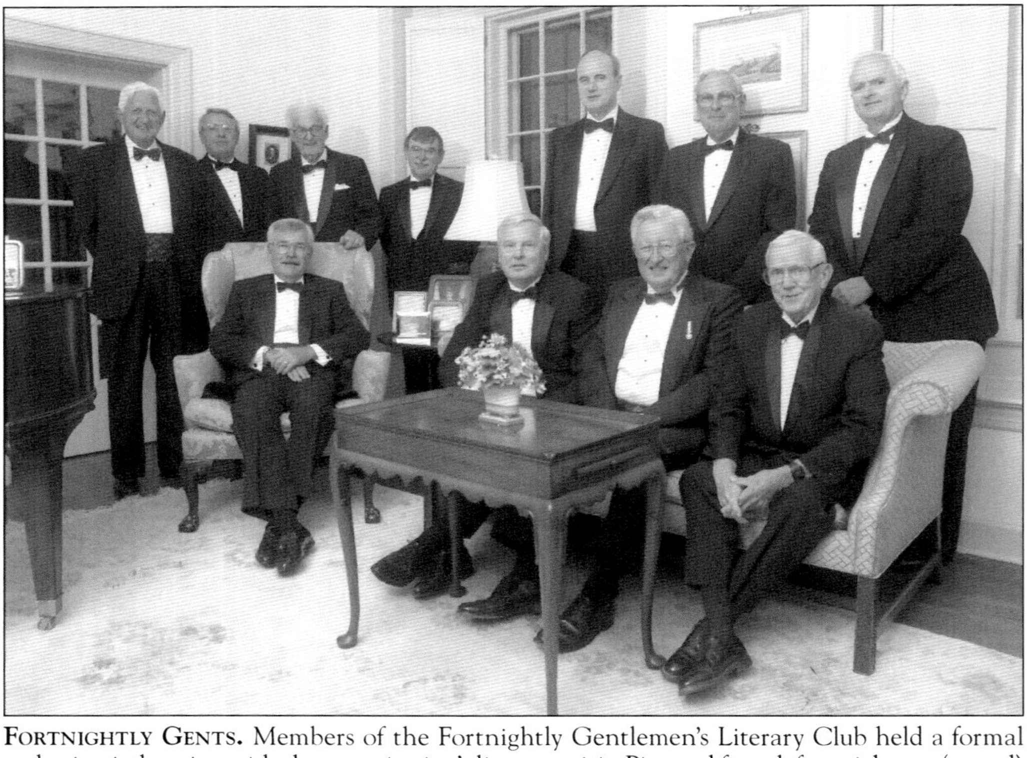

Fortnightly Gents. Members of the Fortnightly Gentlemen's Literary Club held a formal gathering in keeping with the organization's literary spirit. Pictured from left to right are (seated) Bill McKenzie, Joe Cheek, Robert Spiller, and Maxey Harlin; (standing) Herb Smith, Ray Buckberry, Jo "Top" Orendorf, Ron Hatcher, Jerry Parker, Jeff Jefferson, and Howard Surface. At monthly meetings, these bookish gents engaged in spirited discussions on their readings and other topics of the day.

MAGNOLIAS IN MAY. The wedding ceremony of Mia Blevins and Greg Morris was performed at Eastwood Baptist Church by Pastor Greg Hooper at 2:30 p.m. on May 11, 1991. With simplicity and grace, in white cotton lawn and with a bouquet of garden-fresh mixed flowers, this young couple's nuptials were a day of springtime bliss.

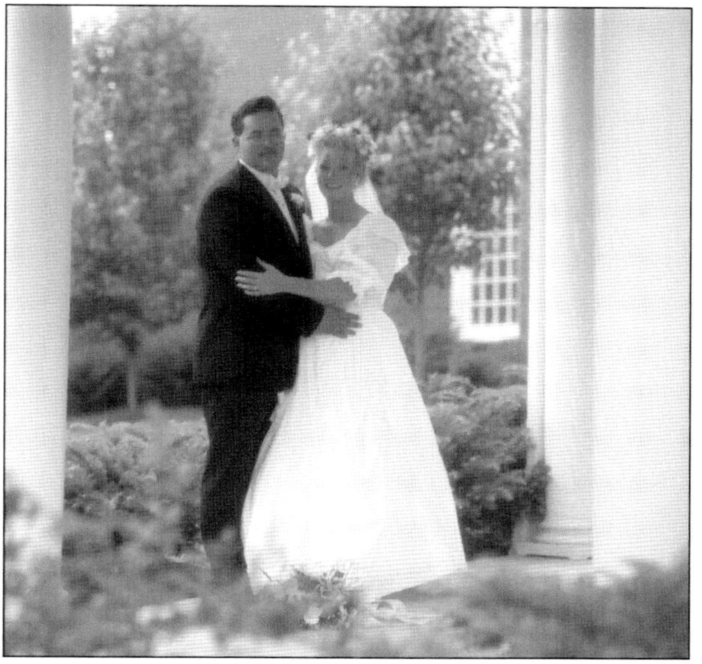

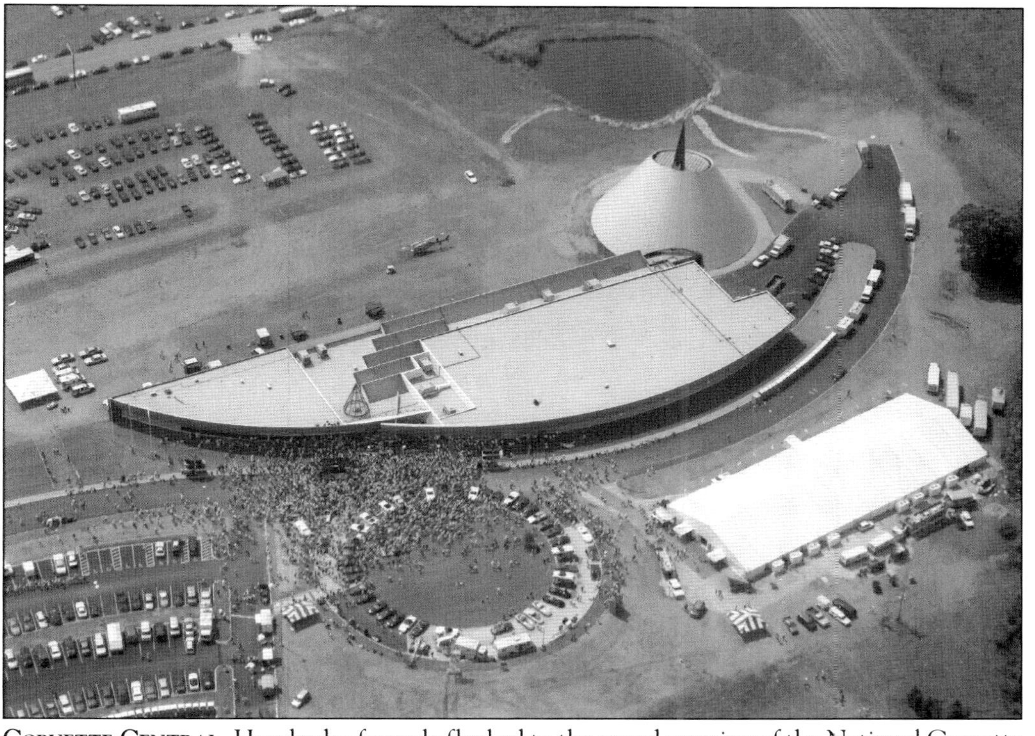

CORVETTE CENTRAL. Hundreds of people flocked to the grand opening of the National Corvette Museum on Labor Day in 1994. As captured from above, the museum is one of the most unique buildings in Bowling Green with its curved design and distinctive spire, which can be seen for miles. It draws Corvette enthusiasts from around the world for special events throughout the year.

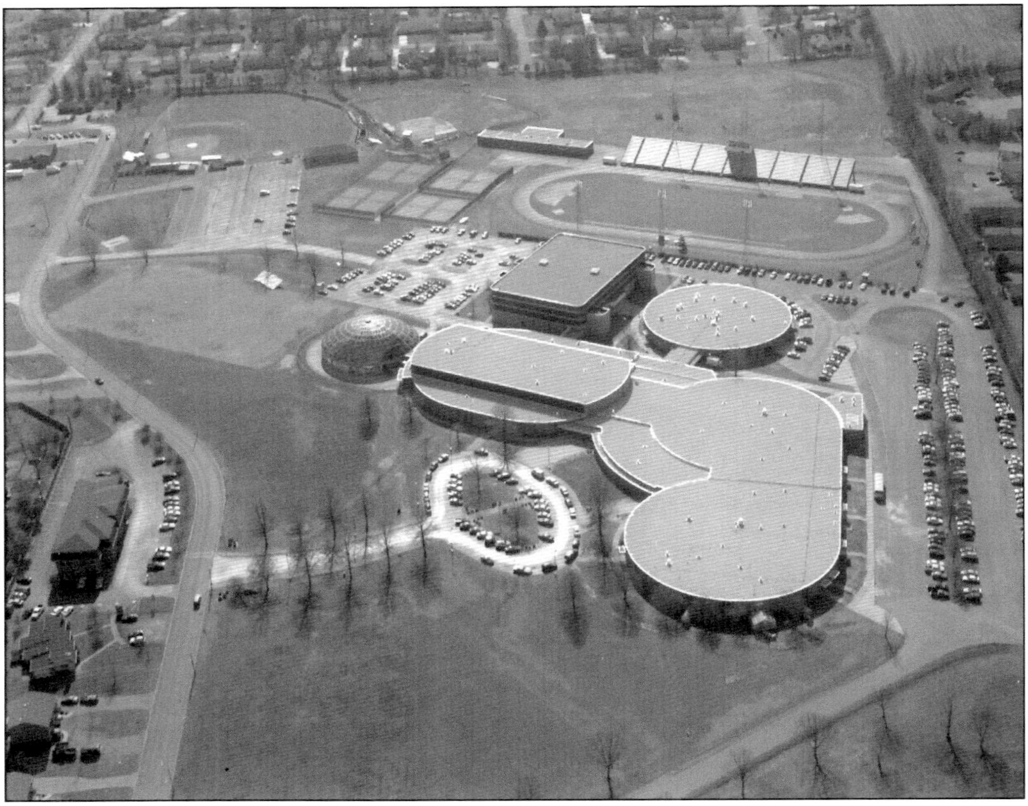

Sky-High Bowling Green High School. Uniquely designed by Joseph Wilk and built in 1971 at a cost of $4 million, Bowling Green High School's architecturally avant-garde interlocking circles, as seen from above, provided students with what administrators hoped would be a never-ending thirst for knowledge.

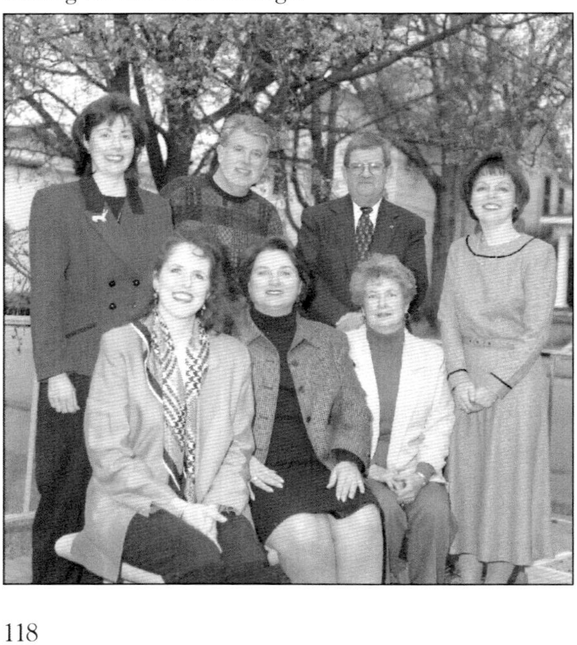

Library Lions. Members of the board of trustees of the Bowling Green Public Library are seen meeting at the main library branch at 1225 State Street. From left to right are (sitting) Portia B. Pennington, chairwoman Ferris VanMeter, and Martha McGuirk; (standing) Amy Wood, Brian Sullivan, Bob Kirby, and director Karen Porter. Avid believers in improved library services for all citizens, these members helped preserve and advance library services in the county. Today a stunning memorial sculpture has been installed at the main branch location in memory of VanMeter's many contributions, and a branch facility at 175 Iron Skillet Court has been named in honor of Kirby's dedicated service.

Norman Rockwell Moment. Pediatrician Dr. Keith Coverdale cared for the children of Bowling Green for over 40 years, seeing several generations from birth to adulthood. A founder of Pediatric Associates, which remains in operation, Coverdale was a reassuring voice to many concerned parents. Merrill Bradford poses with her grandfather in 1995 in this charming re-creation of the Norman Rockwell masterpiece portraying the tender patience of a dedicated physician.

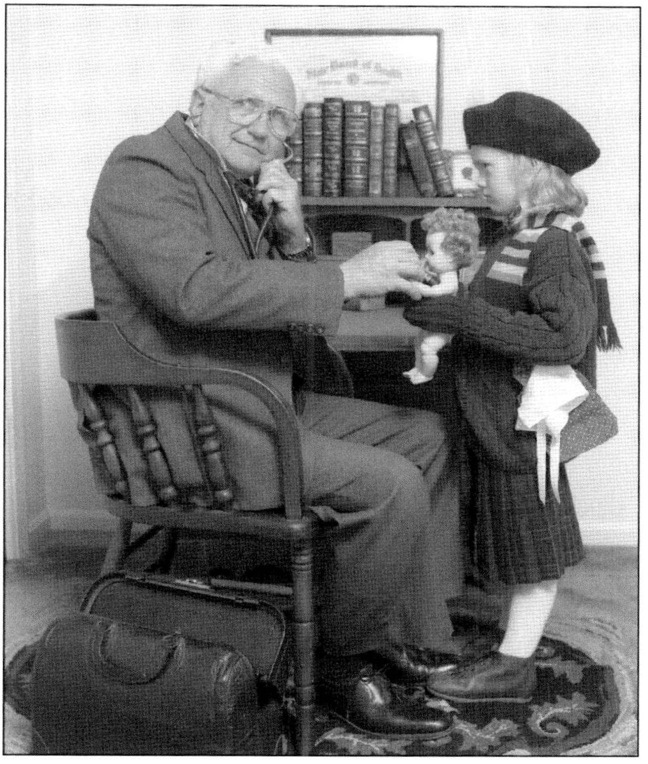

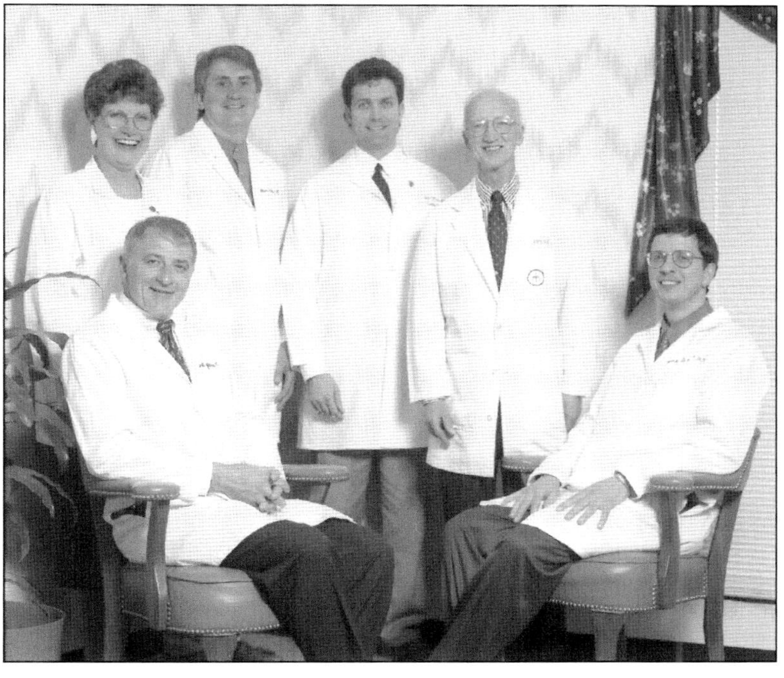

Medical Mavens. Internal Medicine and Associates, a private practice group, opened its office in the 1990s. From left to right, Dr. James Jarvis, nurse practitioner Shala Wilson, Dr. William Moss, Dr. Richard Welch, Dr. Herbert Harkleroad, and Dr. John Gover provided personal health care with an eye to innovation.

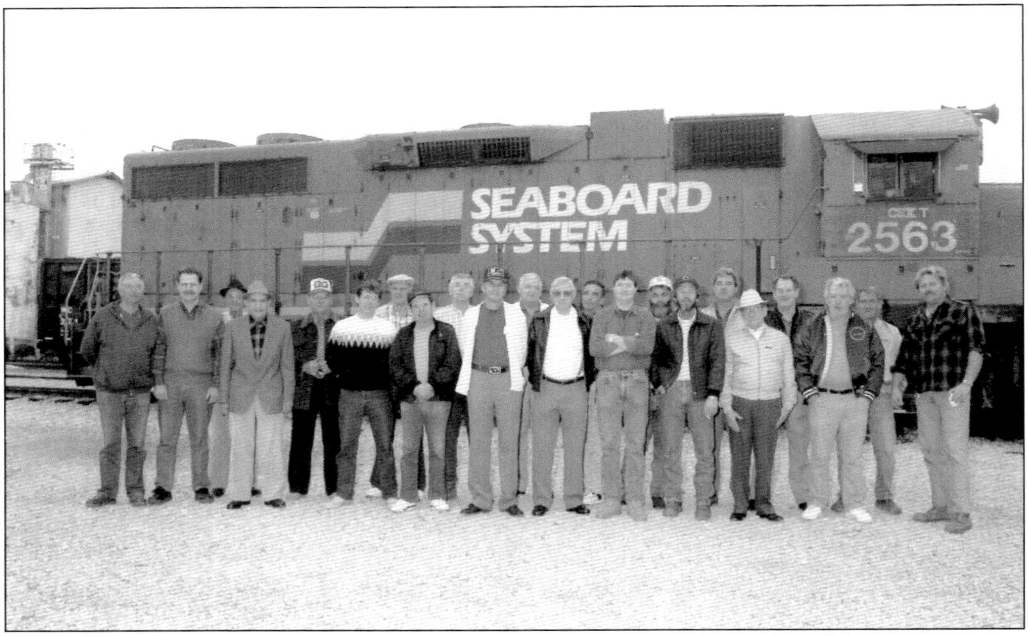

SEABOARD SONS. The men of CSX Railroad gathered in front of a Seaboard System engine at the Louisville and Nashville Railroad depot in 1993. Although passenger trains ceased service to Bowling Green in 1979, the mournful whistle of an outbound freight train can yet be heard on a still summer night.

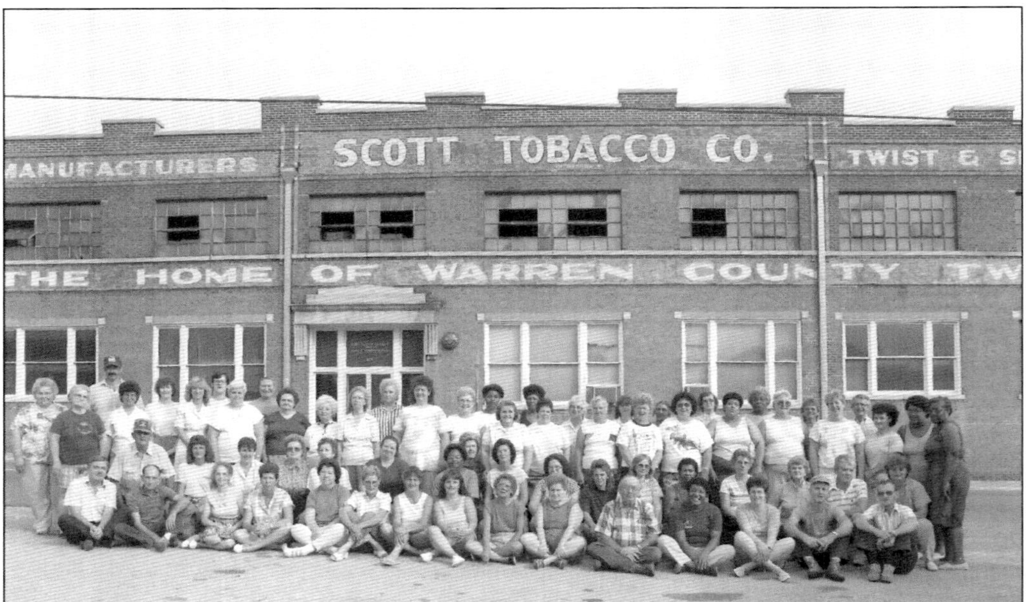

BROADLEAF HERITAGE. Scott Tobacco Company, at 939 Adams Street, was founded in Bowling Green in 1900 and has utilized this historic facility since 1939. Pictured here on July 31, 1990, company staff gathered in front of "the Home of Warren County Twist" to mark their place in Kentucky's agricultural and economic heritage.

Hail Storm Havoc. Memories of April 16, 1998, remain fresh in the minds of young and old alike, who can recount with pinpoint accuracy their whereabouts on that frightening spring afternoon when a violent hail storm hit, causing millions of dollars' worth of damage to homes and businesses and changing the face of the community as bright blue tarps mushroomed across thousands of damaged roofs.

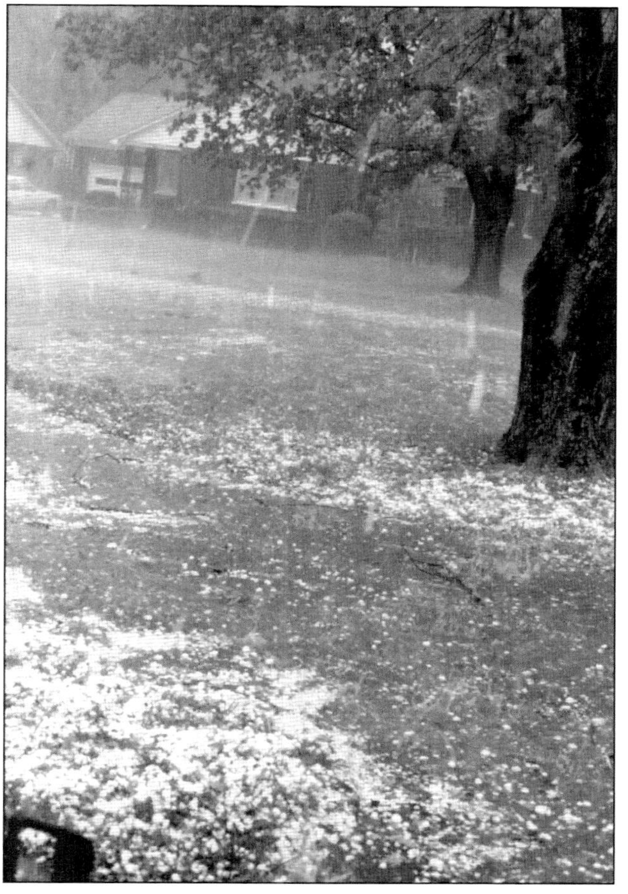

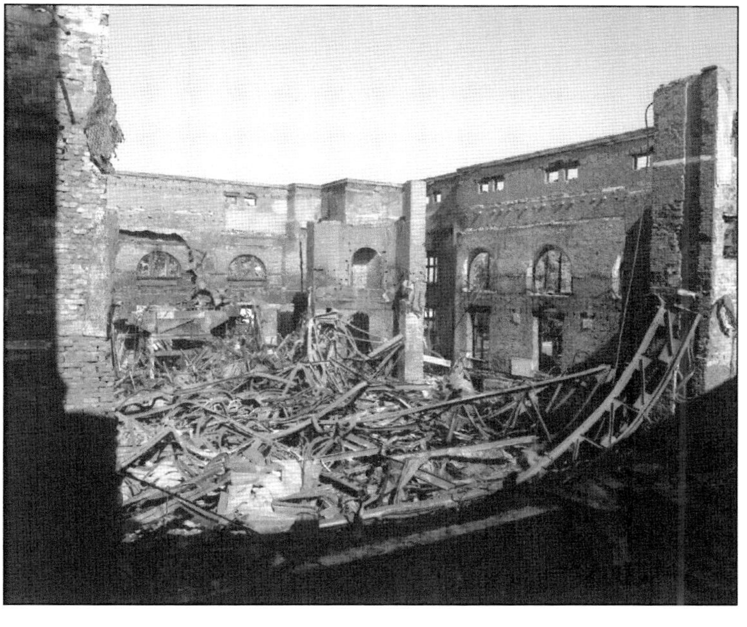

Charred Ruins. The beautiful and historic sanctuary of the First Baptist Church was destroyed by fire on October 14, 1991. With the blaze well underway at 3:00 p.m., distraught parents dashed to the church as the First Baptist preschool and day care was forced to evacuate. Damage was irreparable, and the church embarked on a multi-million dollar rebuilding campaign, which came successfully to fruition some three years after the fire.

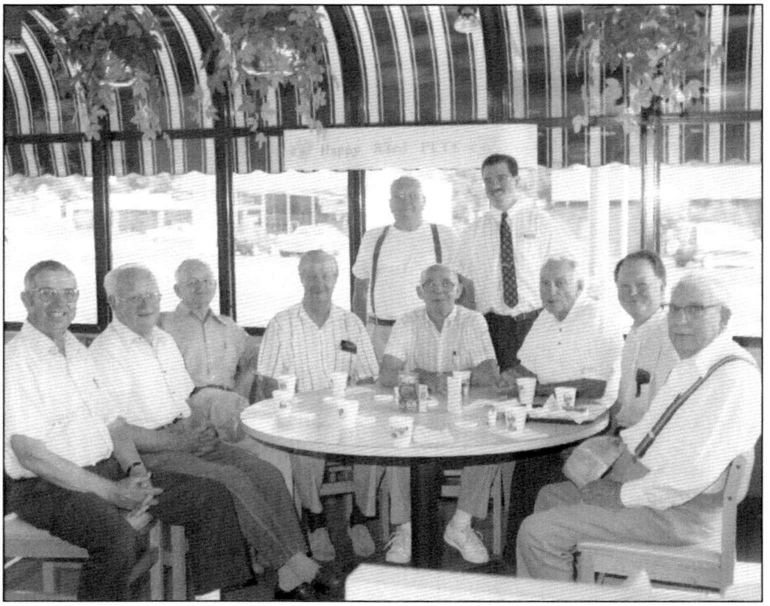

COFFEE KLATSCH. Here, a group of coffee regulars meet at Arby's on the U.S. 31-W Bypass to celebrate Pete Lowe's (standing, center) 83rd birthday. Jovial members of the club who were raising a cup to their buddy are, from left to right, Orville Elkin, Bill Pierce, Roy McKenzie, J. C. Hopper, Ernest "Bud" Lowe, I. H. Sadler, Fred Thurman, W. S. Stone, and Kevin Trowbridge (standing at right).

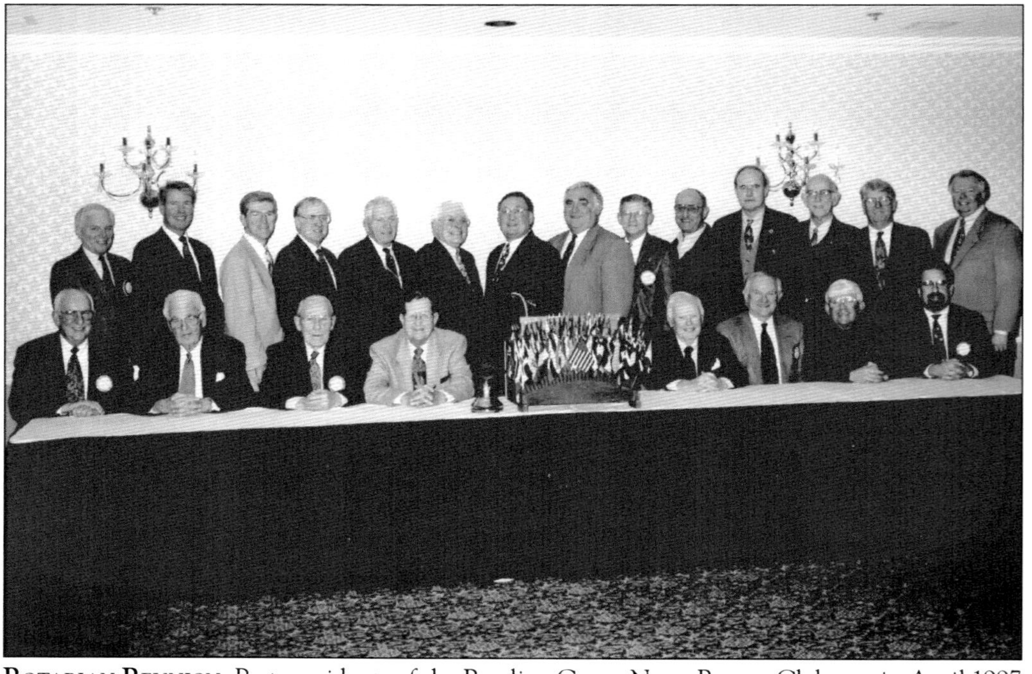

ROTARIAN REUNION. Past presidents of the Bowling Green Noon Rotary Club met in April 1997 to celebrate the heritage of their organization. From left to right are (seated) Ron Shrewsbury, J. T. "Top" Orendorf, Walter Nalbach, Ken Mullins, Roy Gaddie, Carroll Hildreth, Jim Johnson, and Tommy Holderfield; (standing) Chuck Coates, Kenny Wallace, Henry Pepper, Charlie Hardcastle, Lee Truman, Charles Moore, Mike Hepp, Wayne Priest, Rex Galloway, Henry Carlisle, Jerry Parker, Dr. Lewis Graham, Bob Kleier, and Craig Evans. These civic servants joined a long line of Rotarians in the club, which was originally chartered on November 24, 1920, with only 15 members.

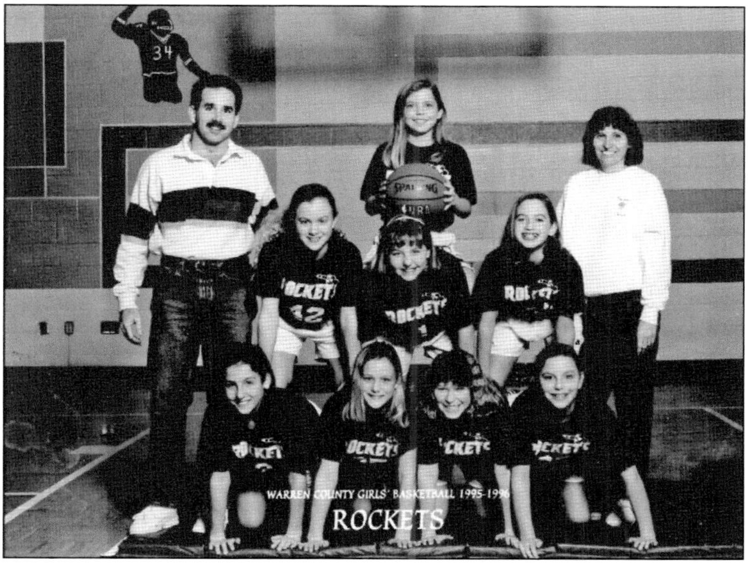

HOOP STARS. The Warren County Rockets celebrated their 1995–1996 season on the court. From left to right are (first row) Elizabeth Cummins, Mindy Coleman, Lindsay Harper, and Ellie Wigodsky; (second row) coach Ken Fitzpatrick, Jenny Larson, Andrea Fitzpatrick, Heather Cole, and coach Beverly Cummins; (third row) Leslie Hazle.

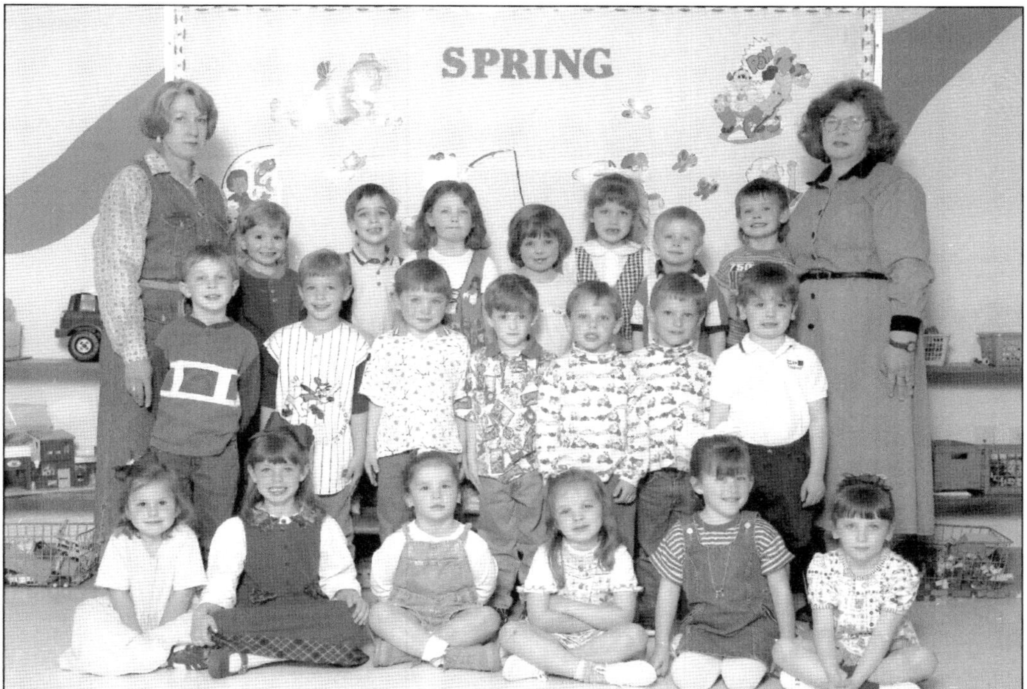

PLAY SCHOOL PLAYMATES. Happy students of the Bowling Green City Play School gathered on April 10, 1997, pausing for a moment from their fun and learning with teachers Mrs. Smith (left) and Mrs. Halter. The inquisitive four-year-olds are, from left to right, (first row) Jacqueline Otis, Chelsey Halter, Karly Gilbey, Elizabeth Collins, Alexandria Nath, and Megan Dugard; (second row) Matthew Geis, Matthew Peterson, Kaleb Harris, Michael Speck, John Magner, Eamonn Magner, and Brandon Moran; (third row) Chase Pardue, Jacob Brennenstuhl, Grace Logsdon, Amy Marie Hitch, Shelby Lawson, Cain Wilson, and Kyle Neal.

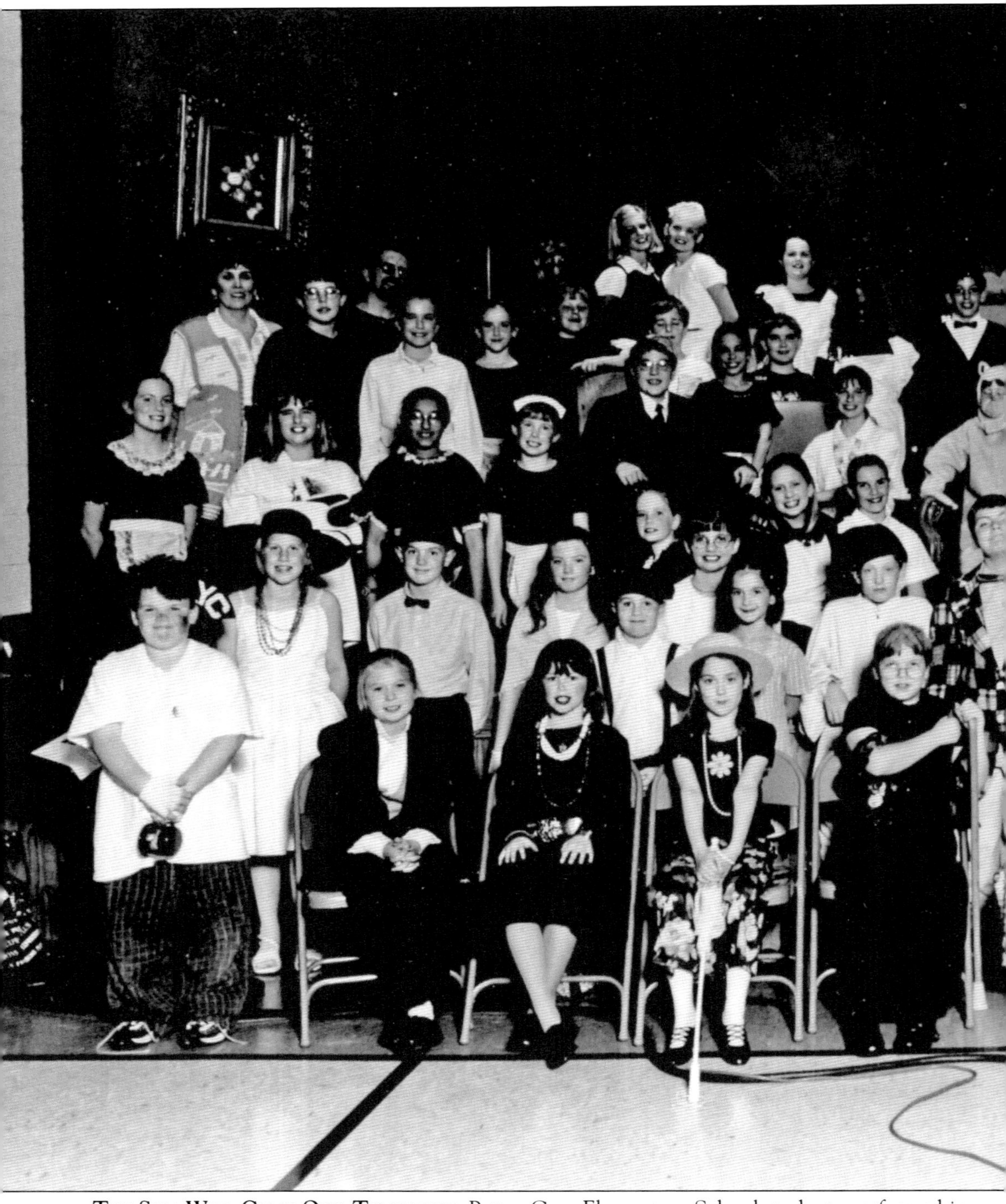

The Sun Will Come Out Tomorrow. Potter Gray Elementary School students performed in director Pat Keller's 1999 production of *Annie, Jr.* on the stage at the school at 610 Wakefield Street. A fitting tribute to hope, optimism, the indomitable spirit that is Bowling Green and America at large, these smiling faces and their vast talents exemplified what is yet to come. As they have

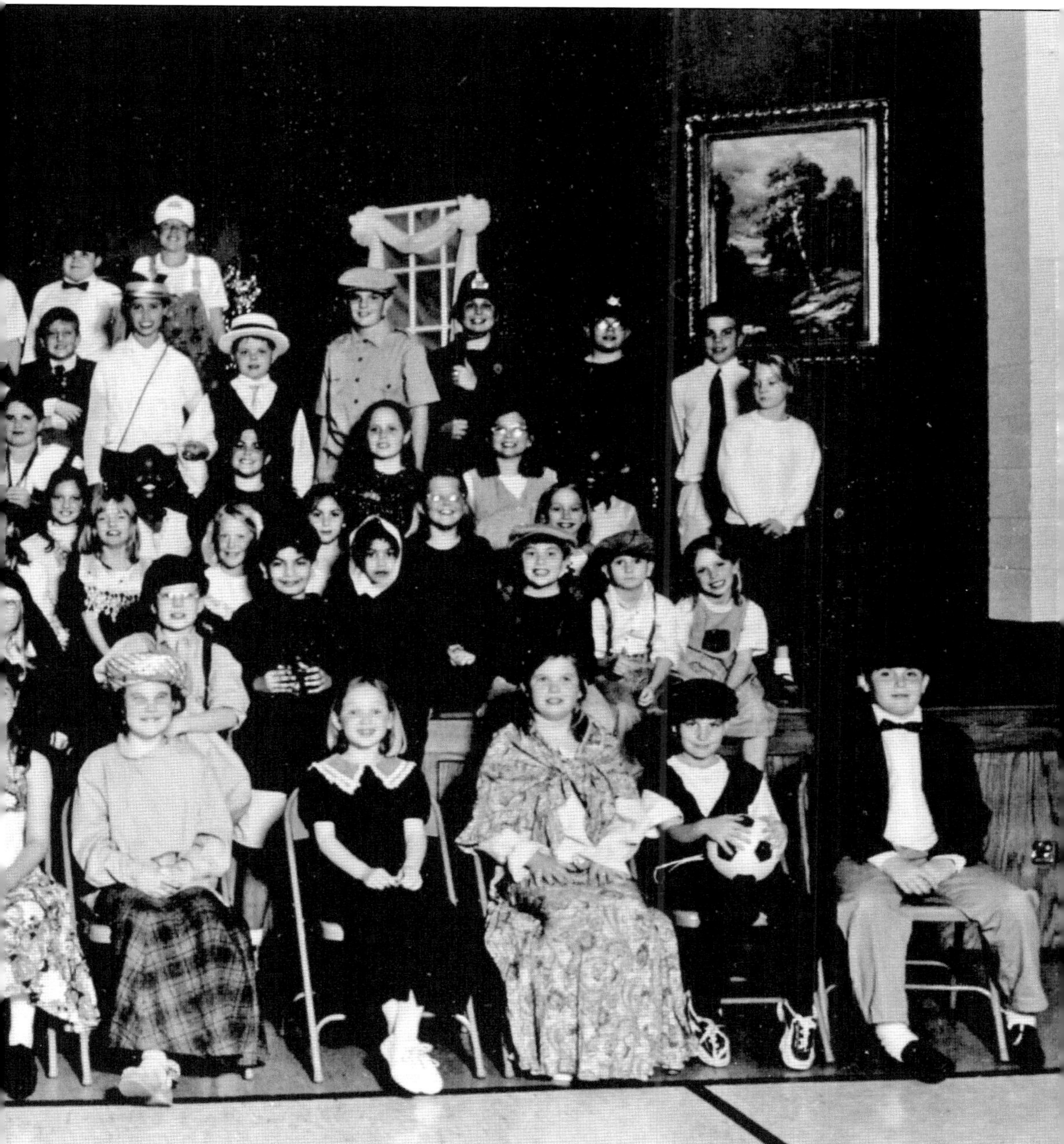

grown and prospered, so has Bowling Green, and these many children and their compatriots across the city are now young adults, taking their place and making their mark on the future. Looking back across images of decades past serves as a reminder that "tomorrow is only a day away."

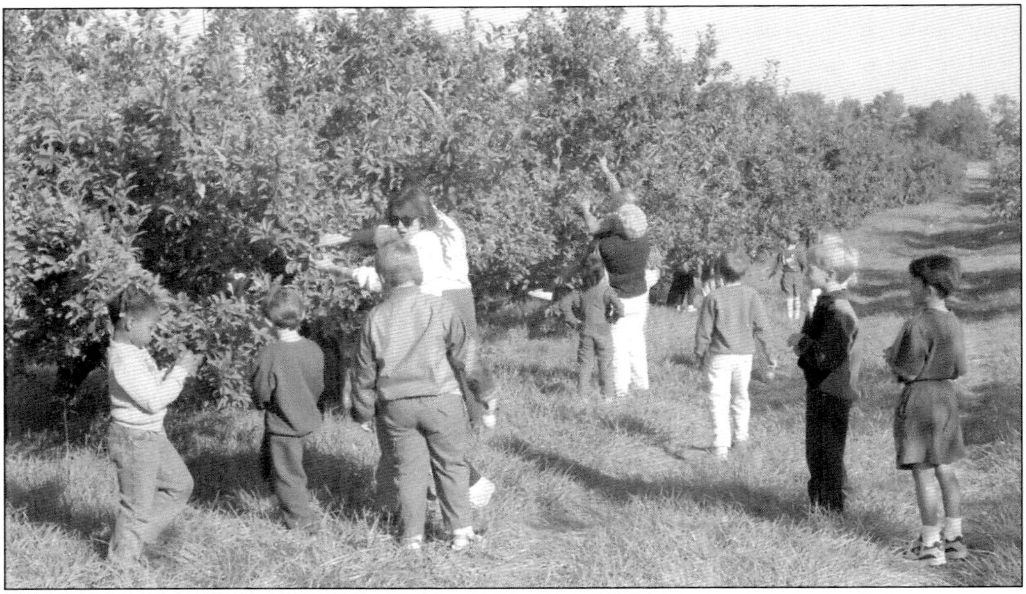

A Day on the Hill. Norma Mercer's first-grade class enjoyed a day "on the hill" during a field trip to Jackson's Orchard. An autumn tradition for generations of Bowling Green children, a day at Jackson's Orchard was filled with icy apple cider slush, hot fried pies, apple picking, and races through a giant hay bale maze. Owned by Bill and Shirley Jackson, the orchard remains a popular Bowling Green attraction and is an inspiring example of a thriving Kentucky agribusiness.

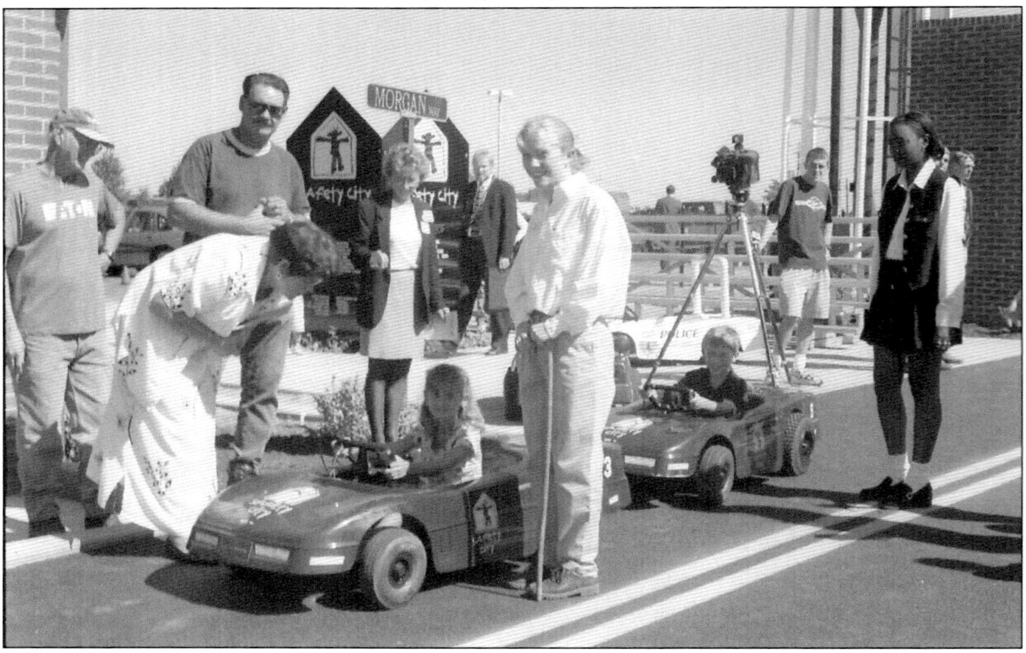

Traffic Stop. Principal Mattie Jane Cobb (left) gave student driver Kathryn Hawkins instruction as Mayor Sandy Jones (back, center) looked on during the opening day of Safety City, constructed at Greenwood High School. Hundreds of elementary school children traverse these "city" streets each year, gaining valuable insight into rules of the road.

ROLLING WATERS. The mighty Barren River, a curving tributary that winds its way around Bowling Green, was an integral part of the early history of the area, providing water transportation for freight and passengers. Bowling Green was a regular stop for steamboats, but the sharp and narrow turns of the river and the onset of modern rail transportation saw the Barren River become a modern-day attraction for the leisure pursuits of canoeing and fishing, while the swift waters keep rolling along through the Kentucky landscape.

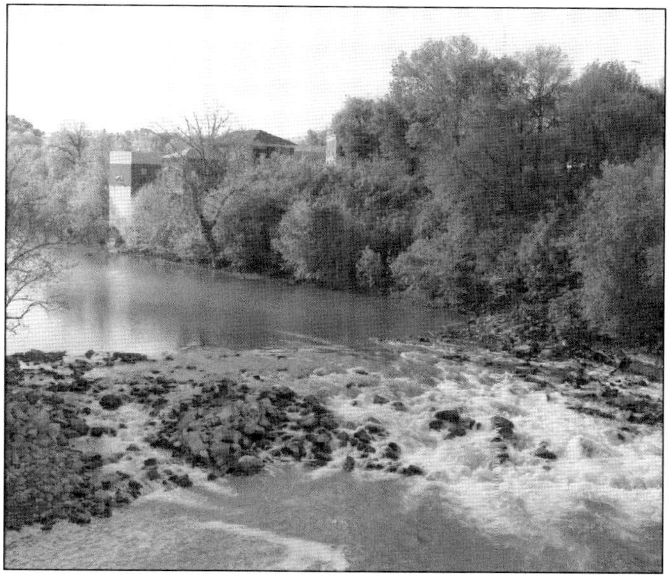

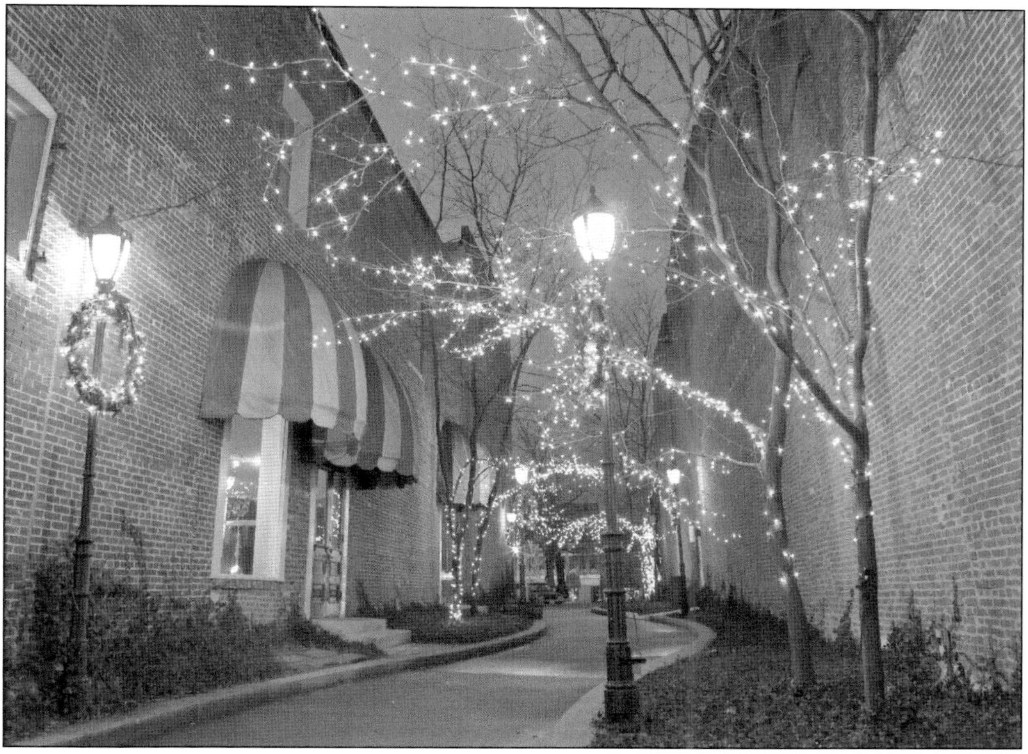

HOLIDAY CHARM. Morris Alley, the picture of downtown Christmas spirit, beckons strollers to meander along its serpentine sidewalk, admiring the sights of twinkling lights and windows dressed for holiday shopping. Thousands of Bowling Green feet have traversed this inviting walkway on their way to the Capitol for show-stopping entertainment or to Fountain Square Park for making memories that last a lifetime. Thousands more will walk this way in memories, and in pictures, yet to come.